The Practitioner Inquiry S

Marilyn Cochran-Smith and Susan L. Lytl

Action,

Talk, and

Text

LEARNING AND TEACHING
THROUGH INQUIRY

Edited by Gordon Wells

Teachers College, Columbia University
New York and London

Published by Teachers College Press, 1234 Amsterdam Avenue, New York, NY 10027

Library of Congress Cataloging-in-Publication Data

Action, talk, and text : learning and teaching through inquiry / edited by Gordon Wells.
     p.   cm. — (The practitioner inquiry series)
  Includes bibliographical references (p.   ) and index.
  ISBN 0-8077-4015-2 (cloth : alk. paper)—ISBN 0-8077-4014-4 (pbk. : alk. paper)
  1. Active learning—Ontario—Case studies. 2. Science—Study and teaching—Ontario—Case studies. 3. Action research in education—Ontario—Case studies.
  4. Developing Inquiring Communities in Education Project. I. Wells, Gordon, 1935.
II. Series.
  LB1027.23 .A26 2001
  372.3'5044—dc21   00-056373

ISBN 0-8077-4014-4 (paper)
ISBN 0-8077-4015-2 (cloth)

Printed on acid-free paper
Manufactured in the United States of America

08 07 06 05 04 03 02 01   8 7 6 5 4 3 2 1

Contents

Acknowledgments

MANY PEOPLE have been involved in the work that is reported in the following chapters and to all of them we owe a debt of gratitude for their participation. First, and most important, are the many students with whom we have explored the potential of the "inquiry approach." Not only have they allowed us to observe, record, and interview them, but in several cases they have also participated as full-fledged coinvestigators. As teacher-researchers, we have all discovered the value as well as the pleasure of learning with and from our students.

We should also like to pay tribute to the support we have received from colleagues, from school and school board administrators, and from the Ontario Institute for Studies in Education (OISE) of the University of Toronto. The project has also been supported throughout by the Spencer Foundation, who provided the funding for the first phase, "Learning through Talk," and was willing to extend their funding for the second phase, ambiguously entitled "Extending Learning through Talk." We should particularly like to thank Dr. Rebecca Barr who, as our Program Officer, helped us to keep on track. We should make it clear, however, that the views expressed in the chapters that follow are those of the DICEP authors and not necessarily those of the institutions that have supported our research.

Regrettably, not all those who are, or have been, members of DICEP have been able to contribute chapters to this book. Although they all had important learning experiences to share, limitations on length made it impossible to include them all. However, as members of the group, they have each played an important part in the development of the understandings and practices that the present authors share and we thank them for their contributions to our discussions. They include: Jackie Alspector, Gen Ling Chang, Jim Giles, Mari Haneda, Elizabeth Measures, Christine Monteiro-Almeida, and Barbara Smith. We owe a special debt of gratitude to Myriam Shechter, who made many of the videotaped classroom observations, organized the transcribing, and conducted many of the interviews. Together with Patrick Allen, she took responsibility for the routine management of the project and, like him, pursued her own inquiries, which added significant additional dimensions to our understanding of communities of inquiry. We should also like to thank the many graduate students at OISE who played a part in the transcribing and coding of the discourse data obtained from classroom observations.

Finally, support of a more personal kind has been unfailingly given by our families, who have provided encouragement as well as allowing us time and space for the many activities that have constituted participation in DICEP: analyzing data, attending monthly meetings, preparing for and attending conferences, writing and revising papers for publication, and, of course, communicating regularly by e-mail. To all, we extend our sincere appreciation for the ways in which they have helped us in our learning and development.

CHAPTER 1

The Development of a Community of Inquirers

Gordon Wells

TRANSFORMATION. That is the chief purpose of education—that all who are involved should transform their capacities to act, think, and feel in ways that contribute to the common good and enrich their own individual lives. To create opportunities for such personal and social transformation is certainly the aim of the authors of this book, both in our individual work as teachers and collectively as members of the Developing Inquiring Communities in Education Project (DICEP). In the following chapters we tell of the changes we have attempted to make and of the ways in which we and our students have developed in the process.

But before we present our individual inquiries, we need to set them in the larger context within which our own efforts are situated for, inevitably, the changes—political and economic as well as intellectual—that have been taking place in our society have influenced the ways in which we have come to think about what we are attempting to achieve. Furthermore, although we no doubt have our own way of making sense of it, this context is itself very similar for teachers in most of the world's more developed countries. We believe this is important because it means that the principles that guide us are likely to be ones that the majority of teachers the world over will share, although the settings and specific issues addressed in our inquiries may not seem familiar. In this introductory section, therefore, I will set out the context and framework within which our inquiries have been pursued.

A BRIEF INTRODUCTION TO DICEP

The Developing Inquiring Communities in Education Project has been in existence for almost ten years now although it has undergone substantial changes since its beginnings in 1991. Started initially with a grant from the Spencer Foundation to carry out a study of "Learning through Talk" in elementary science classrooms, the group has increased in numbers over the years and also in the scope of its inquiries. DICEP now consists of educators from public schools (Grades 1–8) in metro Toronto and the surrounding areas and university teacher educators at the Ontario Institute for Studies in Education (OISE) of the University of Toronto; our current concern is with creating opportunities for inquiry-based learning and teaching at all levels and in all areas of the curriculum. Equally important is the commitment of each of the group's members to inquiring into our own practice and to making connections between the different communities to which we belong. For we believe that lasting improvement in education can come about only through the work of individual teachers and school staffs as they seek, through inquiry into their own practice, to provide optimal learning conditions for the particular students in their care.

A commitment to action research is never easy to sustain, particularly in a climate of change that is politically rather than educationally motivated. During the life of the project, we have seen the introduction of two new K–12 curricula in our province, the second introduced, without consultation, only two years after the first, following an election won by a party campaigning to undo many of the gains made in public education, in the name of "common sense" and reduced taxation. With the resulting imposition of a curriculum that demands breadth of coverage rather than depth of understanding, the introduction of provincewide "high stakes" testing at Grades 3, 6 and 9, and a substantial cutback in staffing and financial resources, the opportunities for thoughtful and innovative teaching have been seriously reduced. However, we are trying not to be disheartened by the reduced room for maneuvers, but instead to treat this new situation as itself eminently worthy of inquiry.

In addition to our commitment to collaborative action research, two features distinguish DICEP from most other school-university collaborative projects. First, the group works with a common theoretical framework, based on the sociocultural ideas of Vygotsky and his followers, combined with an approach to the analysis of classroom interaction derived from Halliday's systemic functional linguistics. Within this framework, the focus of our research is on discourse, both spoken and written, which is at one and the same time the chief medium in which knowledge is coconstructed and evaluated and also the mediational means through which, in curricular activities, students encounter and appropriate the ways of understanding and making meaning in the different academic disciplines. The second distinguishing feature is the democratic basis on which the group is organized; topics for investigation are either chosen by individual teacher members or jointly agreed on within the group. Recognizing that each classroom is unique in its makeup, its context, and its history, we each search for ways of enacting the principles on which we are all agreed in a manner that is appropriate to local conditions. Thus, although we share the emphasis on communities of inquirers or learners with other reform-oriented groups, we have no party line that all must follow, and, in that way, our work remains close to the concerns and aspirations of the majority of classroom teachers everywhere.

As I have already stated, DICEP has undergone far-reaching changes over the years, and in the next sections I will attempt to capture some of this history.

THE EMERGENCE OF INQUIRY: A CRITICAL CLASSROOM EPISODE

The original title of the DICEP project was "Learning through Talk." From the outset, we were certain that the essence of learning and teaching was to be found in the interaction among students and teachers that constitutes such a large part of classroom activity (two-thirds, according to some estimates). At the same time, we were also convinced that the most valuable talk occurs in the context of exploration of events and ideas in which alternative accounts and explanations are considered and evaluated. The question, then, was: What are the conditions that make such talk possible? Is there an overall approach that makes it more likely to occur?

In the first year of the project, we worked with three teachers in a single school, recommended by a school board official. Our invitation to them was to engage in collaborative action research in the teaching of science in order to try to discover what roles talk played in the process. Two of the teachers eventually found out that they were not interested in action research and left the project at the end of the year. However, a third teacher, who joined the project when she replaced one of the original three, was extremely interested. As a language arts specialist who had spent most of her career in special education, she had never been involved in teaching science, and so she was delighted to have someone else with whom to share the responsibility for her Grade 6 science program. Our agreement was that she would collaborate if I would be a coteacher. In practice, this meant that we met together to plan each of the units and, in many cases, forthcoming lessons; in addition, I was a participant-observer in as many of the actual lessons as I was able to attend.

It was an eventful year, full of exciting and challenging insights for both of us, since neither of us had taught science before. For the students, too, it was a new experience, as we placed great emphasis on practical investigation and on discussion of what they were discovering in the process. It was in the last unit of the year, however, that the breakthrough really occurred, when the class was involved in a study of the metamorphosis of a brood of painted lady caterpillars. During the first few days, the students carefully examined the caterpillars as they consumed the "green mush" that had been part of the kit supplied to the class, and they made a number of interesting observations. Then, as the caterpillars climbed, one by one, to the top of their glass cells, adhered themselves to the gauze covering that stopped them from escaping, and spun their cocoons, the students were asked to come up with new questions about this stage in the process.

The Importance of "Real" Questions

How exactly do caterpillars turn into butterflies? What goes on inside the chrysalis while it hangs motionless—as if dead—from a leaf or from the gauze covering of a jam-jar? These were the questions that intrigued Nir when he and two other students talked with me in the corridor outside the classroom. Nir proposed that the best way to find out what happens would be to dissect a chrysalis every two days to see what changes had occurred inside. Since this would involve sacrificing other students' chrysalises, the teacher called a class meeting to consider this proposal, at which the majority argued strongly against it, mainly on ethical grounds. However, Nir was not ready to abandon his idea so easily. After listening to the arguments of his peers, he came up with a compromise: One of the chrysalises had fallen from its anchorage and had been lying for some time, unmoving, on the bottom of its jar. This chrysalis had obviously died, he argued; surely, therefore, it would be acceptable to carry out a dissection on a dead chrysalis. After further discussion, it was decided that if the chrysalis did indeed continue to show no signs of life, it would be deemed to be dead and an autopsy could be performed.

The next morning, after further observation and tests to establish that the chrysalis was really dead, Nir and a group of friends prepared to carry out the operation. As the teacher had insisted, they approached the task in the spirit of scientific investigation. While Nir donned surgical gloves, Alicia held the chrysalis firmly with a pair of forceps. Another student prepared to draw what was revealed, while another took written notes on the proceedings. Finally, the video camera was trained on the operating table in order to record the investigation for the benefit of those who could not get close enough to see.

Taking a scalpel, Nir delicately made an incision along the length of the outer casing. Immediately, one end of the previously inert chrysalis began to vibrate violently. The autopsy was halted forthwith, amid excited reactions from spectators and conflicting views on what to do next. Another class meeting was immediately convened in order to consider the implications of the changed status of the chrysalis: Was it really alive, or was this just the nerves reacting although it was actually dead? Most believed it was still alive, and the question for them was: Could it still recover if it were treated with care, or would it be more humane to put it out of its misery by killing it immediately? Finally, by a substantial majority, it was decided to abandon the dissection and to re-secure the chrysalis in its hanging position in the hope that only minor damage had been inflicted and that it would continue its invisible process of metamorphosis in the normal way. Nir, it should be recorded, agreed with the majority view. Some days later, a butterfly emerged from the rescued chrysalis, but unfortunately, one wing was damaged and it was unable to fly away with the others.

Reflecting on the Observed Events

The episodes just recounted occurred toward the end of the school year in this sixth grade classroom, and for all participants—students as well as teacher-researchers—they marked a significant breakthrough. For the students, "schoolwork" suddenly became a matter of engaging concern: In discussing whether to go ahead with the dissection of the chrysalis, both emotion and intellect were fully engaged. For the teacher-researchers, it was significant in a different way. It certainly confirmed our belief that inquiry-oriented activities could provide authentic and powerful occasions for all to learn. At the same time, it prompted a considerable amount of critical reflection, as we sought to identify the factors that had led to this outcome.

There was no doubt in our minds that the class discussions that had taken place around the proposal to dissect the chrysalis were different in important ways from other discussions that had taken place in the classroom earlier in the year. In debating whether to carry out the dissection, students presented alternative positions and argued for and against them, using explanations and analogies based on cause-effect relationships; they tried to persuade each other of the rightness of their positions, seeking to achieve a consensus on the action to be taken; and they spontaneously responded to each other without waiting to be nominated by the teacher. In other words, their discussion constituted a seriously undertaken collective attempt to solve a problem on the basis of informed consideration of the alternative options.

Initially, it seemed somewhat surprising that the fate of a painted lady chrysalis could be so engaging when other, apparently more intellectually challenging, topics, such as the structure of our solar system or the development of ways of measuring time, had earlier failed to be so. However, as the teacher and I reflected on the relative success of the different science units that the class had undertaken during the year, certain features suggested themselves as potentially significant.

For one thing, over the course of the year, both teacher and students had begun to feel more comfortable with the exploration of issues to which there was no predetermined correct answer. Moreover, the students had also been encouraged to ask questions and to seek answers to them themselves, rather than passively accepting someone else's judgment about what they should know. This active seeking to understand was clearly an important ingredient on the present occasion. Nir's proposal to dissect the chrysalis sprang from a "real" question. He genuinely wanted to know how a caterpillar changed into a butterfly without any intervention from outside the chrysalis, and quite a number of his peers were drawn into his desire to understand.

However, Nir's intellectual curiosity could not have been the only significant factor on this occasion. Earlier in the year, he had been equally interested in the relationship between the earth's daily rotation on its axis and the system of international time zones. But his enthusiasm—and the ingenious way he found of representing his solution to the problem (described in detail in Wells, 1993)—had not then aroused the same sort of animated discussion. The difference here, it seemed, was that Nir's question about the chrysalis and his proposed way of answering it had engaged his fellow students' feelings. Although small and insignificant, the chrysalis was a living creature and might be capable of feeling pain; furthermore, its development was in some ways similar to that of a human fetus. In short, the issue of what action to take was not only an intellectual matter of selecting an appropriate research method but one with profound ethical ramifications about which his peers cared deeply. It was the combination of all these factors, we hypothesized, that had changed the nature of discussion and kept everyone fully involved long after the bell signaled the end of the school day.

Nevertheless, successful though this event had been in all these ways, it still left many unanswered questions. In particular, we were left wondering how events of this kind could be brought about on a more regular basis. At the beginning of the year, such open-ended but focused discussions would have been impossible. What had changed about the classroom ethos that enabled them to happen now? Similarly, if emotional involvement is such an important ingredient of engaged learning, how can a teacher create the conditions for this sort of learning to occur? In the case of the chrysalis, this had not been deliberately sought for; in fact, without Nir's contribution, it would probably not have happened at all. But are there ways of setting up curricular topics so that students will be led into fruitful wonderings of this sort, and are there principles for organizing the classroom regime so that their questions can become the engine that powers the activities that take place? Equally important, how can this more exploratory approach to learning and teaching be reconciled with the requirements imposed by a prestructured curriculum and closely specified learning outcomes?

In general terms, the conclusion that we in DICEP have currently reached is that the force that drives the enacted curriculum must be a pervasive spirit of inquiry, and the dominant purpose of all activities must be an increase in understanding. It is this conviction that underlies all the inquiries reported in this book. However, as we have also come to realize, there is no straightforward, universal method of achieving these goals. Not only will the appropriate strategies differ according to the age of the students and the topics to be investigated but, more importantly, they will depend upon the particular mix of participants that makes up the classroom community, each with his or her interests and aptitudes and a particular history of personal experiences associated with gender, class, and ethnolinguistic background.

Each classroom is thus unique. And so, if teachers are to create communities that work collaboratively toward shared goals while valuing diversity of opinion and personal learning style and, at the same time, are to foster individual initiative and creativity, they also must approach the task in a spirit of inquiry. Not only should the teacher join in the students' inquiries, but he or she should also use these occasions to learn about the students themselves and about the conditions that enable them to develop, both as individuals and collectively as a community. In fact, teacher and students together must become a *community of inquiry* with respect to all aspects of the life of the classroom and all areas of the curriculum.

EMBARKING ON COLLABORATIVE ACTION RESEARCH

This commitment to the creation of classroom communities of inquiry was not where DICEP started. As I have explained, our beginnings were much more tentative and exploratory, with the first year being less than completely satisfactory. In the second year, we decided to try a different approach. Through the M.Ed. program at OISE, we advertised a seminar-workshop for teachers interested in an inquiry approach to science. Five teachers signed up, including the teacher of the class just described. This was the true beginning of the collaborative research group, as all members were volunteers and were committed to carrying out action research. Starting with regular meetings over a period of several months, we read and discussed articles about science, social constructivist thinking, and classroom research. Just as important, we also talked about significant events that had occurred in the participating teachers' classrooms, such as the one described above, and began to make recorded observations and to analyze the transcripts of the talk that occurred.

One article that we read had a particularly strong influence on our thinking: "Learning to Teach by Uncovering Our Assumptions" by Judith Newman (1987). Newman encouraged us to be open to being surprised by "critical incidents," including well-laid plans that went awry and activities that took off beyond our expectations. As she suggested, by reflecting on the mismatch between our expectations and what actually transpired, we had a basis for thinking and acting differently on future occasions. Such reflection on our practices together, based on video and audio recordings, also helped us gain a better understanding of the principles underlying effective learning and teaching.

In the course of these meetings, a number of things became clearer. First, if classrooms were to become places where students were actively and enthusiastically attempting to construct answers to questions that were of real interest to them—rather than simply going through the routines of "doing school"—more would be needed than the introduction of prepackaged inquiry activities, taken from teachers' manuals or downloaded from the Internet. Useful though such materials might be as starting points, they, too, would have to be used by the teacher in an exploratory manner, with a willingness to depart from them in response to students' developing interests and a desire to find out how to stimulate such interests where they did not emerge spontaneously.

Second, from viewing and discussing videotapings from participants' classrooms, we became convinced that a great deal hinged on being able to change habitual patterns of interaction in the classroom, with their built-in assumptions that it was teachers, not students, who were entitled to ask questions and that such questions should be ones to which there were correct answers, already known by the teacher. These assumptions stifled genuine exploratory discussion; they also contradicted the message we were implicitly trying to convey, namely, that really interesting questions rarely had simple answers and that, for this reason, it was well worth considering alternative proposals and carrying out research to put them to the test.

However, it is one thing to see what needs to be changed and quite another to find ways to achieve the hoped-for results. Not only do schools, as institutions, have established patterns of organization—from the arrangement of furniture to unrelenting timetables—that make it difficult to depart from traditional practices, but both teachers and students have been enculturated into roles and routines that are often hard to break. When the way forward is not known in advance, it takes courage as well as imagination, and a willingness to make, and learn from, mistakes. In some cases, pressures from outside the schools further add to the problems experienced, as the demands for greater accountability increase and parents express uncertainty about approaches to curriculum that are very different from those that they themselves experienced.

All these considerations underlined the need for us to adopt an explicit action research stance in our attempts to introduce inquiry into the classroom and prompted us to extend the scope of our collaborative endeavors. This we did in a number of ways. First, in requesting a continuation of support for a second three-year phase of the project, we undertook to explore how inquiry could be introduced in other areas of the curriculum, in addition to science. Second, we undertook to add a focus on written discourse, but treated as a complement to spoken discourse rather than as a separate activity. And third, we agreed to invite other classroom teachers to join the group, in effect more than doubling the total number of members. By 1996, there were 10 teacher members and also a number of graduate students in addition to the 3 university researchers.

But the most important innovation was a change in our whole approach to constructing the proposal requesting support for the second phase of our research. Traditionally, proposals for research in education are written by university researchers, who not only formulate the questions to be addressed but also specify the target population to be studied and the methods to be used in data collection and analysis. We argued, however, that if the research is to be truly collaborative, none of these issues should be decided by the university researchers alone; they should be negotiated among all the members of the group, once it had become established. It was with some trepidation that we put forward these arguments for an open-ended investigation, and it was no doubt with some uncertainty on the part of the funding institution that they approved the proposal. Phase 2 began in the school year 1994–1995.

BUILDING COMMUNITIES OF INQUIRY

It would be misleading to suggest that collaborative action research is straight-forward and free of tensions, a point that is made clear in this volume's con-cluding chapter by Monica McGlynn-Stewart (see also Newman, 1998). Our attempts at collective planning and decision making have not always been easy, and there have been occasions when the commitment made to the fund-ing agency to carry out a systematic study of discourse was felt by individual members as a digression from their own research interests, if not as an ac-tual imposition (McGlynn-Stewart, 1998). However, two actions taken early in the second phase were important, in more than symbolic ways, in estab-lishing this new form of school-university collaboration. The first was the decision to have a rotating chairperson for our monthly meetings, with the agenda for each meeting being constructed by the incoming chair on the basis of proposals received from all members of the group. The second was the choice of a new name for the project, chosen through an extended process of discussion in meetings and via our e-mail network.

The name finally chosen, Developing Inquiring Communities in Edu-cation Project, made clear the breadth of our concerns. It also emphasized our conviction that inquiry was not only relevant to learning in schools; it applied equally to university classrooms, to preservice and in-service teacher development and, most important, to the work of our own group. In the chapters that follow, there are references to the ways in which we have benefited from occasions of collaborative knowledge building within our community, including informal discussions immediately following a class-room event, collaborative interpretations of videotaped episodes, responses to individual reports of work-in-progress presented at our monthly meet-ings, joint preparation of conference presentations, coauthoring of papers for publication, as well as the ongoing dialogue via e-mail.

At this point it might be helpful to describe in more detail the way in which one of our group investigations was chosen, taken up in individual inquiries, and explored collaboratively within the group. In order to con-struct this account, I went back and reviewed the minutes of our monthly meetings, transcripts of recordings of two of our meetings, and the e-mail discussion that took place around the theme chosen for investigation—in all, several hundred pages of data. Where I have included verbatim quo-tations from this material, I have used pseudonyms for the contributors.

Tracking the Development of a Group Investigation

At our meeting in June 1995, after a year in which we had pursued "indi-vidual inquiries with mutual support," it was proposed that, in the coming year, we should work on a shared topic. The minutes note that this proposal received enthusiastic endorsement by the group, and there was considerable interest in exploring "journal writing." By the September meeting, however, the enthusiasm for focusing on journals had abated considerably, and we were unable to agree on a common focus.

Then, starting on the evening of the meeting and continuing over the following weeks, a vigorous discussion ensued in the medium of e-mail. The initial contributions reemphasized the desire to find a common focus:

> I think that our individual inquiries have been great, but there were many times last year when I really wished that we could discuss issues in more depth—both personally and via e-mail. While we are all well-read, thoughtful individuals and we contribute a great deal to each other's inquiries, I think there's a power to collaborative work that we haven't even begun to explore. . . . Is there a way that we can come up with a topic that is broad enough to include everyone's interests, but specific enough to allow us to: make our research plans together, discuss details, share theoretical literature, and maybe come up with some group findings? (Martha, 21 Sept.)

> I support Linda's argument that whatever we do should tie into our present experiences and be of benefit to the students that we teach and to our own personal inquiries. I like the idea of using DICEP to further the students' learning by sharing with them the observations and comments we generate from samples of their work. (Bill, 22 Sept.)

> . . . the theme of "Learning through Writing" and also the aspect of community. I, too, would like to explore the possibilities of "homing in" on this theme and finding some ways to collaborate as a team and do some "knowledge building" together. (Veronica, 22 Sept.)

A few days later, the discussion was significantly advanced by a two-part message from Linda, a teacher in an inner-city school. In the first part, she suggested we consider two specific questions and added her reasons for proposing them:

> 1. How is writing (or written discourse as some might wish to frame it) used as a tool for learning and/or thinking and/or understanding and/or social action in each of our classroom communities?

2. How would or could I systematically conduct an inquiry on an aspect of whatever my answer is to question 1?

I feel that if our contributions are to be significant, one aspect of our efforts could be reconceptualizing & reseeing practices and theory. Individually and as a group we are not only committed but thoughtful educators. What emerges from our responses to the two questions and the process will be, I bet, exciting because we have some very exciting & significant practices going on in all our classrooms as well as common patterns & trends because we share common learning-teaching beliefs & theories. Our practice is theory in action, and this will enable us to strike & identify common "plans." Last but not least, this process will enable our "plans" to emerge and be rooted in practice which in turn is subjected to joint inquiry, conversations & reflections. (27 Sept.)

In the second part, Linda described an event in her Grade 6/7 class that illustrated her suggestion:

I have noticed that [in class discussions] it was often the same few who would participate enthusiastically while the rest sat & listened. Yet inside me I know that there is the possibility that the latter have things to say. . . . I conjectured that perhaps if writing is used as a tool for what I call "rehearsal thinking," would our oral discourse be one in which more will participate as well as more substantive? My conjecture, in part, is due to my beliefs in the value of writing and, in part, to experiences as a teacher & learner. So I decided to use writing as a tool for individual thinking before embarking on a class discussion.

   I asked my students to complete the following prompt "Science is . . . . " in their learning logs. I also informed them that they would be asked to read what they wrote to the rest of the class.. After hearing everybody's responses they would have the opportunity to add two sentences to their original responses.

   The consequences were amazing. First the pool of ideas surprised me. They reflected some very solid understanding of what science is or is not but more significantly the follow-up discussion had everyone participating. They were responding to each other, debating & offering counter arguments or examples. The level of our oral discourse was indeed sophisticated verging on philosophical, for example, Marta asked, "Is language science?" What do I make out of all this?

It also provided the less confident, like some of my ESL kids, a chance to "see their own thinking" & therefore feel more confident in being able to "read out their thoughts" rather than having to respond not only spontaneously but at the turn-taking speed of oral discourse. Another is that writing slowed down own's thinking, making it more deliberate & intentional allowing one the "space" to be more thoughtful, making one's thinking visible for review & changes. Very significantly, writing provided everyone a "same-time" turn & therefore increased dramatically the pool of knowledge which linear turn-taking in oral discourse does not.

Also, my intention behind the provision of the opportunity to add two more sentences to one's own ideas, having heard from others, is to model the recognition of how our knowledge is often coconstructed & that this is in fact valuable. (27 Sept.)

This example met with an enthusiastic reception. Consequently, building on the various suggestions that had been made, I prepared a first draft of an approach we might take to the two questions that Linda had proposed. This plan was sketched in very general terms so that it could be included in members' individual inquiries. At the same time, it indicated a focus on writing, not as finished product, but as a tool to be used in some superordinate activity. It also indicated an expectation that action and talk would be intimately connected to the written text. The plan was approved at the October meeting, and individual members outlined the ways in which they intended to put it into effect in the contexts of their programs.

Space does not allow me to describe in detail any of the very interesting projects that were carried out under this umbrella research theme (but see Hume, Chapter 6, and Haneda & Wells, 2000, for some examples). They included writing in activities related to literature, math, science, and history; writing carried out collaboratively as well as solo; and writing on Post-it notes, in the form of webs and charts, as well as in logbooks. Over the next few months, a major part of each of our monthly meetings was given over to individual members presenting reports on their investigations, often including video clips, examples of students' writing, and transcripts of extracts from discussion. In turn, these provoked wide-ranging discussion in our group, in which important insights were gained about the relationships between action, talk, and text, and connections were made to related activities in our different classrooms. For example, a presentation at the December meeting had included a description of how students were responding to a story read aloud, in writing and in discussion, using the cues "retell, relate, and reflect" (Schwartz & Bone, 1995). The discussion that followed produced this insight on the role of the teacher in classroom response:

You have this high incidence of "reflecting" and "relating" in your oral discussion. I think it is [specific to] your class, because I don't think it's a given that that will happen in any class, because your key word . . .—you say to them "Some of you might have some thoughts about that." You use the word "thoughts" and everybody starts to say "I think ." That's a very powerful suggestion, because when you give that prompt, you're actually scaffolding them and engaging priorities, whereas if I were a teacher who never used that kind of prompt, then I think the children would be operating at a very different level. Whereas in writing, they do not have that sort of scaffolding. They're on their own. So it's only over time that they engage a lot of higher order thinking in the oral mode and only slowly that it comes across in writing. So I think the role of the teacher talking, her role leads to a lot of reflection and the children being able to relate to it. (Linda, 4 Dec.)

In the same meeting, the issue of the tendency for the teacher to act as the hub in discussion—both nominating speakers and providing a follow-up to their contributions – surfaced as one that needed to be made the subject of future action research. In fact, this became a central theme for Zoe Donoahue's inquiry (Donoahue, 1998a, 1998b). It also became a focus for systematic analysis of the discourse data collected across all members' classrooms (Nassaji & Wells, 2000). As is apparent, the decision to adopt a common theme had valuable consequences for the group as a whole, as well as for individual members.

Spreading the Word: School-Based Inquiry Groups

Most of the chapters that follow describe the inquiries carried out by individual members of the group, either solo or in collaboration with one of the university members. Naturally, these are specific to the concerns of particular classroom communities and to the developing professional and personal interests of the teachers concerned. This brief overview would not be complete, however, without mention of the third dimension on which we have attempted to build communities of inquiry, namely, with teacher colleagues working within the same institutions.

There is little doubt that long-term change and improvement in the ways in which educational institutions function requires more than the innovations introduced through the actions of individual staff members, although these can certainly have beneficial effects beyond the walls of their own classrooms. Numerous attempts have been made to bring about change through reform initiatives introduced from outside. Some of these have achieved substantial results—as long as the external change agents continued to provide leadership and support. In the long term, however, for change to become institutionalized it must be appropriated by those who are involved on a continuing basis, and enacted in the moment-by-moment decisions that make up daily classroom practice.

Several DICEP teachers were successful in initiating communities of inquiry among their colleagues although, interestingly, the goals of the different communities as well as their members' reasons for participating varied considerably from school to school (Shechter, 1998). In some cases, the motivation was principally the members' desire to improve their individual teaching practices (Hume, 1998), whereas in others the goal was to change or coordinate practices on a school-wide basis (Donoahue, 1996). Independently of the success achieved by the different groups, however, what these differences emphasize once again is the importance of recognizing the diversity of learners' interests and motives and of making these the basis for working towards a mutually acceptable and productive mode of collaborative inquiry.

CONSTRUCTING A COMMON FRAMEWORK FOR INQUIRY

In our work over the years, the DICEP group has continued to find the writings of other teacher-researchers to be a valuable source of ideas, and we have been helped by the writings of such educational action researchers as Carr and Kemmis (1983), Elliott (1991), and Hubbard and Power (1993). We have also read and discussed chapters and articles that enabled us to deepen our understanding of a social constructivist approach to education (Moll, 1990; Vygotsky, 1978), activity theory (Engeström, 1991; Leont'ev, 1981), and systemic functional linguistics (Christie & Martin, 1997; Halliday & Hasan, 1985; Lemke, 1993). Chapter 10 reviews much of this work, in particular those developments in ways of thinking about knowing and coming to know and the roles of discourse in these processes that we have found particularly helpful. Although each of us has drawn on a wide range of additional reading for our own investigations, we have also attempted to develop a common framework for analysis and discussion that draws on the sources mentioned above. In this section, I explain briefly how this framework helps us to think about our action research in creating communities of inquiry.

The impetus to develop this framework came generally from the need to explain what we were attempting to do when writing for other educators. But the specific occasion was the need, in the fall of 1996, to respond to a letter from the funding agency's program officer who was responsible for our project. She asked us: Just how do the various parts of your project fit together, and how are your specific inquiries contributing to the understanding and improvement of education? Composing a response to this question was a task that we tackled collaboratively over several months, again using e-mail as well as discussing drafts in our meetings. The following paragraphs are based on the reply that was eventually sent to the program officer.

A Model and Rationale for Educational Action Research

In much policy-based discussion of teaching, it is common to talk about practice being driven by theory. What is envisaged is a hierarchical relationship, in which experts outside the classroom develop the theory, which is then formulated as recommendations that teachers are expected or required to implement. However, this view of the relationship is neither appropriate nor desirable (Stenhouse, 1975) and the history of reform efforts has shown it to be quite unrealistic (Fullan, 1992). One reason for this is that every classroom is unique in respect to the persons it brings together, the resources available to them, and the constraints under which they operate. This means that any theory of pedagogy or curriculum necessarily has to be adapted and modified according to local conditions.

There is, however, a much more fundamental reason for the failure of top-down reform, namely, that the relationship between academic theory and the practice of teaching is much less direct than the implementation model implies. The theory that guides teachers' practice is typically based much more on personal practical knowledge (Connelly & Clandinin, 1985) and on professional wisdom than on the findings of university-based research. It is also heavily imbued with values and is integral to a teacher's personal identity. Although the theory may be tacit rather than explicitly formulated, it nevertheless influences what aspects of classroom life a teacher treats as most important and provides her or him with a point of reference in decision making and problem solving. For this reason, we refer to this practice-based orientation as the teacher's *vision*. If educational theory is to have an impact on practice, it must enter into discourse with individual teachers' visions, as it is this vision that guides their daily practice.

However, a further problem lies in the traditional assumption that the relationship between theory and practice is unidirectional. In our view, theory should not only seek to influence practice, it should also grow out of and be informed by practice. One way in which this can happen is through critical investigations of the relationship between vision and practice carried out by practitioners in their own classrooms. In this sort of investigation, it is not theoretical generalization that is the principal object in view, but rather an improved enactment of vision in practice and an increased understanding of the ends and means of education, as these are realized in the particular conditions of the teachers' own classrooms. In this context—as we have found—theory is most useful as a set of tools for systematically describing and interpreting the data derived from observation of practice.

These, then, are the four components of our conceptual model : *vision, practice, theory,* and *data.* The following paragraphs spell out in more detail the ways in which we have put them together to describe our conception of educational action research. Then, in several of the following chapters, readers will find examples of the ways in which we have interpreted them in the actual conduct of our inquiries.

Vision. Although we might each express them somewhat differently, the goals at which the members of DICEP aim include:

- Creating communities characterized by inclusiveness, equity, and caring, as well as by intellectual achievement
- Giving a high priority to knowledge building and understanding through inquiry, while not neglecting the routine processes and skills needed to engage in them
- Encouraging collaboration between teacher and students, as well as among students—valuing and building, whenever possible, on students' contributions to the activity in progress, so that knowledge is coconstructed, rather than unilaterally delivered
- Broadening interests and recognizing and valuing the contributions of experts beyond the classroom—bringing the classroom community into a two-way relationship with communities beyond the classroom (local/worldwide, practical/intellectual) by participating in their practices
- Acknowledging and taking into account that, whatever the activity, the whole person is always involved (body, mind, feelings, values)
- Providing for the growth and self-determination of each individual as well as for the development of the classroom community as a whole

Practice. While we can work toward agreement about the vision, we necessarily differ with respect to the specifics of practice because of the unique combination of participants and conditions with which we each work. This highlights the crucial difference between vision and practice. Vision is essentially abstract and synoptic; practice is dynamic, realized in the successive decisions and actions of unique individuals and communities in relation to the possibilities and constraints of their specific material, social, and intellectual environments. Although there is clearly a relationship between vision and practice, it is not a simple one, such as is suggested by the term *implementation*. However, it is toward understanding this relationship, as well as toward optimizing the learning opportunities created in practice, that our individual and collaborative inquiries are directed.

Theory. Theory can be looked at in two ways. On the one hand, a theory is an artifact created in the process of knowledge building in collaboration with others, including thinkers of the past whose ideas live on in their writings. From this perspective, it is produced in, and is the outcome of, attempting to make sense of the diversity of one's own and other people's particular dynamic experiences with the help of a model that attempts to explain by reference to more general categories and relationships. On the other hand, a theory is a tool for use in action. From this perspective, it is only valuable to the extent that it enables us to better understand and plan for the situations we find ourselves in so that we are able to act more effectively. As a tool, it has two functions. First, it provides a systematic means for interpreting the data derived through observation of practice and through the collection of related artifacts of various kinds. And second, the theories we construct in collaboration with others give greater explicitness and coherence to the personal visions that guide our practice. Furthermore, theories are improvable objects, and as educators, we are committed to improving the theories that we use to interpret and evaluate our practice as well as the practice itself.

Data. Like theory, data are also artifacts; they are outcomes of specific activities that, deliberately collected, represent some aspect(s) of those activities. They are thus evidence of the nature of practice. Their value lies in the fact that, like written texts, they continue to exist after the activity is over and can therefore be revisited and analyzed from perspectives derived from theory. In our case, the data we have collected consist of videotapes of classroom activities, written texts of various kinds, interviews, e-mail discussions, and tape recordings of parts of our meetings.

Data stand to theory rather as practice stands to vision. Where vision and theory tend to be abstract and general, practice and data are specific and dynamic. However, there is another way of considering them: theory and data, considered as a functional system, can be thought of together as a tool that mediates understanding of the relationship between vision and practice. That is to say, by using theory to analyze and interpret the data we collect in our inquiries, we are able to evaluate how far our practice matches our vision and, on that basis, to plan necessary changes; at the same time, the increased understanding achieved leads to clarification and enrichment of the vision. This process will, we hope, become clearer in the following chapters.

Spelling out this conceptual model gives substance to the procedural model of action research proposed in earlier work (Carr & Kemmis, 1983; Wells, 1994) inasmuch as the four components just described map directly onto the four "moments" in the cycle of action research: *plan, act, observe*, and *interpret*. At the heart of the resulting framework is individual and collective understanding, where *understanding* is construed as "knowing that is oriented to action of personal and social significance and to the continual enriching of the framework within which future experience will be interpreted" (Wells, 1999). These relationships are represented in Figure 1.1.

One of the strengths of this overall framework, we believe, is that it was constructed on the basis of what the DICEP group was already doing. In that sense, it is theory growing out of practice and, at the same time, illuminating practice. Maria Kowal, who was not able to take part in the original discussion, subsequently commented as follows:

> For me, as well as being descriptive of our actions and way of looking at research, [the model] enriches the notion of teacher-researcher. Many others have described action research cycles (e.g., Lewin, Kemmis and Carr, McNiff) but the components—vision, practice, theory, data—show that the teacher-researcher is not just following the action research cycle but is a contextualized individual, with a belief system which influences the action research cycles. S/he is contributing to and constructing theory, based on practice and the data collected. For me, this is a much richer construct of the teacher-researcher, and more accurate of what we have experienced. I think too, that in terms of "research" in general, it adds more legitimacy to the notion of teacher-researcher. (e-mail, 26 Jan. 2000)

An important feature of the model of action research is that the relationships it represents are not unidirectional. As several authors in this volume note, investigations of practice can lead to clarifications and enrichments of vision, and analyses of data can lead to development and/or modifications of the theory, as well as vice versa. In this way, the model rejects the traditional direct hierarchical relationship between theory and practice by substituting one that more adequately captures the complex dialectic among the four components and that better expresses the ethos of collaborative knowledge building that characterizes educational action research carried out in communities of inquiry. Equally important, each

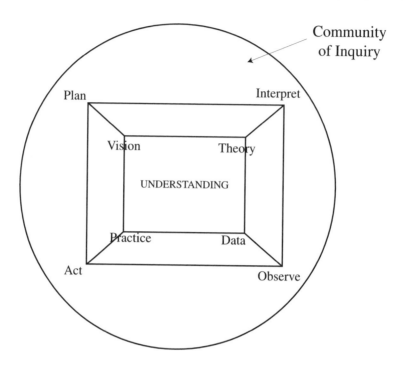

Figure 1.1. Model of Action Research

individual member decides both on what question to investigate and on where to enter the cycle.

Our hope is that, by sharing the framework that we have constructed for our research as well as by presenting some of the results of our inquiries, we can contribute to the dialogue among educators about how best to achieve their vision in an effective and responsible manner. At the same time, we hope that this collection of reports of teachers' action research will open up a more productive interchange between educational practitioners and those who have the responsibility for setting educational policy and overseeing its enactment.

OVERVIEW OF BOOK

The remainder of this book is divided into three parts. The first two parts consist of individual reports, organized in terms of the ages of the students involved. The third part provides the theoretical background for our work and also a retrospective review of the DICEP project. This section can be read first or last or at any point in between.

Two central themes run through this book. These are our attempts, through practice-based inquiry and reflection, to answer two overarching questions:

- How can teachers create and sustain communities of inquiry in their classrooms?
- What kinds of discourse promote and extend inquiry and enable participants to transform their individual and collective understandings?

Part I explores these questions in the context of the primary grades. Zoe Donoahue investigates the particular contribution of regular class meetings to the building of community in her second grade classroom, and also in Grade 2, Mary Ann Van Tassell describes her early attempts to use children's questions to develop an inquiry orientation in her science program. Greta Davis combines both these perspectives as she compares the discussions that occurred in her Grade 3 class meetings with those that followed her serialized reading aloud of a novel. In the final chapter of this part, Gordon Wells investigates a three-way discussion of a science experiment, in which he was involved as a visiting teacher, and seeks an explanation of his failure to give due credit to the contributions of one of the students. By analyzing nonverbal as well as verbal behavior, he shows how important a role the former plays in face-to-face interaction.

Part II concerns work with older students in the intermediate and secondary grades. Like many other DICEP teachers, Karen Hume also started with science and the part played by discourse in her students' learning. In order to complement the hands-on investigations her students carried out, she created the "knowledge wall" as a public arena in which they could explore their questions through the medium of dialogic writing. Maria Kowal tackles inquiry in history and explores the effectiveness of a simulated Supreme Court Land Claims Hearing to enable her students to gain a deeper understanding of the issues at stake. Monica McGlynn-Stewart focuses on an exploration of leadership with high school students; as she found, students at this stage do not all take easily to an inquiry-oriented approach, and she had to go through several cycles of action research to find ways of meeting their needs and concerns. Not all students value discussion either, it seems, even in Grades 6 and 7. In response to the objections of one such student, Karen Hume invited those students who were interested to engage in a coinvestigation of the features of their class discussions that were proving either helpful or unhelpful, and she reports what they came to understand in the process.

Part III provides two kinds of commentary on the preceding sections. First, Gordon Wells develops the argument for the inquiry approach the DICEP group has adopted, by bringing together key ideas in current thinking about learning and development and the roles that collaborative meaning making play in these processes. Although not explicitly referred to in all the preceding chapters, these ideas have frequently been discussed in our monthly meetings and in our e-mail conversations and, in these ways, have become the orienting assumptions that underpin our individual inquiries. Then, in the final chapter, Monica McGlynn-Stewart presents a retrospective review of DICEP. She posed the question "What has it been like to be a member of DICEP?" and then compiled the answers she received from her teacher colleagues. As might be expected, she found that members' experiences of participation included frustrations as well as satisfactions. However, the fact that the group still continues and plans to embark on further collaborative projects is strong evidence that collaborative action research is not only rewarding in itself, but it is also a way of being in the classroom that allows us to continue to work to improve our schools, even in the face of external constraints.

PART I

Inquiries in the Elementary Grades

CHAPTER 2

An Examination of the Development of Classroom Community Through Class Meetings

Zoe Donoahue

CONDUCTING RESEARCH into my classroom practice has become an integral part of my teaching over the past 10 years. Inquiring about questions that intrigue me was initially a requirement for master's level courses. Then, through an action research course near the end of my studies, I was fortunate to meet up with others—classroom teachers, a research officer, graduate students, and university professors—who were interested in forming an action research group and continuing their inquiries once the course finished. Over the next few years our membership changed and expanded, and a name was decided upon: Developing Inquiring Communities in Education Project (DICEP).

One year, we decided that the group's research focus for the whole year would be on the development of community in our various settings. At the time I was teaching a Grade 2 class of 28 children. My school was located in an upper-middle-class neighborhood. Almost all the children spoke English as their first language. There were about 650 students in the school, and the population was stable from year to year. The children in my class displayed a range of behaviors, abilities, and learning styles. Several children had been labeled as gifted, and a couple had identified learning disabilities. Some worked independently, while others needed a great deal of teacher direction. Some were very responsible; others were learning to take greater responsibility for their behavior.

THE CLASSROOM AS A COMMUNITY

> I believe a community of learners is formed as learners come to know each other and value what each other has to offer. We commit to sharing responsibility and control, establishing a learning atmosphere that is predictable, yet full of real choices. As we learn through action, reflection and demonstration, the focus is on being problem posers as well as problem solvers through the process of inquiry.
> —Kathy G. Short & Carolyn Burke, *Creating Curriculum*

During 14 years of teaching in elementary schools, the idea of the classroom as a community had become central to my teaching. For that reason, the focus that our group had chosen was of great interest to me. At the beginning of each year, I consciously try to establish a strong classroom community in collaboration with the children. I hope to build a community that is unique and possesses special characteristics. The children need to know that their voices will be heard and that their ideas and opinions will be asked for and valued. The atmosphere must be supportive of children who have various strengths and interests and are at different levels of development. Each child must know that he or she is a respected member of the community, with an important role to play.

Our community aims to be a community of inquiry, where children make choices, ask questions, and find answers, and where we work together to reflect on and improve ourselves and the classroom program. I attempt to realize my vision in my choice of classroom practices. Children choose the books they read, their own topics for story writing, and where they will sit each day. Along with their parents and me, they set goals each term and, during interviews, they take an active role in discussing their progress. Each week they complete a written self-evaluation that asks for their thoughts and feelings about their learning and our community. The children keep a literacy portfolio with work samples that tell about their development as readers and writers. They examine their work, reflect on their progress, and set further goals. Children are also encouraged to take risks and to support one another in their endeavors. I have always felt that class meetings play an important role in helping us to achieve this vision of a community of inquiry, so I welcomed the opportunity to look closely at the relationship between class meetings, my classroom practices, and the development of my vision of a classroom community.

CLASS MEETINGS: HOW AND WHY

Class meetings have been a part of my classroom routine since they were introduced to me during an in-service series during my first few years of teaching. Since then, they have occurred in my Grade 2 classroom for about half an hour on the last day of the school week. The meetings are never canceled, so that the children can depend on their occurrence, and they take place on a weekly basis, so that we can celebrate what we have done, rather than meeting only when there are problems.

The meetings are divided into three parts. First, the children celebrate *positives*—something they enjoyed, are getting better at, or that has gone well. Then they list *reminders*—anything they need to remember to do relating to routines, special events, or bringing items to and from school. Next we deal with *business* items—something the children would like to change or start doing, a question, a problem, or a situation that has been bothering them.

Both children and the teacher can raise business items for discussion. The person who has the concern explains the situation, and everyone brainstorms solutions. If the issue has two sides, several children are invited to express their feelings about each viewpoint. When necessary, a vote is taken. I resist contributing my ideas or opinions, except when an issue involves safety, is very serious, or is nonnegotiable. We also look back at the previous week's agenda to follow up on business items and to evaluate how well what we decided to do is working. We then rediscuss items that need our attention. Over the first part of the year it usually becomes apparent that there are three different kinds of business items: those problems that can be solved with a definite answer or consequence; those that have a number of solutions that can be tried; and those with which we will constantly be wrestling.

This year, as in the past, I scheduled our inaugural class meeting on the first Friday of the school year, so that the children would begin to see the meetings as an important and regular part of our week. Initially, some children seemed surprised that their input would be sought and did not seem accustomed to thinking about and reflecting upon their school experiences, making joint decisions, and solving problems collaboratively. After a few weeks, however, most children were eager to contribute their thoughts and feelings. Somewhat further into the school year, they trusted that class meetings and the classroom community were a safe place where they could raise concerns, make plans, and solve problems.

Class meetings fit well with my philosophy and vision for a classroom community because they provide opportunities for us to reflect on and celebrate what we have done and learned about each week; they are also a time for us to raise issues and concerns and solve problems together. Nelson (1981) emphasizes that "learning and practicing problem solving skills [at class meetings] is a benefit for students that will serve them in every important life endeavor" (p. 133). Class meetings "provide the best possible circumstances for adults and children to learn the democratic procedure of cooperation, mutual respect, and social interest" (p. 132). Developing these skills and working with these values as a class became an important part of our work together as a community of learners.

As Wells writes in Chapter 1, "the force that drives the enacted curriculum must be a pervasive spirit of inquiry, and the dominant purpose of all activities must be an increase in understanding." At class meetings, the children ask and seek answers to their own questions, and these questions are those to which the teacher does not know the answers. In collaborative endeavor, they have an opportunity to use their knowledge to solve problems. The children are emotionally involved because the questions are theirs. Those who are "experts," who have had more experience in discussing issues and generating possible solutions, can lead the others in this process. The teacher, too, can provide scaffolding and help the younger members of the community take part in problem solving. This is a time when "teacher talk" does not prevail; rather, the children initiate topics, discuss, and make decisions. We work together to find answers to the children's questions and together build increased understanding that contributes to the development of our community.

FOCUSING AND PLANNING MY RESEARCH

My questions, within the DICEP focus on community, were about identifying the important characteristics of a classroom community and about the values and expectations that are important when a classroom community is being formed. I wondered if I might find answers to my questions by examining our weekly class meetings.

In order to examine the topic of classroom community through class meetings, I decided to videotape them and to analyze the minutes that I kept of the meetings. Eventually, my data consisted of the videotapes and written minutes of 25 class meetings between September and April. Minutes were kept of each meeting on large sheets of chart paper. Some teachers have the children take responsibility for the role of secretary, but in order to keep the meetings moving, I recorded the minutes myself. The charts would hang on hooks at our group meeting area, so that the past week's sheet could be referred to between meetings. Because they were hanging in view, I hoped that the children might reread the charts and that further thought might be given to what we had talked about.

A number of elements that are important in classroom communities became apparent as I analyzed and categorized the items from our minutes: participation at class meetings, celebrations, volunteers and student teachers, attitudes toward schoolwork, work habits, behavior, routines, care of the environment, respecting the property and work of others, and social issues. As I analyzed the children's comments, I became aware of areas of the classroom program that were successful and others that needed to be changed or improved. Using class meetings to reflect on and improve the classroom program was also an important characteristic of our community.

Participation

When I watched the videotapes of our meetings, I realized that a small group of boys was listing most of the positives. I wanted our community to provide every child with an opportunity to participate and wondered how I could give the quieter children a protected space in which to talk. When my concern was raised at a DICEP meeting, a colleague suggested that the children sit in a circle, rather than in a cluster, and that all have a turn to list a positive or to "pass." We tried this and I noticed an immediate difference, as the more vocal children thought of better quality contributions when they knew they would have only one turn, and the quieter children knew when their turn was coming and had a chance to prepare what they wanted to say. In time, the children decided that those who passed should be given a chance to think further and to contribute a positive after we had been around the circle once. Watching our meetings on tape helped me involve more children in our meetings and strengthened our sense of community. Every child knew that his or her voice was valued and important; inviting all children to have a turn demonstrated our faith in their ability to make a contribution to our community through class meetings.

Volunteers and Student Teachers

On a number of occasions the children listed the participation of parent volunteers and student teachers in our community as a positive. In our school we were lucky to have student teachers who worked in classrooms over a period of several months, and to have a strong and committed group of parent volunteers. It was easy to take this extra help and support for granted, and the children's positive comments reminded us all how much richer and more interesting our community was when other adults could plan for and work with the whole class, small groups, and individuals.

The children's comments led us to discuss, at class meetings, ways in which we might thank volunteers and student teachers. We decided to write thank-you letters, to have surprise parties for student teachers, and to hold a Parent Appreciation Tea at the end of the school year. In turn, I reflected on how our community is more complete and better able to meet the needs of each child when other adults are involved with and helping to care for all of the children. For the next year, I planned to think of other ways to involve volunteers and student teachers in the life of our classroom.

Celebrations

Throughout the year the children mentioned special events, such as holiday parties, our Parent Appreciation Tea, and Open Houses at the end of a unit of work, as positives. In turn, we used class meetings to collaboratively plan this type of event, including details such as food, decorations, and activities. As the year went on, the children would suggest that we schedule a special event and they began to take greater responsibility for both the planning and the running of our celebrations. These events had, of course, been enjoyed by all as they occurred, but having a place to plan them and to reminisce about them after the fact demonstrated how important celebrations, such as bringing closure to units of work and thanking classroom volunteers, were to the life of our community.

Attitudes Toward Schoolwork and Work Habits

After we had been together for about a month, the children started listing their attitude toward schoolwork as a positive. I interpreted this as a sign that they were beginning to feel the positive energy that is generated when everyone is involved with and interested in classroom activities. Reading workshop, a time at the beginning of each day when everyone reads silently, was often mentioned as a positive, and it was a time of day when I felt a strong sense of community. Each day I took great pleasure in scanning the room and watching children reading, nestled in corners, sitting on chairs with their chins in their hands, and lying on their stomachs on the carpet. It had taken some time to get to the point where every child was able to choose books that he or she could read quietly and independently for half an hour, without talking or leaving their chosen spot. The children's comments at class meetings illustrated their strong sense of efficacy about reading workshop and helped me see how important a consistent and successful morning routine can be toward the development of community.

The children also commented positively about their work habits. Work habits listed as positives included working hard, understanding assignments, bringing back homework, listening to instructions, moving away from distractions at group time, choosing seats responsibly, working independently, and concentrating. Their comments helped me see how the values and expectations that we talked about and practiced on a daily basis were becoming embedded in our sense of community.

Discussions about work habits were also part of the reminders and business sections of class meetings. The children reminded one another to ignore people who were asking for attention in inappropriate ways, to listen to one another, to move away from distractions, and to enter the classroom quietly when others were working. But reminders were often not enough, and issues relating to work habits would need to be placed on the agenda as business items.

An ongoing problem throughout the year was what children might do when someone was distracting them at group time or during a quiet work period. The children raised the issue as a business item and brainstormed a number of ideas that others could try. Discussing this issue led us to talk about how everyone in the community has a right to concentrate and learn without interference—an important value. I hoped that children would remind each other about our discussion when they were in the midst of telling someone to stop bothering them. Discussing problems as a class and listing possible solutions brought issues to a conscious level and was, I hoped, a springboard for children to be more articulate and assertive when stating their feelings to others.

We continually recognized and celebrated our successes and collaboratively dealt with problems as they arose. Our community was partly defined by the children's wonderful attitude toward their schoolwork and their developing efficacy about their work habits, and this was revealed during class meetings.

Routines

Routine matters were often mentioned during class meetings. This was understandable, as a great deal of time was spent at the beginning of the year establishing and encouraging children to follow routines, as well as discussing the need for them. When the children listed a routine as a positive—for example, the way that everyone was respecting our schedule for taking turns sitting on the couch—it also served as a reminder about the routine. Responsibility for remembering and reinforcing routines was shared by all members of the community.

Reminding each other about routines at class meetings also became a way for the children to work together on problems. Early in the year the children had missed most of a gym period because they could not work together and make a quiet line before we left the classroom. This experience was not lost on them and every week, beginning in Week 8, someone mentioned lining up quietly for gym as a positive. Significantly, we did not have a similar problem until Week 25, months later.

The children needed to understand and respect the reasons for having routines, and class meetings were an excellent place in which to collaboratively set up routines, negotiate and decide upon new routines, or make changes in routines as the need arose. Nelson (1981) stresses that "children will come up with the best solutions, and are most willing to cooperate when they are involved in the solutions" (p. 141). Early in the year, I let the children know that any routine with which they were unhappy could be discussed during the business part of the meeting and changes, if appropriate for them to decide, could be voted upon. They also learned that any decisions made at class meetings could be reversed at a later time.

An initial routine that we worked together to establish related to the children's choice of seats. I feel strongly that children should choose their seats each day, so I explained to them on the first day of school that this was a nonnegotiable routine. Within that routine, however, the children discussed how they would go about choosing their seats, when they would be allowed to change seats, and what they might do if two children laid claim to the same seat. Interestingly, once our routines were set, there was no record of us dealing with this issue again at a class meeting.

A second routine that we needed to establish collaboratively at the beginning of the year related to how the children would take turns sitting on the couch at our rug area. For the first few days, there was a sign on the couch telling the children that they could not sit there until we had decided upon a turn-taking system. At our first class meeting, the children decided that they wanted to form permanent "couch groups" and that each group would have a rotating turn to sit on the couch for an entire day. A couple of months later someone suggested, during the business part of the meeting, that we make up new couch groups. This happened again every couple of months. Negotiating these initial routines together was important in setting the tone for problem solving and joint decision making in our community.

Some problems were not solved as easily. An ongoing routine issue about which the children debated on a monthly basis was whether the communal pencils should be stored in one cup at the rug area or in caddies at their tables. We had started the year with pencils in the caddies, but the children soon voted to keep them in one cup. A couple of weeks later they had voted to use the caddies again. Despite the results of the vote, a group of children still wanted the pencils to be kept in one cup, and each month (we agreed to look at this issue only once a month), one of them would ask that we have yet another vote on this issue. Before the vote, several children from each side would be invited to state their position. When it came time to vote, I would ask the children to cover their eyes, as there is pressure to agree with a friend's vote when they can see one another. The group was persistent, but the pencils still remained in the caddies for the rest of the year. I do hope, however, that a message was conveyed to the children about how we can debate about and negotiate routines in our community.

During the first day or two of school, I used to ask for the children's input to create a list of classroom rules specifying how we should treat each other, work together, and care for the classroom. This year, I decided to do this work collaboratively with the children once our community had been together for a few weeks. At our fourth meeting, the children spontaneously listed many reminders about how they should work together in the classroom and how they should treat one another. That weekend I reflected on what they said and decided that this would be a good time to create the chart listing classroom rules.

We did this work together the following Monday, using the minutes from the meeting for reference and phrasing each issue in a positive way. Our chart was referred to for the rest of the year by both students and teachers and had a tremendous impact on the development of our community, giving us common standards for behavior and common language that we could use when talking to one another. Right away I noticed children admonishing each other while pointing to the chart: "Remember, keep your hands and your feet to yourself!" By creating this chart together, I felt that the children had more ownership of our community expectations. The ideas came from their class meeting reminders, so the list reflected ideas that were important to them.

Throughout the year, the children used class meetings as a place to initiate new routines in response to problems and situations they perceived as being unfair. They wanted systems in place so that everyone would get a fair share of turns on the computer, using the floor blocks, and turning the song book pages when they were singing along as I played the guitar. The issues were raised as business items, several possible routines were suggested, and a vote was taken. The children had a vested interest in following the routines that they created. They were necessary routines, designed to fit their needs, and could be changed or modified as needed.

The children's many comments about routines throughout the year made me wonder if they were beginning to realize how important having consistent and meaningful routines is toward the development of a cohesive community. Class meetings gave children the power to change, modify, and suggest new directions in the classroom. There was a legitimate forum for them to voice their opinions and vote on issues and ideas. They also had the security of knowing that I would make some decisions about non-negotiable issues. Class meetings provided us with the time and the opportunity to reflect on, add to, and, when necessary, modify and change our routines, and our community was stronger as a result of this work.

Care of the Environment

Issues relating to the care of the classroom environment, tidying up and keeping the classroom library organized, were mentioned as positives early in the year. This was another example of positive comments becoming reminders and self-fulfilling prophecies. Caring for the environment was a responsibility shared by all members of the community, and the children were proud of their efforts. This group was so good at noticing what needed to be done and working together to do it that I did not suggest that we assign classroom jobs, as I had always done in the past.

There were times when we needed to discuss issues about cleanliness, but I was usually the one to raise them. For example, the children had an ongoing problem keeping their coat hooks in the hall outside our classroom organized. Solutions were discussed several times over the year but unfortunately this was not a problem that troubled the children, and it was never resolved to my satisfaction. Issues at class meetings that were resolved most effectively were those that were initiated by and important to the children.

Respecting the Property and Work of Others

Partway through the year, as a business item, the children expressed concern that some of their classmates were not respecting others' work, specifically their creations in the block area. First, children expressed how they felt when their constructions were knocked down, then solutions and rules were brainstormed. In this case, the children decided to set a consequence for those who didn't follow the rules. This was an issue that needed to be revisited for several weeks running, as the problem persisted. The situation did improve, but was never completely settled. A similar situation occurred when children's pencils and erasers from home were taken by other children. It was important to our community that we persist in addressing such issues that were important to the children. Respecting others' work and belongings was a stated community value through discussions and problem solving at class meetings.

Social Issues

Class meetings were also a time when children could ask for help with social issues. Children would briefly explain the situation that was troubling them, but there was a firm rule that others could not be mentioned by name. Not mentioning names kept the focus on the problem and on generating solutions, and made the problems more relevant to everyone, not just to the children who were directly involved. Children frequently needed prompting to move from the problem to finding solutions; they tended to want to repeatedly restate their feelings and to encourage others to echo their views.

At times, a problematic social situation would arise during the week that I felt could wait to be solved. I would ask that child to write a quick note about the problem and place it in our suggestion box, which we would open at class meeting at the end of the week. Waiting to solve a problem often helped to defuse the situation, and then the children were better able to discuss what happened and brainstorm solutions more rationally. Nelson (1981) describes this as a "cooling off period" (p. 134).

Two areas that we discussed at length were bullying (what it is, why children do it, how to deal with it) and friends (what makes a good friend, how to resolve problems with friends, why friends exclude each other). These discussions were not focused on finding one solution to a problem, but were more a time for all members of the community to share their feelings and possible solutions that they had perhaps found successful themselves. This broad type of issue might be raised by me, when I noticed similar types of social problems arising with a number of the children. Empathizing with others and realizing that everyone has similar problems and feelings around social issues made us a stronger, more caring community.

REFLECTING ABOUT AND MAKING CHANGES TO THE CLASSROOM PROGRAM

When I analyzed the minutes of the meetings, there were a number of comments that fell into categories defined by curriculum areas. Many of these comments told me what the children enjoyed learning and doing as a community. Two daily occurrences that were often mentioned as a positive were the calendar routine and a morning cloze-type message that was written by me on chart paper, where words, capitals, or punctuation were intentionally omitted and later filled in by the students as a whole class activity. From the children's comments, I realized that these two daily routines had become an integral part of our community. As well as enjoying the activities, the children seemed to understand what they were learning from them. Our sense of community was strengthened as we celebrated our enjoyment of learning and conducting daily routines together.

As a result of what I had learned from analyzing the children's comments, I was very willing to accept a suggestion that was made in the following year. A child proposed that children who wished to might have a turn to lead the class in the calendar routine or to write the morning message and lead the group in filling in the blanks. Almost every child was interested in taking a turn, and having the children take on the role of teacher was tremendously powerful. The children seemed to have developed an appreciation for what is involved in leading and teaching the whole class, and it was fascinating to see them model their teaching styles after me and after one another. For the following year, I planned to ask the children if they could think of other ways in which we could all be both teachers and learners.

As I looked over the children's comments in each curriculum area, it became apparent that there were changes that I could make in the classroom program. An example was the spelling program. The children's comments were mostly in the context of how they were learning to spell commonly used words and how they were using posted spelling resources in the classroom. Their limited comments about the spelling program caused me to think of more interesting ways to engage and involve the children in learning about spelling on a day-to-day basis. I also asked the children for their input, as I wanted them to know that the way we did things and the way they were learning were negotiable and that their comments and ideas would be considered and tried out.

During the business part of the meeting, the children were specifically invited to suggest changes to the classroom program. A frequent request was that we have more time for activities of their choice, for science, for writing workshop, and for gym classes outside in the playground. I took this opportunity to explain how the schedule was designed, and what the choices and limitations were as I decided how we would spend time in a balanced way over the course of the six-day cycle. Consequently, there were changes we could make, such as scheduling more time for writing workshop on occasion or going outside for gym more often, but the children also learned that there were things we could not change. Whenever possible, I wanted to explain the rationale and process behind the decisions that I made and to give the children appropriate input. Having open discussions and approaching these issues cooperatively was the spirit that I wanted to prevail in our community.

Children could also suggest something totally new that they thought we should start doing. One child suggested that we have a science table with a rotating focus of experiments and objects, so we set up several different activities in which children could participate during activity times. Another child suggested that we go tobogganing during one of our gym periods, and we did. Sharing the responsibility for initiating new ideas and seeing that their ideas could be implemented were important characteristics of our community.

As well as showing me what was important to the children in our classroom community, hearing what they felt was going well prompted me to reflect on my own teaching and helped me plan a program that was more effective and motivating for the children. An example was the feedback that the children gave me on the science program. At over half the meetings, the children told me how they enjoyed hands-on activities, such as planting seeds and making a hot air balloon, and learning new information and skills, such as making predictions, observing, learning from nonfiction books, and making "jot notes." I knew that I was on the right track with science and planned further experiences from which I believed the children would get just as much pleasure. Their feedback illustrated whether they were valuing and seeing the learning that was occurring in our activities, and their input helped me plan future activities.

Throughout the year, the children gave me ongoing feedback on curriculum issues and this led me to continue, modify, add to, or stop certain practices. The children came to better understand the process a teacher goes through when designing classroom programs, and they were able to share in some of the decisions with me.

EACH COMMUNITY IS UNIQUE

After I had analyzed the minutes and examined what was important to our classroom community, I decided to ask the children directly about community to see how their perceptions fit with mine. In one weekly evaluation I asked, "What makes our classroom community special or unique?" I felt that a sense of community would be related to seeing the classroom as having special characteristics. Many of the children's comments did, in fact, echo themes from class meetings.

The children mentioned their work habits and attitudes: They were "good at things," "smart," "listening better," "learning a lot," and "getting our work done." Someone wrote that "every day we get a little better at something." Curriculum areas were also listed: "We read good," "the novel [that is read to the class each day] is special," "we do write really well," "our math is special," and "our quiet reading makes our class special." The classroom environment was also mentioned: "We have a couch in our class," "the things on the walls are special," and "we have plants in our class and we take care of them."

Being different, or a perception that we did things differently, was an important part of our uniqueness, according to the children: "Our class is special because we do things different." What made us different was that "we're the only class who has writing workshop" and "discussion after novel" and that "we got to publish our books." We were not, in fact, the only class that did these things, but it seemed important for the children to believe that we were.

Evidence of the characteristics of a strong community was seen in the children's comments about teachers and friends. Student teachers and their regular teachers were listed as being special: "We have nice teachers" and "We have student teachers." The children reported that they "have lots of friends," "are nice to each other," "like to work together," and "don't fight." Someone wrote, "we are lucky to have all these kids," and someone else wrote, "our friendship makes our class special."

The children's comments about our unique community confirmed for me that the characteristics I had discovered from analyzing class meeting minutes were important and apparent to both the children and to me.

WHY WE HAVE CLASS MEETINGS

I had always intuitively felt that class meetings were an important part of the week, and I was even more convinced of their value after examining their connection to community. I wondered, though, whether the children liked class meetings and what they felt we accomplished through them, so I asked them about this on their evaluations. Previously, seven children had mentioned class meetings as being part of what makes our class special: "because we get to remember all the special things that we did that week." Children also thought we had class meetings "so we can get together," "to get better at school," "to make our classroom a better place," "to help run our class," "to know what's happening," and "for learning." Positives were a part of class meeting so we could "discuss what we've done over the week," "so we have to think of things we're getting better at," and "to remember all the good things that happened." Reminders were important so that we could "remind people to do things" and "remind us of things we're not supposed to do." We talked about business items "to sort things out in the class," and "to make things different each week."

Twenty-one children said they enjoyed class meetings, four said they sort of enjoyed them, and three said they didn't. The children who liked the meetings said they enjoyed learning, discussing, and listening to others talk. Their comments echoed the comments made about why we have class meetings; they seemed to both understand and enjoy the process. Those who didn't like class meetings said, "I can't think of anything to say," "we just sit and talk," "I don't like some of the comments," and "it's boring because we sit for a long time." It was encouraging to hear that most children liked and valued class meetings.

INVOLVING THE CHILDREN IN TEACHER RESEARCH

Studying our community through class meetings gave me the opportunity to involve the children in my research, and doing this, I believe, strengthened our sense of being a learning community. At the beginning of the year, I explained to the children that I was going to be examining our class meetings and that I would videotape them each week. At this point I didn't know what I would discover, but was sure that collecting and examining the data would lead to some insights about our classroom community. The children seemed quite flattered that I would think their comments were important enough to videotape. Some children even got into the habit of checking to be sure that I had the camera set up and turned on each week!

I agree with Nancie Atwell (1991) when she writes that teacher-researchers can "serve as models of thoughtfulness for our students" (p. 8). Therefore, as my research evolved and I began to have a sense of what I was finding out from it, I shared my thoughts with the children. I told them when I was concerned about the lack of participation by some children and how the new idea of taking turns around the circle came from a member of my research group. After we successfully tried out the idea, one of several students who were e-mailing me from home wrote and told me he thought we should continue with the idea of "going around the circle."

The children were curious about what I would say when I presented my findings at an out-of-town conference, so I told them what I would be speaking about. Upon returning, I talked to them about what I had learned from presenting my findings and from attending other conference sessions. I repeated some of the comments and questions people had asked at my session. Marian Mohr (1996) believes that it is important that "teacher-researchers learn in front of their students, demonstrating and discussing the processes that a researcher—a learner—goes through. Their students watch this learner at work and see not only what there is to learn, but ways to learn it" (p. 119).

Karen Gallas (1994) writes about making one's research more "visible" to the children she teaches. "[The children] understand that while I am a teacher, I also study what is happening in the classroom. It makes their actions as learners more important and more powerful" (p. 18). Like Atwell (1991), I hope that my children will remember me "as an adult who learned in public, as a researcher" (p. 8).

CONCLUSION

The members of a classroom community need regular opportunities to collaboratively build values and expectations and to celebrate learning. I believe that class meetings played a critical role in the development of community in our classroom. They provided a regular opportunity for the children to express their feelings about their learning and our classroom. We had a weekly time to air and deal with problems and to decide on plans, changes, and new initiatives. Class meetings can really set the tone in a classroom community. Ours was a community where we asked and found answers to "real" questions and learned about one another through an activity that was meaningful and purposeful.

Looking at the data from class meetings helped me see how classroom practices were contributing toward my vision for a classroom community. Analyzing the data helped me see how well my vision for our community was being enacted and how changes in practice were made. Throughout the year, the children were a part of this dynamic process.

Meeting monthly with members of DICEP and having the opportunity to present my work in progress and hear others' reactions to it is an important part of my research. Our meetings are a time to reflect on our practice and how well it informs and relates to the theories in which we believe.

Class meetings can really set the tone in a classroom community. An experience that made me realize this happened on a day when the children were not managing well and I was in a terrible mood. It was time for class meeting, and I felt like canceling it although I knew I couldn't. By the time we had finished listing the positives I was in a much better frame of mind. Class meetings forced the children and me to focus on the good things that were happening in our community, even on a bad day. I cannot imagine my classroom community without class meetings, and I now firmly believe that they can both tell me about and help develop our classroom community.

CHAPTER 3

Student Inquiry in Science:
Asking Questions,
Building Foundations,
and Making Connections

Mary Ann Van Tassell

> Understanding starts with a question, not any question but a real question. A question that because it is real does not remain detached from us. A real question supposes that a real person (i.e., a questioner) is asking about some domain of experience (i.e., an object). Said in another way, a real question expresses a desire to know. This desire is what moves the questioner to pursue the question until an adequate answer has been found (i.e., made). Desiring to know opens ourselves to experiencing what is new as new and the already known as renewed under new aspects.
> —A. Bettencourt, *On Understanding Science*

I HAD RECENTLY joined DICEP when I encountered the above quotation. I had volunteered to take part because I was feeling dissatisfied with the type of science program I was delivering and the DICEP group was proposing to focus on learning and teaching in science. Over the next two years, this quotation served as the impetus to an investigation that led to a significant modification in my approach to teaching science in the primary grades.

JOURNEYING TOWARD MY OWN QUESTIONS

I teach a split, first and second grade class. The science curricula for the grades are separate, each grade having a separate science period each week. So Barbara Galbraith, the other Grade 2 teacher, and I combined our Grade 2 students so that we could teach science together. We teach in a coeducational, independent school, which is centrally located in the city of Toronto. This population is reflective of the public school student population in the area in which the school is situated. The 20 students in each of our classrooms are diverse in their learning styles and developmental levels, ranging from emerging to independent readers and writers. A small percentage of the students have identified learning disabilities.

The students had always been asking questions in a formalized way as part of our program. At the beginning of a new unit, we would have the students record in their Learning Logs what they knew already about the topic and any questions they had pertaining to the topic. After a brief period of sharing these ideas and questions, we would proceed with activities that explored what we, the teachers, felt to be important about the topic.

Bettencourt's words reverberated in my mind, nudging me to look more closely at the use of student questions. We were approximately three weeks into our study unit on the states of matter, and their questions had not yet been consulted. In the past, Barbara and I would have had the students return to their records of "What We Know" and "What We Want to Know" at the end of the unit in order to move toward closure by having them reflect upon "What We Know Now." Any questions that had not been answered would be given little, if any, attention. So, were the questions they had recorded in their Learning Logs "real," or were they merely fulfilling a teacher expectation?

Growing out of my readings and thought-provoking dialogue with colleagues in DICEP, whose wonderings were close to my own, I started to formulate the following questions for my inquiry:

1. What do I, as teacher, do with students' questions in science?
2. Does the pursuit of individual questions in science create a valid learning situation? If so, how?
3. How can I make the doing of science relevant to their knowledge, so that it is not only "hands-on" but "minds-on" as well?

And later,

4. How does this type of approach to science learning shape my perspective on science learning and teaching?

5. How do I resolve a tension between students doing science and my desire for them to know scientific concepts?

TRYING NEW APPROACHES: A LOOK AT THE DATA

The first part of our unit on solids, liquids, and gases was coming to a close; so far, the students had explored properties of each state. Before continuing onto the next section, exploring changes from state to state, we returned to the questions and statements the students had recorded initially about what they knew. They were asked to think about what they now knew and to add any new information they felt relevant. They were also asked to think about any new questions they had. As I observed the children during this time, Melanie commented to herself, "I sure know a lot now. Look at the only thing I had written before." She then proceeded to record information she now knew about the properties of solids, liquids, and gases. Next they formed small groups of four and shared this information and their questions. They were to decide upon one statement and one question for their small group to share with the rest of the class.

The group I am observing in the transcript below has a conversation while sharing their statements, and I intervene, asking Alice to clarify her meaning (see Appendix for transcription conventions).

1   ALICE: (reading from her Learning Log) "A solid is a solid because it takes up more space than liquids or gases"
2   Ms. V: Okay . What about one small grain of salt? Does that take up more space than a glass of water?
3   ALICE: Oh . . . maybe that's not what I mean . . SOME solids are bigger
4   Ms. V: Or are you talking about shape?
5   ALICE: Yeah . I mean they're solid and liquids and gases go all over
(Alice revises the statement she has written and reads it to the group.)
6   ALICE: "A solid is a solid because it keeps its shape and gases and liquids don't"
7   KATHY: But liquids and gases have shape
8   ALICE: No, but solids keep their shape ON THEIR OWN and liquids and gases don't
9   KATHY: Oh yeah, I see what you mean . solids have their own shapes just on their own

10   ALICE: Right . Okay then, should we use mine? (to read to
        the class)

During the above episode, the students were sharing their learning
with others, that is, making it public. In so doing, they had to make their
personal understandings clear for others, and this opened a path to discussing and consolidating their knowledge. Getting into groups and discussing their statements, then finding one they wanted to share with the
other groups, forced the students to be specific and precise in their reflections about what they knew now. Not only did they think about what they
knew now, but about what they still wanted to know.

Barbara and I had decided that we would give more attention to their
questions than we had in previous years. We were both beginning to see
that, if their questions were to be personally meaningful, they should play
a role in the shaping of our study of solids, liquids, and gases from this
point onward. On large chart paper, we wrote down the questions they
were still asking:

Why is liquid wet?
Why did solids, liquids, and gases come to our earth?
Why do gases float up?
Can you sometimes see gases?
What were the first solids, liquids, and gases?
Can there be gas in liquid and liquid in gas?
Where do gases come from?
Can we use up or run out of solids, liquids, and gases?

Barbara asked the students how they thought we might go about finding the answers to these questions. Their suggestions were:

Look them up in the dictionary.
Watch movies.
Ask a scientist.
Look in special magazines.
Get a librarian to help.

No students mentioned conducting investigations of their own. It was
not until Barbara prompted them that someone suggested doing an experiment to find out. I was surprised that the children didn't suggest this as a
viable method on their own. I felt that the absence of this option on their part
provided even more reason to give them an opportunity to investigate with
their peers the questions they were still asking about solids, liquids, and gases.

I was reminded of an article in which the authors had researched and compared the kinds of questions that students ask and the value these different questions hold for learning. The authors speak of a "cognitive apprenticeship" existing between students and teacher "where master and apprentices pursue the same goals, rather than a contrived apprenticeship, in which the cognitive goals for the students have already been achieved by the teacher" (Scardamalia & Bereiter, 1992, p. 32). Perhaps we were on our way to a "true apprenticeship" that provided a balance between teacher and student input.

A discussion of the above questions led us to eliminate several that did not lend themselves to investigation. We were left with four questions:

Why do gases float up?
Can we sometimes see gas?
Can there be gas in liquid and liquid in gas?
Can we run out of solids, liquids, and gases?

The students then formed groups of four or five and developed a means to go about investigating the question of their choice. In the following days, students came prepared with demonstrations that they had agreed would help answer their group's question. The group that is presenting in the excerpt below is examining the question: Can there be gas in liquid and liquid in gas? They have brought a balloon and put water in it, explaining that this demonstrates water in air. As they stand before the class, Brad, Derek, Garth, and Zena explain to the group that they now have water in air because simultaneously there is air and water in the balloon. Bruce LePaige, an intermediate grades science teacher has come to observe and offer input, motivated by his own interest in seeing younger elementary students establish a more open, questioning approach to science before they reach his classes. During the student demonstration, Mr. LePaige questions them further:

19   Mr. LeP: Is that showing liquid in air? Is that showing water in the air?

20   Brad & Garth: Yeah

21   Mr. LeP: Think so? Okay, do you have any balloons? (taking balloon) What you've done really is taken a balloon and something else, anything, (getting a piece of chalk) a piece of chalk . . Okay, you had a balloon and put water in it—or a piece of chalk (blows up balloon with chalk in it) Has the chalk gone into the air? (shakes chalk around, kids are shaking heads "no") Mrs. Galbraith, shake yours up a little bit . . so what do we really have?

22   KATHY: Something in a balloon
              (Laughter)
23   MR. LEP: That's absolutely right
24   Ms. G: You can feel the water sloshing around
25   MR. LEP: Yeah, but it hasn't gone into the air. Can I use the
              board? Okay, when scientists speak about having water
              in the air, what we really mean is it's inside between the
              air molecules . . Who knows what molecules are?
26   BRAD: They're little bits of space
27   ZENA: They're teensy things, they're microscopic
28   MR. LEP: Molecules are the smallest piece of something we
              can have . . so if we want the smallest piece of air—a
              molecule—it would have some stuff in it
              (Draws a diagram of air and water molecules, explaining
              the composition of water in air as two hydrogen and one
              oxygen molecules)
29   MR. LEP: (throws piece of chalk in the air) So there really
              isn't a piece of chalk in the air . . it hasn't disappeared
              into the air

From here, the students proceed to show air in water. Using a straw,
they blow air into the water. The group observes the bubbles and comments
that the bubbles are "jumping" and "popping" when they reach the surface of the water. Mr. LePaige probes their thinking a second time:

54   MR. LEP: Do you think that showed air in water?
55   STUDENTS: (several say yes)
56   MR. LEP: Yes? Okay, think back to what we just did with the
              water . . remember the picture I drew?
57   LAURA: It <air> didn't quite go into the water because inside
              the bubbles there was air and it wasn't in the water, it
              was in the bubble
58   MR. LEP: Exactly . Okay, everyone stand up for a second and
              I'll show you what it's like . everyone stand so shoulders
              are touching . . This (pointing to group) is our jar of
              water . I'm one air bubble coming out the end of the
              straw (pushes his way through the group). What hap-
              pened to the water?
59   STUDENTS: (several say it spread)
60   MR. LEP: Okay, it spread . . it got pushed aside by the air
              bubble, right? Okay, that's what happened with the
              straw in the water . . we had all this water here (draws

diagram of water and straw in the jar) . . we blew air
into it, it came down, and air formed bubbles . . . The
bubbles came up, and I was a bubble and what did I do
to you, the water?

61   STUDENTS: (several say he pushed them)
62   MR. LEP: So what did water look like on top?
63   STUDENTS: Bubbling/Jumping/Popping
64   MR. LEP: It looked like this (drawing) bubbling up and
popping . the air couldn't go this way, this way, or this
way (pointing to sides of jar in diagram) because of the
jar . . the only way it could go was up . so it pushed the
water up and when the air bubble was gone, the water
went back down
65   KATHY: So it (the demonstration) doesn't really show it (gas
in water)
66   MR. LEP: So it doesn't really show air in water . . air in water
is really the same idea as water in air . . These are really
tricky things to understand
(Pause)
67   MR. LEP: Now air, especially oxygen, in water is very
important. Why do you think oxygen is important in
water?
68   KATHY: Oxygen goes in water so fishes can live
69   MR. LEP: That's right, fish breathe oxygen just like we do . .
The stuff we need in the air is oxygen . it makes us
breathe, it makes us live . . Fish take in oxygen through
their gills . . That oxygen isn't big bubbles, it's mixed in
so you can't see it . it's molecules
70   KATHY: For the first <question>, water in air, a humidifier is
<an example> because water is in the air and it looks
exactly like a cloud

Throughout the demonstration, the children were involved in sorting
out the question of gas in liquid and liquid in gas based on what they were
seeing, as were the teachers. My goal was to understand what the group
was actually showing and if this matched the question they were asking. I
believe Barbara's goal was similar. We never really reached an answer, but
we had come to a greater understanding of the question. The children were
thinking about what they knew about solids, liquids, and gases as they tried
to determine if this was indeed an answer to their question, as demonstrated
by Kathy's final comment (line 70) when she wonders if a humidifier is
connected to the question of water in air.

When Bruce puts a piece of chalk in the balloon (line 21), when he throws the chalk in the air (line 29), and when he has the students act as water and he acts as an air bubble (line 58), he is helping them to think about what they saw from a new perspective. He assists in extending their knowledge and he challenges their belief that this really is showing liquid in gas and gas in liquid. By listening to the students' comments and observations, the teachers are able to help the students delve deeper into what they are seeing.

By the end of this lesson, I had begun to wonder if this was an issue of semantics as well, if the students' perception of *inside* was what they had, in fact, shown. It seemed to me that the group had defined *inside* as we (the teachers) would define *in*, as sharing the same space. And so, I posed this issue to the group, and we shared our thoughts with the students:

1   MR. LeP: We could say in one way this brush (picking up an
     eraser) is *in* the air, but we can't say it's *inside* the air,
     mixed in with the air

2   Ms. G: And maybe that's what we have to do . . I think this is
     a good lesson to be clearer about what we want to know
     . . We need to think about our questions when we're
     writing them up and determine what it is we want to
     find out

3   Ms. V: That was one thing I don't think we talked about . . I
     didn't realize until now what we meant by *inside of*

4   Ms. G: Right, this is a good lesson for me because sometimes
     we think we know what the other person is trying to
     find out and we really don't and maybe you (the chil-
     dren) had a different idea than what Ms. V thought you
     had . . Perhaps we need to talk about it more at the
     beginning, about what it is we are really trying to find
     out

In retrospect, Barbara and I agreed that it was precisely because there was exploration and subsequent discussion that we were able to come to a clearer understanding of the question being asked. I do not think it would have been possible, or at least not nearly as valuable, to have reached consensus about what was being asked before making an attempt at answering the question. Because we had explored and discussed, we were all able to understand the question more clearly.

I can relate this to my own inquiry into the science program. It wasn't until I began investigating the science program in a structured, deliberate way that I began to understand what I was asking. Even then, it wasn't until I had spent time reading, discussing, trying new things out, observing, reflecting, and writing, that I really began to understand more clearly the questions I was asking and the direction in which I was heading in my own study. This process was common to all DICEP members. The support and feedback offered by DICEP members was significant to the clarity and sense that I made throughout this inquiry. These activities are all part of the process of understanding. Bettencourt (1990) speaks of one aspect of this process of understanding as "use." He says:

> We do not understand and then use, but we understand as we use and we use as we come to understand. The process of constructing understanding is thus, not only circular, but also endless. (p. 5)

My involvement in DICEP was an important link between my classroom practices and the understanding I constructed.

The discussion in our classroom had moved into a new, very important area of science: understanding and becoming clear about what one is asking. If there had been more time, it would have been interesting to send the group back to explore their question further with the new knowledge they had gained. I feel we were coming closer to a "true apprenticeship." Gordon Wells (1995) speaks of the value of student inquiry in this regard when he says:

> For it is when the learner is engaged in an activity that has become imbued with his or her own purpose that he or she most benefits from the model provided by a more expert co-participant; by the same token, it is when the teacher's guidance and instruction are contingent upon the learner's conception of the goal to be achieved that they are most properly characterized as assistance. (p. 250)

I felt my role as teacher had shifted from "one who knows already" to "one who is wondering along with the students." Really, having achieved the right answer to the question was not what was important or even considered as the goal of the discussion, but rather "having a go at an answer," "giving it a try," was what was most exciting and interesting.

As Bettencourt said, "Not just any question, but a real question," and it wasn't until we began to give the students' questions some weight that their questions became real. Once we started to do something with them, they began to be real. And the students began to see that they could "have a go" at an answer. Over the next few weeks, interesting things began to happen, subtle things. A few students ventured to bring in science "tricks" they had tried out at home, hoping for further explanation or understanding from the group or wanting to show what they had come to understand while doing them at home. Others would posit ideas or make connections to their known, experienced worlds as we studied other things. For example, Barbara's class had just finished a geometry lesson on lines, and Barbara was about to read a book when one student piped up, "Look, Mrs. Galbraith, divergent lines!" as he pointed to the book opened in a "V" in her hands.

They seemed to be making connections in other areas, or maybe we were becoming more aware of the connections they had been making all along. Most likely, it was a combination of the two. We were changing, and this was affecting student behavior as well. The changes in our approach to science had influenced the wider classroom environment. Barbara made a significant observation when we were reflecting together on these changes: "The carryover is not in knowledge, but in the kinds of questioning or thinking they are bringing to other lessons. In the process [of trying new approaches in science], *my* questions or approaches [to questioning] in other areas are changing."

MAKING SENSE: UNDERSTANDING THE CHANGE

One of the most challenging things for me to do was to let go of my control, my sense of responsibility that I must teach them the scientific concepts. I am beginning to understand that what we were offering students was opportunities to make sense of their observations in light of what they already knew. They were involved in the cyclical, endless process of understanding about which Bettencourt has written. For example, the children and I were involved in a process of making sense of new experiences (i.e., the bubbles in water) in light of what we knew about liquids and gases. We were able to make use of new information (i.e., Bruce's input) and make greater sense of the question being asked.

This process of coming to understand is linked to what I understand to be the root of sociocultural theory, namely, that learning is largely a social endeavor. Through questioning, exploring, discussing, and reflecting with others during the course of the science unit, the learning became more meaningful and exciting. The students were freer to make sense of new situations, based upon what they already knew and with the help and support of more experienced learners—the teachers. The students were able to "make the meaning their own" when the learning situation was imbued with their purposes and driven by real questions. As Eleanor Duckworth (1987) observed, "Once the right question is raised, they [learners] are moved to tax themselves to the fullest to find an answer" (p. 5).

I originally thought that it would have been much more effective to make use of the students' questions right from the start of the unit. However, upon closer examination, I now feel differently. I believe the knowledge they acquired during the first three weeks of the investigations influenced their ability to pose and pursue questions that would further their understanding of the concepts.

Eleanor Duckworth (1987) raises this point in stating:

> Making new connections depends on knowing enough about something in the first place to provide a basis for thinking of other things to do—of other questions to ask—that demand more complex connections in order to make sense. (p. 14)

The role of the teacher, then, becomes one of assisting students to extend and deepen their knowledge when their own knowledge is not sufficient. The teacher is most effective when she can meet the student where the student is and offer the assistance needed in helping the child to make the learning his or her own.

A FURTHER LOOK AT QUESTIONS

The impact of the new approaches Barbara and I had taken was lasting. As we entered into a new school year, we took with us an excitement and interest in continuing the use of an inquiry approach to science teaching and learning. When I first thought of using the children's questions as the basis for inquiry and learning in science, I imagined it would be pretty straightforward: that posing questions and pursuing answers would be relatively simple. I had not anticipated that there would be many challenges and stumbling blocks along the way. However, the questions have never come easily for me in my own professional inquiries, so I really shouldn't have expected that the questions would come any easier for my Grade 2 students. As I entered into the second year of investigating my science program, I found myself continuing to wonder about their questions, how they were formulated and how this type of approach to science learning and teaching affected their growth. I remained a member of DICEP as well, feeling that my involvement in this professional community offered support, discussion, prodding, and joint knowledge building that assisted me in my own pursuits.

Another factor that influenced my continued interest in student questions was the group of Grade 2 students that we had the second year. In general, the group's reading and writing skills were not as sophisticated as the previous year's group and the group dynamics were a greater challenge. Barbara and I wondered how they would be able to handle the challenges of inquiry. The support we would need to provide for this group would be different from the support provided to the previous year's group.

At this point, I began to think more closely about the cognitive skills involved in pursuing an inquiry. Skills of social interaction, cooperative problem solving, reflecting, and writing needed to be developed further with this group. Building on our discoveries in the previous year, Barbara and I felt it would be important to give them many opportunities to pursue questions jointly with us, so that we could provide modeling and support before having them pursue their own questions in a more open context. These decisions were influenced by Vygotsky's (1978) notion of the "zone of proximal development" (ZDP) in which more able learners assist less able learners with tasks they are not yet able to conduct independently until they are ready to take them over themselves (p. 90).

And so, during the first two terms, Barbara and I conducted many inquiries with the students together: posing questions and conducting whole group inquiries, helping the students to build connections and extend their knowledge. In the third term, we felt the students were ready to take over more responsibility and decision making around the types of investigations and questions they would pursue.

In the third term, we decided to do a unit on air. We began by brainstorming everything that they connected to the concept of air. We organized the information into a web, with the word *AIR* in the middle. Next, the children wrote down questions they had about air. Both Barbara and I were surprised with the outcome. Many children struggled with writing questions, and the questions that were proposed were:

Where does air come from?
Who first invented air?
Why can't we see air?
Is there air in outer space?

The questions were mainly ones that would not lend themselves to inquiry. Barbara and I had thought we would proceed with investigations the following week, but we realized their knowledge of air and its various roles in human activities was limited. I was reminded of the article by Eleanor Duckworth quoted in the previous section, regarding background knowledge, and I knew there was a foundation that needed to be established on which more independent student-inquiry could be built.

Over the next month, Barbara and I planned a series of experiments for the students to conduct that would expose them to different principles of air movement and its uses. The first experiment involved a balloon under a stack of books. The students put the balloon under the books and tried to blow it up, observing what happened to the books as they did this. In the group discussion that followed, a chart of what the experiment told them about air was created. We assisted the students in making connections between what they had observed and the attributes of air. These comments were compiled into a chart:

Air is strong.
It pushes.
It squashes.
It can be compressed.
Air expands to fill space.

They were then asked to think of different objects that take advantage of these attributes of air. With the help of the teachers, the students were extending their knowledge beyond the observations they had made. Each discussion that we had with the students over the next few weeks was imbued with one purpose: to help the students make connections between what they were doing and observing and what this told them about principles of air and how these principles are used in natural and human-made objects. It was very challenging for both Barbara and me to help the students make sense and reach deeper understandings of what they were experiencing, in part because we felt our own knowledge was somewhat uncertain and limited. So we were engaged together with the students in trying to understand our experiences in an organized way.

I videotaped these sessions and transcribed the discussions. At first I was perplexed and troubled, feeling that they went all over the place and lacked clarity. However, upon closer examination, I began to see that the business of making meaning is not always clear-cut and straightforward. It involves a lot of messing around with ideas and fumbling for words or clarity. I came to see the value of the conversations as I read an article by Gordon Wells in which he quotes M. Lampert on discussions and learning in mathematics:

> This means we do not proceed as if whatever the teacher says, or whatever is in the book, is what is assumed to be true. It also means that lessons must be structured to pursue the mathematical questions that have meaning for students in the context of the problems they are trying to solve. And this means that lessons are more like messy conversations than like synoptic presentations of conclusions. (quoted in Wells, 1999, p. 157)

As with mathematics, the same can be said of our discussions in science. The discussions revolved around the challenges of furthering our knowledge of air and how these principles were connected to our existing knowledge. What follows is an example of one such "messy conversation" during the follow-up discussion to the balloon and book experiment, as we were trying to list the attributes of air:

18   JAKE: Um . . the air when it came in, it made the balloon get squi- squish . . like get bigger and bigger . it's like a whole bunch of people in a balloon and they get all squished up so they want to get out . . and then it just tries to pop the balloon

19   Ms. G: Oh, okay so you're saying that you kept blowing air into the balloon?

20   JAKE: Yeah

21   Ms. G: And you blew more . . . and you were pushing the air more into- okay . . I get the idea . . that you were squashing the air into the balloon and the balloon was filling up with air

22   JAKE: Yeah

23   Ms. G: Well, what would happen if you let that balloon go?

24   JAKE: It would zoom all over the place

25   Ms. G: Yeah, but what would happen to the air? Why would it zoom all over the place?

26   ALICE: Because the air would be coming out

27   Ms. G: Out of the balloon?

28   MELANIE: And it would be pushing it, because it would be wanting to get out and the balloon is going there because all the air is coming out and that's what is making it go because it's power
(Many start talking at once)

29   Ms. G: I can only hear one person at a time Put your hands up . . Melanie, finish what you're saying

30   MELANIE: The air is trying to get out and it makes the balloon go

33   Ms. G: All right, the air is trying to get out of the balloon and because it's trying to get out of the balloon it made the balloon go . . Okay . . . Zena?

34   ZENA: That when you blow up a balloon and then you put like . . that the air- the air comes out of it . . . and the air is holding the balloon up in the air . .
Since you took it out (your hand off the end) all the air is

coming in so it pushes this way (to the left) but the air
wants to go this way (to the right) so then the balloon
goes down and loses-

35   Ms. G: The air wants to go which way?

36   ZENA: That way (pointing to the right)

37   BRAD: Out of the balloon?

38   ZENA: Yeah, but the balloon wants to keep the air in

39   Ms. G: The balloon wants to keep the air in?

40   ZENA: Yeah

41   JAKE: Umm . . I'm not so sure because the balloon doesn't
want ***
(Others start talking)

42   BRAD: The air wants to come out of the balloon because the
books are moving down on the balloon so it wants to
come out . . instead of going in, but it can't come out
because you're blowing more air in

43   Ms. G: Okay, and what did that do?

44   BRAD: It sort of lifted up the books

45   Ms. G: Okay . (going back to list) so we- we- . . now did
we- . we talked about it <air> being (reading from the
list) "squashed, compressed, expands to fill space" . . All
right, that's one more thing we didn't add then . it lifts
things, right?

Throughout the excerpt above, the students are engaged with the
teacher in trying to make sense of what they experienced, as they attempt
to connect it to new concepts. The students are not just thinking of the experiment, but rather are accessing all their previous knowledge regarding
air and its behavior. In line 18, Jake is trying to make an analogy between
air and people, applying the same principle to both in order to get his idea
across. In the course of trying to explain in scientific terms the role of air in
something they are all familiar with—letting air out of a balloon—several
make "messy" attempts as they struggle to convey their ideas.

As the students continued to conduct different experiments, our charts
of "What Air Does" and "Things That Use Air" grew. These two charts,
and the questions behind them, guided our initial investigation into air as
we built the foundation. We would return to our charts after each experiment and revise or add to them in light of newly acquired knowledge.

Connecting experience to knowledge had been a concern of mine from
the start of my inquiry last year and was behind one of the questions I had
initially posed. How can I make the doing of science relevant to their knowledge, so that it is not only "hands-on" but "minds-on" as well? An essen-

tial component of inquiry-based learning is the "so-what?" What do my observations tell me? How does this new knowledge connect to what I think I already understand? This transformation of knowledge, or appropriation, on the part of the learner is an essential part of inquiry-based learning. It can also be the most taxing and challenging part, and this is where teachers can be of great service to their students. Gordon Wells (1999) writes of this essential component in describing the role of the teacher in inquiry:

> Their role is to help the learner to understand the significance of the activity as a whole and of the constituent actions and artifacts that mediate its performance and, while taking responsibility for the organization of the overall structure, to involve [the learner] as fully as possible, providing help and guidance with those parts of the activity that he or she cannot yet manage on his or her own. However, this assistance is seen as only a temporary "scaffolding," the purpose of which is to enable the learner to become a fully competent, independently-functioning participant. (p. 137)

Helping students build a foundation before pursuing individual projects provided an excellent opportunity for the teachers to help students make connections, with the hopes that in their individual inquiries they would start to use the developing tools needed to make further connections with increasing independence. Together, the skills of observing, recording, discussing, reflecting, and transforming were being modeled and supported by the teachers. And all these skills would be further developed and utilized as they pursued their own questions.

The questions the students asked a month after beginning the unit were quite different from their initial questions. They were more specific to the questions the students were still pondering, questions that had grown out of their experiments and our subsequent discussions, questions like: How does a hovercraft work? Why are airplane wings shaped differently? How does a parachute work? Why do hot air balloons need hot air? and How do airplanes fly? We categorized these questions together into groups and then the children selected a question to pursue through constructing an object that would help them find answers.

MAKING CONNECTIONS: A FURTHER LOOK AT SOCIOCULTURAL THEORY

As I now understand, the questions students ask are an important component in the framework of an inquiry approach to science teaching and learning. The questions help to provide focus and purpose to an investigation, guiding it along. Sometimes, these questions are slow in emerging, and it takes a variety of opportunities for exposure to a topic to help the questions emerge. Upon reflecting after the first year's investigation, I noted that the students' questions were valuable and had taken on personal meaning after they had had initial exposure to the topic. This view was confirmed in the second year of my investigation.

Questions are the seeds that have to be nurtured and cared for, that need to be provided fertile soil in which to grow. Teachers are responsible for providing the fertile soil—the context—nurturing the questions along as they germinate and begin to grow. In a study of the effects of collaborative inquiry on minority students' learning, Rosebery, Warren, and Conant (1992) speak of the benefits of pursuing questions:

> By pursuing their questions, students work toward goals that are meaningful to them, and, often, to the larger community (which can encompass the classroom, the school, or the outside community). They learn that there are alternative investigative paths to a problem and that many different questions can be pursued at any given point. And, importantly, they learn that there is not necessarily one solution or answer to a given problem. (p. 63)

Teachers attempt to provide the context relevant to the students' learning purposes and the support needed as students transform their knowledge and take over tasks. The value of creating and developing a foundation along with the students cannot be underrated. I came to see that it takes time for questions to develop and that young students need the support, encouragement, and modeling of their teachers in order to transform their learning. I am encouraged to see that it is possible for students of all ability ranges to be involved in their own inquiries in science. We found that we were indeed able to work within a structure similar to the previous year's, but that our roles as teachers required different things of us because of the specific needs of this group.

Within an inquiry-based framework, scientific literacy is not seen as the accumulation of isolated facts and procedures, but as a way of thinking and coming to know relevant to the scientific community at large. Rosebery, Warren, and Conant (1992) write that

> to become scientifically literate, students (and teachers, too) need to be enculturated into the ways of making sense that are characteristic of scientific communities. They must learn to use language to think, and to act as members of a scientific community. (p. 65)

By using an approach to science learning and teaching in which students develop and investigate their own questions, teachers and students alike can enter into the scientific community and begin to use and appropriate its tools. This is not to say that the tools of the scientific community are exclusive, but rather that, when students are encouraged to pursue their own questions in science, they are engaged in the process of doing science within a personally meaningful context. They are not learning about science in a context that is unconnected to their world and experience. What they gain through their experiences in science will be connected and transformed as they work in other areas as well.

MORE DISCOVERIES: A LOOK AT MY ROLE AS LEARNER

For me, as a learner, the most difficult and taxing moments are the "so-what?" times. I can see and sense the success of the new approaches I am taking in science by the interest and enthusiasm of the students. However, making sense of the changes, discovering how they transform, challenge, or support my existing beliefs about learning and teaching is the most difficult moment in inquiry for me. I also believe it is this struggle to make sense that makes teacher research so exciting and valuable. It requires more than observing, reading, reflecting, note-taking, discussing, or writing alone. Most important is a moment when all the threads are brought together to form a newly woven cloth, a moment when connections are made and meaning transformed that moves me onto further learning and understanding. My involvement in a community like DICEP provides a supportive context within which to reflect upon my own learning. Through sharing ideas, theories, and data in our monthly meetings, I am given the support necessary to make those connections and move further along.

Each time I have been involved in a classroom-based research project, I have come to appreciate and affirm the role it has played in my professional development. My understanding of what it means to be a teacher-researcher has deepened. I appreciate more fully how necessary it is to have a motivating, personally generated question. I have also come to value and recognize the importance of seeking out questions, and laying the groundwork so that questions can emerge. In my own research, I start out with a vague notion of an area I wish to investigate and, through observation, reading, discussing, and reflecting, I find that the questions begin to emerge. The work is rewarding, relevant, and full of opportunities for professional growth because it is essentially connected to my professional life as a teacher.

In addition, I have also come to value in a deeper way my membership in different communities and their interconnectedness. My relationships with the students I teach, with my coworker, Barbara, with my colleagues in DICEP, and with the broader educational community (through reading) are all enhanced and more meaningful because of my involvement in research projects. After having explored the importance of children's question in science, I have made an important realization regarding my role as a learner: one aspect of teacher research that makes it distinctive and valuable is the pursuit of a real question. And in pursuing these real questions, I find myself on the cyclical and endless path of coming to know and asking further questions. Also, I recognize that the business of investigating questions and making meaning is challenging work and I must utilize a variety of components to keep the cycle spinning.

Little did I know when I started to investigate my science program that it would lead me into the areas where I now find myself. My learning and questioning have been greatly enhanced by my membership in the different communities in which I participate. I am journeying toward a greater understanding of the importance of reflecting and making meaning for one's self. I echo Melanie's comment, made during her reflection on what she knew about solids, liquids, and gases after three weeks of study: "I sure know a lot now. Look at the only thing I had written before."

CHAPTER 4

A Comparison of Student-Led Discussions: Class Meetings and Novel Discussions

Greta Davis

As I EMBARKED on the new school year, I envisioned a Grade 3 classroom that would be inclusive, caring, and equitable—a community of inquiry in which knowledge was collaboratively constructed through the validation of student contributions, not delivered solely by the teacher. This vision had evolved over several years through my own experiences as an action researcher in my classroom, from my graduate studies, and from my participation in DICEP. By becoming involved with other adult learners, I experienced firsthand the value of collaboration, conversation and inquiry, in practice as well as theory. As a result, I began to investigate and emphasize these elements in my own classroom.

VISIONS, QUESTIONS, AND ACTIONS

My previous investigations had involved listening to and reflecting on student discussions concerning science experiments and the books they were reading. With teacher colleagues, I had explored issues which surfaced through student comments and questions and, in the process, discovered how discussion provides an opportunity for students to collaboratively develop an understanding of a topic by talking through ideas together. I had also discovered that these discussions allowed me, as teacher, to form a much richer awareness of the students' current level of understanding. From reading Vygotsky (1978), I had learned that language is fundamental to thinking; as he explains, it is through talk with others that the means for higher level thinking can be appropriated and constructed as a personal resource. And in Gallas's (1994) work, I had been intrigued by the complexity of children's conversations; they revealed that, given the opportunity, students could take initiatives to explore and make sense of complex issues beyond prescribed learning expectations. Taken together, these experiences led me to believe that a closer examination of my own classroom discussions could provide me with a better understanding of my students' meaning making and that this knowledge, in turn, could assist me in improving my current practice.

I also wanted to explore the development of community. I wondered how I could make my classroom more equitable. How could I give the students a greater voice in its development? In the past I had always enlisted the students in the creation of the rules that govern our daily classroom practice, but their role ended there. This year I wanted to expand their involvement in the daily decisions that create community. I wanted to work from their understanding because this, in my opinion, would be a preferable way of creating a collaborative community and of guiding student learning. After some reading and discussion with colleagues, I decided to introduce classroom meetings. I wanted a forum that would promote dialogue and empower students. Classroom meetings seemed like a good starting point because they allow students to negotiate and develop the daily routines while acquiring both academic and social benefits through student-led discussion (Bien & Stern, 1994; Murphy et al., 1991).

In addition to class meetings, I hoped subsequently to engage the students in whole class novel discussions, an area in which I had some previous experience. I was interested in learning how conversations would evolve in the class meetings as compared with the more curricular context of novel discussions. By comparing the two formats, I hoped to uncover similarities and differences in the patterns of the dialogue, to discover what impact these student-led discussions would have on the community, and to identify what my role was in creating such a forum. This chapter is an account of my journey toward developing community and, in the process, greater skill in my craft. First, I describe the class meetings, then the novel discussions. I conclude by comparing the two types of discussions.

CLASS MEETINGS

My Grade 3 class consisted of 27 students, drawn from diverse cultural backgrounds. Class meetings were initially held every week, beginning in September. The meetings were a time for brainstorming, negotiating, and creating plans of action. Items discussed during this time were, in general, initiated by the students. When an issue was brought to my attention during the school day, I encouraged the students to write it down and put it in our suggestion box for a future class meeting. Their suggestions formed the agenda for our meetings, although as a community member, I also occasionally submitted agenda items.

We met as a whole class, seated in a circle on the carpet. The meeting would commence with an invitation to comment on the agenda, and then students would be free to contribute their thoughts and opinions, one at a time. They did not raise their hands to be nominated but waited for an opportunity in the conversation to speak. I wanted their talk to parallel a natural conversation as much as possible. The meeting usually concluded when all agenda items had been discussed, but on occasion, agenda items were carried over to the next meting due to time constraints. All of the meetings were videotaped to provide a record of the talk so that it could be revisited and analyzed.

Changes in Practice

After participating in and observing a few class meetings, I began to formulate questions such as the following:

- What are we learning in class meetings?
- How do the children feel about class meetings?
- Can class meetings be made more positive so we aren't just solving problems?
- Who is doing the talking?
- How can a greater equity of voices be achieved within the discussions?

As my questions evolved, the types of data I collected grew to include not only transcripts of videotaped meetings, but also small group interviews and students' journal entries. Analysis of the data in light of these initial questions led to my personal reflections becoming more than just a look back on the day. I found myself questioning and reflecting on my current teaching practices. This, in turn, led to discussions with colleagues about their current practices and some modifications to my own. Finally, I made the decision to analyze the transcribed data more systematically in order to understand its implications for my vision, for my actions, and for theory.

I began my analysis by examining the agenda items of our meetings. This revealed that the focus of our class meetings was solving problems in our classroom community. Bien and Stern (1994) found a similar problem-solving focus in their class meetings. We dealt mainly with issues such as stealing pencils in the classroom, handling people who bother us, and cutting in line at recess. The agenda items read like a series of complaints in need of solutions.

While I was pleased that the students were solving problems in our community, I also wanted them to celebrate the positive aspects of our classroom. Many good things were happening, and I felt that recognition of this fact was important in the building of a community. So, after the first few meetings, I incorporated a sharing time at the beginning of class meetings. During this time we went around the circle and each student had an opportunity to say what he or she had enjoyed about the week or something at which they felt the class was doing well. We called this time "community circle" (Gibbs, 1994). Students enjoyed this addition and it gave our meetings a positive starting point.

Over time, the nature of the agenda items changed. They became less focused on solving behavioral problems and more concerned with negotiating classroom routines, such as the organization and frequency of class meetings, the setting of monthly reading goals, and the inclusion of spirit days. In one meeting, which focused on the negotiation of free time in the classroom, we decided to hold classroom meetings every two weeks rather than weekly in order to ensure that free time was also a valued part of our community. This did not imply a devaluing of the meeting time, but rather a reorganization of the classroom events to meet the needs of the community—a process that teachers usually undertake. In this case the students were empowered to negotiate these decisions.

My next step in working with the data was to tally the contributions made by students in order to determine who was talking. The data revealed that, in the early meetings, one-third of the students were engaging in the discussion. I wanted to increase the potential for student voices to be heard. The addition of the community circle already encouraged increased student contributions in the beginning portion of the meeting, but I wanted to extend this to the regular meeting. In the second month of class meetings, I began to post an agenda the day of our meeting and gave the students time in groups of four or five to talk about the agenda items prior to bringing the issues to the large group.

This strategy could have actually decreased the number of participants contributing if I had just asked a representative from each group to report on the small group discussion. Indeed, this is what I had done in the past in an attempt to share students' ideas. However, this time I was hoping that trying out their ideas in the smaller group and hearing those of others might encourage more students to contribute to the larger discussion. This seemed to be successful, inasmuch as over a period of three months, we moved from having one-third of the class contribute to having three-quarters of the class contribute ideas. This is not meant to imply that students had to speak. My attempt was to increase the opportunity for students' voices to be heard and validated in our community.

As I further examined the data I realized that, although I had a record of what had been decided in the meetings, this record was not visible to the students. I wanted the students to be able to see, as well as hear, the contributions they were making to our community. Because I wanted to empower student voices as much as possible, I nominated a student in the class to record discussion ideas and write a summary of what we decided on each issue during the meeting. Not having the pen in my hand, I was not viewed as the expert, but I remained a member of the ongoing discussion. This record allowed students and visitors to our class to see how, together, we were forming the norms of our community.

The Changing Role of the Teacher

Analysis of the data also revealed the number and types of contributions I was making to the discussion—a full third of the talk. Wells (1996) believes this type of conscious attention to speaking may change the way teachers intuitively respond during class discussions. I definitely found that my examination of the transcripts affected my contributions. Armed with an awareness of the frequency of my participation in the discussion, together with a record of the types of comments both I and the students were making, I reduced my contribution to one-fifth of the talk. Analysis of the subsequent meetings revealed that my comments became less directing and took more of an initiating and summarizing role with respect to the agenda items under discussion.

I believe that, in the beginning, it was important for me to have a considerable role in the talk. I needed to guide the students in developing a familiar structure for our meetings. I needed to model appropriate ways of listening, responding, and questioning as well as to encourage problem-solving and decision-making strategies. By modeling the language and strategies for them, I ensured that students could begin to appropriate these tools. This was my role in the early stages of the class meetings.

It is important to note that I did not organize separate activities to instruct my students in social skills, such as attentive listening, turn taking, and responding to others' comments, as I had done in the past. I modeled them as I participated in the discussion. When students were not pleased with the manner in which certain members were contributing, we discussed the issue. For example, when turn taking was raised as an issue by the students, we discussed why it was important and how to secure a turn appropriately. Based on my experience, the class meetings were more motivating than an artificial role play of social skills. Since the meetings were of interest and concern to the students, in order to take part they had to appropriate the skills necessary for their voices to be heard. In this way, social skills developed as a result of engaging in self-directed discussions, and their evolution was one of the benefits of participation in a collaborative community.

While it is important that the teacher provide the model initially, as I did, students can and do assume this role as well. Over a few months, the children gradually began to assume my role by questioning each other for clarification, and I was able to assume a more silent role in the process. If time had permitted, I would have extended the sharing of control by appointing a student chair for each meeting. I believe that, over time, the students would have been able to carry out the process with minimal teacher support.

The Children's Voices

My next step in the investigation was to interview the children because I wanted to know how they felt about the process and what they thought was being accomplished. The students viewed the class meetings as something that made our classroom special. They felt the discussions gave them a say in the running of the classroom, an opportunity few of them had experienced before. I believe this opportunity helped to increase the students' sense of ownership in the development of our community, as some of their comments show:

> You get to express your feelings and what you want.

> It's like you get special privileges.

> Class meetings are great because our class is able to make our own decisions.

> The class will do better in the year than if just the teacher was making the decisions because not everybody would like that because, well, the class would be pretty boring.

They saw class meetings as being "about problems in the classroom" as well as an opportunity to celebrate "good things." Acknowledging success in our classroom routines helped to reinforce our developing classroom norms, an important step in the building of community. Many also felt that class meetings provided them with a forum to get help with recurring problems.

The students also recognized value in the opportunity to construct knowledge together rather than in isolation. Vygotsky (1978) believes that the learner achieves more success in collaboration than he or she would alone. The students supported this belief as they commented on how other people affected their own thinking and how together they generated more possible solutions to problems:

> It's good because it makes more ideas.

> Sometimes when the other person is talking you forget what you were going to say, [but hearing someone else] sort of makes you think more about what you are already thinking about.

Their comments also showed that they realized there were social skills that needed to be learned and used in order for the meetings to be successful:

> You learn that other people should get a turn.

> People are waiting their turn when the person is in the middle of their talking.

> They're listening to each other.

> Once you get into talking no one is going to interrupt.

The students didn't just learn that these skills were important; they also put them to use in conversation. For example, over the course of three months, the frequency of overlapping talk decreased. Although it still occurred occasionally in the later meetings, students were much more willing to allow one voice to prevail and did not persist in talking at the same time as someone else. They were learning the importance of turn taking in conversation.

Several students also discovered that these new conversation and problem-solving skills could be extended beyond the classroom and used to mediate difficulties among family members. One student said, "Class meetings can even help in your family 'cause, um, some people usually get in a fight in my family and now I can help them talk." Murphy and colleagues (1991) also concluded that the skills learned in class meetings extended beyond the classroom to other areas of the children's lives. As Barnes (1976) emphasizes, making this link between educational knowledge and knowledge needed for action in everyday experiences should be an integral component of all learning. Thus, through their voices and actions, the children reinforced my belief in the value of developing a collaborative classroom community and in the impact it could have on other areas of their life.

A Common Language of the Community

Through an analysis of the successive transcripts of our class meetings, I also saw a common language developing over time. Words and phrases that had been introduced in earlier meetings were being used by the students during subsequent meetings. They were also appropriating a common language by verbalizing the classroom and school norms that were included in our posted classroom rules.

The following is a partial transcript of our initial meeting. It illustrates my attempts to help guide the conversation in order that we could together arrive at a plan of action. *Italicized words* reflect terms previously introduced and discussed in the classroom.

> TEACHER: What do we do when someone says something that
>   makes us mad?
> JAMES: *Say stop it* and if they keep on doing it tell the teacher
> TEACHER: What else?
> JILE: *Please stop doing that, it hurts my feeling*
> X: *Get some help*
> TEACHER: What should happen to people who aren't following the
>   rules?
> JAMES: Send them to Ms. Night (vice principal)
> TEACHER: Any other suggestions? Should we put up with people
>   calling us names?
> ALL: No
> MEL: *Walk away . . first tell them . use your words . ignore*

It took several meetings before the students began to make connections between the agenda items and their own experiences outside the classroom. However, the following transcript from a later recorded meeting illustrates how the children are beginning to do this, as they assume a greater role in directing the conversation. Although they are still suggesting classroom rules as potential solutions to problems and using the developing language of the classroom to negotiate the conversation, they are also expanding the talk to include personal experiences from outside the classroom in order to support or challenge potential solutions. Moreover, the length of most contributions has increased, and in some cases, children are beginning to provide some justification for their suggestions. They are truly concerned about how to get along successfully with others and are discussing means for handling such situations.

TEACHER: Okay we are going to start with our first item on our agenda and that is the issue of not getting along . . Any suggestions that might help someone who is having that trouble in our classroom?

BRAN: You should *keep your hands to yourself* 'cause you might hurt someone and then you'll get hurt and then they'll get hurt and you're both just hurt

JAMES: If you *tell them to stop* and they don't stop go to the teacher and if they still don't stop after the teacher's told them then go to the office for help

ELLY: Or else you could *talk to them* by yourself . go to your friends that are with you and can help you explain it

SHANE: I think if someone is bugging you, um you should just *um talk it out* and if they don't stop, you should just *walk away* from them

JOHN: I think if somebody's bothering you and you *tell them to please stop* and they don't, just *don't bother with them* anymore

AL: I think if they are bothering you and you told the teacher and the next recess they are bothering you, go to their homeroom teacher

JAMES: You mean their own class?

AL: Mhmmmm

SHANE: I think if they don't stop bugging you, you should tell the teacher and they'll say stay away from each other

MEL: If they keep bothering you, you should hide and don't play with them

CHRIS: I think that when somebody's bothering you, you *walk away* and if they follow you, you go back and don't tell the teacher but *say what you would like them to do and what you didn't like and what you want them to do instead*

SHANE: What Chris just said if they keep on bothering you, you should run away

CHRIS: But Shane if you keep on running away, right-

JAMES: They'll still be following you .. maybe you should tell the teacher because they might stop and if they don't stop you could tell them you're going to report them and if they still do it report them

STEVE: What if they catch up to you before you get to the teacher?

JESSY: When you get home you can like tell your parents and they can help by going to the house and talking to parents

JOHN: Maybe if someone's bothering you just leave them alone and then later they might want to be your friend

AL: I had a problem at my old school with Jerry after when he started bothering me .. After when I got off the bus with my friends, what we used to do is, see we had the same baby-sitter, right? . so we ran down the street, 'cause he knows where my house is but he doesn't know my baby-sitter, right? We went to my friends house and I ran inside . he was walking past, right, like he started walking slowly . You see you can just- can just walk inside your friend's house and they can help talk to him

CHRIS: I can remember once they were bugging me and a bunch of my friends a lot . We passed a dog and he ran away

MARK: I think you should fight back, just um *deal with them with your words* and if they still do it tell the teacher and if they still do it tell the principal

AL: Mark, what do you mean by "fight back"?

MARK: Fight back by *using your words*

JOHN: If it is after school tell your parents

STEVE: What if they still do it?

BRAN: If you fight them, you're the one who's going to get in trouble *'cause if you fight them someone is going to get hurt*

The development of a common language, the changing role of the teacher, and the predominance of the children's voices are all evidence of a developing collaborative classroom community.

NOVEL DISCUSSIONS

In the second term, I introduced the practice of novel discussions. The conversation format was similar to that of class meetings, but the discussion focused on issues raised by students about story content. The discussions provided an opportunity for students to talk about responses to the book, to ask questions as well as to clarify peer responses, in a manner similar to Raphael and McMahon's (1994) experiences with book talk. I read aloud the novel, *Julie's Tree.* I chose this novel because its characters were similar in age to my students; it dealt with friendship, an important issue at this age; and it had a plot that naturally led to the engagement of the students in predicting future events. The book was also one that the majority of my students would struggle to read independently. Chambers (1988) found in his experience with read-alouds that the choice of book was paramount.

Each day, I read a chapter from the novel to the whole class as the students were seated in a group on the carpet. When the chapter was finished the students moved into the familiar circle formation used for class meetings. At this point I invited students to speak about story events, and they launched the topics of discussion. In contrast to the class meetings, there was no posted agenda for novel discussions. Because they were introduced following a few months' experience with class meetings, the children were prepared not to raise their hands but to wait for an opportunity in the dialogue to speak. Our discussions generally focused on making and debating predictions, and on developing explanations of story events and characters. The discussions varied in duration from 15 to 35 minutes and were concluded when I sensed that the children were having difficulty in attending to each other. Each one was recorded and then transcribed.

Negotiating Connections: The Teacher's Role in Novel Discussions

As I discussed in relation to class meetings, there are conscious changes that a teacher makes while engaged in ongoing action research. These include the facilitation of new learning through guided activities, plans to modify subsequent discussions, as well as decisions made while actually engaged in the conversation. The transcribed dialogue was invaluable in helping me plan for future learning and make decisions about how to proceed with future discussions. With novel discussions, however, I wasn't simply listening for opportunities to pull back as I had done in class meetings, but I focused more on making contributions that would advance the discussion in new directions.

The issue is not *whether* to intervene in the conversation, but *when and how* to do so. In both types of student-led discussions, making these moment-by-moment decisions about when and how best to intervene in order to guide and to assist student learning requires a combination of knowledge, skill, and intuitive judgment that can only be gained through engaging in the discussion. An understanding of the students' previous learning experiences and an awareness of connections that need to be made to facilitate future learning are paramount. This involves working in the students' "zone of proximal development" (Vygotsky, 1978).

An example of this occurred when a student made a private comment at the end of a chapter but did not contribute it to the discussion. He said, "Why do authors do that? Why do they just end it there?" He was referring to the manner in which the author had concluded the chapter. A child had fallen out of a tree and we did not know what happened until the next chapter. Since his question was not followed up by peers in the ensuing discussion, at the end of the discussion, I directed the conversation back to his comment, and we embarked on a brief discussion of an important element in an author's craft—suspense.

> TEACHER: John, did you want to mention what you said when we finished today's chapter?
>
> JOHN: Stories always end at the good part . it always ends at the good part . it never goes into the bad part . like someone's calling, "Help, Help" and it's very interesting . the ending is always interesting
>
> AL: A hanger
>
> JOHN: Yea, it leaves you hanging
>
> JILE: It's like a TV show . it gets to a scary part and it goes to commercial
>
> CHRIS: And like maybe they do it because they want to make you make up your own story
>
> ELLY: They might be wanting to do that so that some people might always want to get the book so they know what it's going to be about
>
> AL: I think they just want to keep you keep on reading the book
>
> JAMES: She got what I said
>
> TEACHER: Have any of you tried to end your stories in an interesting or suspenseful way?
>
> ALL: Yeah (it's hard)
>
> TEACHER: I think John has raised an interesting issue about how writers think and write and it is one which we should explore further

The discussion had already been very lengthy that day so it was concluded there. However, by intervening in the discussion, I had gained a new understanding of the children's notions of suspense as a writing tool. I made plans to incorporate lessons that week during language time that would focus on finding examples of suspense in the text and discussing how the children could make use of this technique in their own writing. I needed to enlarge their understanding of suspense beyond what they had already verbalized and connect it to the practical experience of writing. Making links between reading and writing are goals of mine as a teacher, but I believe that it is more valuable when the initiation of the topic comes from the children themselves. This gives them ownership which, in turn, contributes to the development of community.

While part of my role is a commitment to support students' efforts to make their own answers to the specific questions that intrigue them, I also have a responsibility to help both individuals and the community as a whole to develop an understanding of the overall themes in the novel. This was an area with which I had always struggled as a teacher. I had been frustrated with novel sets accompanied by teaching manuals that outlined specific comprehension questions to address. It was only when I began to turn control over to the students through novel discussions that I was able to help students make connections from books to larger themes in our everyday lives.

Analyzing the Talk

As I analyzed the transcripts, I noticed that some predictions the students had made earlier in the novel held true while others were contradicted by later events. I wondered if they would be able to identify patterns in their own predictions. I also wondered if the students would be able to see how their understanding and beliefs about characters and events changed over the course of several chapters or, in some cases, remained the same. I decided to highlight this kind of talk for the students by transcribing their predictions on chart paper.

In writing them out, I began to uncover the wealth of knowledge that they were bringing to the text. The following is an example of their beliefs about the old woman in the story during the first five chapters of the novel. In the actual chart, I color-coded the ideas to represent the chapter to which they referred. The ideas are written in the order in which they emerged over the course of five discussions. I have not used verbatim quotations because I tried to combine similar contributions into one statement.

> The old woman is there to protect the tree.
> I think she's a witch because of the cat she has.
> She's going to kill the tree with a spell.
> She will capture Julie and her friends. Maybe she will kill or boil
>   them.
> She's going to cast a spell to save the tree.
> The old woman is going to die.
> She isn't a witch. She just wants to get her cat back.

> She is going to call the police on Julie and her friends.
> Maybe she's the one who made Sandy fall.

After doing this, I realized that the children were drawing on past experience with other stories to develop an understanding of character. For each character in the story, there were children whose predictions indicated a belief that the character was good or a belief that the character was evil. This opened up a new avenue for us to explore as a class. I was able to help them retrace their own perceptions of good and evil and discover where the perceptions had evolved from. On a subsequent day the children worked in small groups to categorize the characters as good or evil with justification for their decisions.

As can be seen from the predictions above, justifications that occurred naturally in the novel discussions were based on beliefs such as owning a cat makes an old woman a witch. These types of connections, which students had made to prior literary experiences, possibly including fairy tales, might not have been evident to me if the discussion had not been transcribed. The children were already using beliefs of good and evil to guide their predictions, but they needed the teacher to help them progress toward a broader understanding of good and evil that they might not have achieved on their own. We were able to explore and discuss how past literary experiences affect our interaction with books and our own writing as authors. Examining the talk enabled me to plan activities that would scaffold or support the students in extending their understanding beyond their current level. I was a learner alongside them. I was thinking in new ways. This was evidence again of an evolving collaborative community.

The Children's Voices

Chambers (1985) suggests that when children discuss books, with all of them listening to each other and responding to what they hear, they not only take on each other's thoughts—that is, they make other people's thoughts their own—but they also begin to think things they couldn't have thought in any other way. The children were able to comment on this process in our interviews. In such reflective discussions, students begin to develop a metacognitive perspective on their activity, as well as a language for talking about this "inner landscape" (Bruner, 1986). Such reflective thinking plays an important role in community building.

As in the class meeting interviews, students commented on the value of opportunities to construct knowledge together by listening to each other's ideas. Their comments also demonstrated an awareness of the impact of collaboration on their own thinking:

Talking gives more ideas.

It gives a lot more things that we can say 'cause we will be thinking and using some of the words they used or using the same sentences they used by adding more things.

I learn that people say different things and then after, you think of an idea that piggybacks on them just a bit.

The students were asked what value they saw in novel discussions compared to their previous experiences involving the writing of story summaries and the answering of questions. Many felt more was learned from novel discussions because greater emphasis was placed on their ideas:

When you get a piece of paper with questions it's like you're just doing questions but in talking you need more stuff in your head so you know more when talking.

In novel discussions you are listened to more.

I think talking is better (than writing) 'cause if you're doing questions you get ideas but then you run out of ideas.

Novel discussions are better (than writing) because you might have more ideas and that might not be on the page that you have.

Chambers (1985), in his work with children and literature, discovered that children are natural critics but that we don't know this because we don't listen and ask the right questions. Similarly, Gallas (1995) found the science questions she posed were not as interesting as the paths down which her students' questions took her. Novel discussions give students an opportunity to raise and explore their own questions. As teachers, we are sometimes quick to judge that a student does not understand when they cannot answer our questions. Turning the discussion over to the students is a means of opening new doors to understanding for all members of the community.

COMPARING THE DISCUSSIONS

Coding revealed some distinguishing features of the dialogue. Class meetings involved generating suggestions and negotiating possible solutions to problems. In novel discussions, time was spent advancing predictions of story events and characters and providing some justification for the thinking. Despite distinctions in function, however, the two kinds of talk mirrored each other with examples of coconstruction. Conscious connections referred to by the children as "piggybacking" on other peoples' ideas were most common in the novel discussions, for example:

I have something to say to Chris about what she said at the end.

I like what Jile said but . . .

I want to piggyback on Jessy because when she said . . .

I want to add on to Bran . . .

Connections to others' ideas did begin to occur in the class meetings, but they took longer to develop and occurred less frequently than in the novel discussions. Novel discussions, it is true, did occur later in the year, after experience with class meetings, but that does not seem to be an adequate explanation of the difference. The difference between the functions of the two types of discussion also seems to be important.

When asked to compare class meetings and novel discussions, the students viewed the two types of discussion as very distinct. "They're different because one is about problems in the classroom and one is about the book." Indeed class meetings dealt with social issues whereas novel discussions focused on story content. Several students also felt novel discussions were more challenging because memory played a significant role in the ability to contribute to the conversation: "Class meetings are like discussing problems in the classroom so they're easier to do because you don't have to remember things."

In order to challenge someone's prediction in the novel discussions one needs to have a recall of the story events, whereas in class meetings a student could simply rely on previous personal experience. In the interviews many of the students indicated that the former type of recall was difficult and that this prevented them from participating as actively as they did in the class meetings. It therefore seems important to provide opportunities for discussion in a variety of curriculum areas so all students can develop a voice in the community.

The Value of Student-Led Discussions

The practice of student-led discussion in the classroom, in the form of class meetings or novel discussions, is important both for the construction of knowledge and for the development of community. Our community evolved as we talked. As we engaged in discussion, tools of conversation were appropriated, conversation skills such as listening and turn-taking became established norms, and decisions regarding routines redefined our daily practice. The agenda items were additional evidence of the evolution of our community. Over time we dealt less with solving behavioral problems and focused more on determining what our community should look like. The data, the children's voices, and my changing role are evidence of this evolution of community.

Metacognitive growth was very evident in the students' interviews as they discussed what they had learned from student-led discussions. Grade 3 students were able to articulate how peer contributions had impacted their own thinking. They knew that they were coconstructing an understanding of issues that they could not have done alone, and they saw the importance of conversational skills in the process. This metacognitive understanding would not have occurred in a more traditional, teacher-led discussion.

CONNECTING VISION, PRACTICE, AND THEORY

Newman (1987) believes everything we do as teachers is founded on our assumptions about learning, teaching, and knowledge. This inquiry proved her right. But it also confirmed her further claim about the need to challenge our assumptions. For I found that the collection and analysis of data was paramount in examining my assumptions about how I teach and how students learn. It was only when I examined the transcripts of the discussions that I discovered how complementary and interdependent the two types of discussions were. Had I not had a record of the dialogue, I might not have discovered the benefits of student-led discussions, and I would not have developed my current understanding of my role in the process. Such knowledge informs future practice. I now see the practice of student-led discussions as a central part of all aspects of a classroom community. Without a record of the discussions, or without an understanding of Vygotsky's theory, I could not have examined my current practice. This highlights the relationship between vision, practice, data, and theory. The four elements are continuously interacting as one engages in action research.

At the same time, my analysis of the data also led to my improved understanding of sociocultural theory. I realized that, even in the way I participated in the conversation, I was modeling my vision of learning for the students. I was enacting my belief that I did not have all the answers and that by listening to each other we could learn more together than we could ever learn by engaging in traditional teacher-student conversations. I also learned that social skills evolve as the community unfolds. In the past, I had spent a great deal of time having students role-play social skills prior to engaging in collaborative endeavors, but I now know that such artificial situations are not necessary. Indeed, this is inherent in Vygotsky's theory of learning through social interaction, but it was only by examining my own practice that I came to this understanding.

The discoveries of this action research only renew the cycle of questions and possible future investigations into other types of student-led discussions. As this journey concludes, another waits to begin. The essential ingredient in this process is the teacher's willingness to improve his or her own craft and to share the experience. By embarking on such journeys, the learning of all community members is enriched.

CHAPTER 5

Learning to Pay Attention to Other Modes of Meaning Making

Gordon Wells

SOME YEARS AGO, I was visiting the classroom of one of my DICEP colleagues in a multicultural, inner-city Toronto school. In fact, it was my first visit to that particular classroom, and my intention was to begin to get to know its members since I was expecting to spend many more days with them, for the teacher and I were planning to investigate ways of adopting an inquiry approach to work in science. As an additional way of obtaining a feel for this classroom community, I also set up a video camera and left it running as I moved around from group to group. The camera, I thought, would give me a second perspective, as it would "see" events in a way that a participant cannot. As I am going to explain, however, it did much more than that. For what was captured on that videotape has significantly changed my understanding of learning and teaching; it has also helped me to develop as a teacher-researcher.

QUESTION: CAN LIGHT BEND?

The events I am about to recount involved Jasmin and Alex, two Chinese Canadian students, as they worked together on a science experiment. Like the other children in this third and fourth grade classroom, they had recently started to explore phenomena of light and color, and on this particular morning, they were following the class teacher's instructions to find a question that they would be interested in exploring, selecting from the variety of materials that she had made available. Along with mirrors, batteries and bulbs, colored acetate and paints, and so forth, the teacher had also brought in a number of books, some of which included suggestions for experiments to carry out. It was from one of these books that Jasmin and Alex had chosen their topic and, as the camera recorded, during the first part of the morning they prepared and carried out the suggested experiment.

Briefly, this required them to take a cardboard box, in this case a shoe box, and cut two narrow vertical slits about two centimeters apart in the middle of one end. Having placed a jam jar of water in the middle, they were to direct a flashlight horizontally through the slits so that the beams would pass through the jar of water. This, they were informed, would cause the beams to bend, a phenomenon that they should be able to observe by looking at the bottom of the box between the jar and the end of the box opposite the flashlight, where they would see that the beams of light crossed. In the book, these instructions were accompanied by a schematic representation of what they should see.

Once they had chosen their topic, Jasmin and Alex assembled the materials and, in order to "see the light crisscross," they took the experimental setup under the teacher's desk (having first draped coats at back and front to keep out the natural light). Then, after having satisfied themselves that they were able to reproduce the crisscross effect, they were anxious to share their success with others. This was the stage at which I went to join them. At that point, however, I did not know what they had been doing as, until then, I had been visiting with other children.

As I sat down at the end of the small table at which they were working, Alex was standing facing me at the other end and Jasmin was on my left; the shoe box was on the table between us, with the end in which the slits had been cut facing me. I started by asking the two children to tell me about the question they had been interested in and what they had found out. This they did in considerable detail, showing and describing what they had done. (The conventions of transcription will be found in the Appendix.)

2   JASMIN: Well we had . well first our question was . can light–
        does light always shine straight– straight forward?
        (gesturing strongly with right hand moving horizontally
        from right to left)

3   GW: And does it?

4   JASMIN: No . 'cause it sort of bends . 'cause before when we
        <set this> light there–

5   GW: Yes
6   JASMIN: -we saw it right through there and it was very dark .
        when it was covered it was dark and it was just a torch
        and we put it right there (showing where they held the
        flashlight. As she speaks, Alex moves to stand beside her
        and also shows where they shone the light) but it
        couldn't be right close to it <u>because</u>
7   GW: <u>uh-huh</u>
8   JASMIN: it would be too bright and straight
9   ALEX: It was just too straight
10   JASMIN: And so we put it too- we put it very far and then
        there was no light and so we kind of moved
        <u>it</u>
11   GW: <u>So you</u> had to get it just the right <u>distance</u>-
12   ALEX: <u>And it</u> got
                 ***
13   JASMIN: <u>At first we</u> did this and then we- and then we did
        this (showing how they varied the position of the
        flashlight)
14   GW: Yeah
15   ALEX: And here was criss-cross

What this transcription is unable to capture, unfortunately, is the enthusiasm with which the two children described what they had done, although this was very apparent from their intonation (notice also the overlapping turns, marked by underlining), their frequent gestures, and excited
facial expressions.

Jasmin and Alex were obviously convinced that they had seen the
beams of light cross, but I played the role of skeptic. In the full light of the
classroom, the crisscross was not apparent, and in any case, I wanted to
see whether they could explain as well as describe the phenomenon that
interested them. "How do you KNOW that the beams of light cross?" I
asked, with heavy emphasis on *know*. "We saw it," replied Alex—entirely
reasonably—and Jasmin continued:

40   JASMIN: Because it just shines through . and it um comes out
        <through there> and then it <comes to> this part (point-
        ing) and it sort of makes . a-
41   ALEX: -a crisscross

But I still claim to be unconvinced, and when they have finished describing what they saw, I push again:

48   GW: And I can see two little lines of light there How do I
          know . that it isn't- that that line- (referring to the slit on
          the left) that that <u>line there-</u>
49   ALEX: <u>Hey the lines cross</u> (excitedly, as he
          looks at the bottom of the box)
50   GW: -isn't going to the . line on the left? (= vertical bar of light
          projected on to the left side at the far end of the box)
          You're telling me . that the light that goes in there .
51   JASMIN: Yeah
52   GW: -crosses over and shows on the right
53   JASMIN: Yeah
54   GW: How do I know that? How can you show me?

Alex obviously considers that seeing is believing and shows little apparent interest in my too subtle distinction between causing and explaining the phenomenon. But Jasmin rises to the challenge, and after pondering for a moment, suggests that the bending of the beams of light is caused
by the jar of water. Still I persist: "How can you . SHOW me . how can you
PROVE to me that you're right?" To prompt her, I ask what would happen if she were to cover one of the slits through which the flashlight is
shining. Jasmin does this and we observe that the bar of light diagonally
opposite on the far end of the box has disappeared. She then tries covering
the other slit and again the diagonally opposite bar disappears.

Alex, who has been standing by, immediately sees the connection.

92   ALEX: If you cover that strip-
93   JASMIN: -it's that one that covers see?

But he doesn't find it easy to recast his understanding in the more
scientific terms that I am angling for.

106   GW: Good . OK so now what does that prove?
107   JASMIN: That proves that water- no-
108   ALEX: -light criss- criss um
          cross
109   GW: That's right that's- the beams of light crossed over . so
          that when you <u>covered the-</u>
110   JASMIN: <u>But you also </u>have to find the rays to
          make it . *
111   GW: What would have made it do that?
112   JASMIN: The water- the water that was in the jar
113   ALEX: I think it's the JAR

Whether or not he really believed it was the jar, Alex's difference with Jasmin clearly called for a further experiment to settle the matter. An empty jar was substituted for the full jar and the finger test repeated. This clearly "showed" that it was the water and not the jar that caused the beams of light to bend, and both Alex and Jasmin seemed to understand the significance of this empirical demonstration.

Following this episode, the two children enthusiastically explained what they had been doing to the Vice Principal, who happened to have come into the classroom. They also shared their work with their class teacher, though much more briefly. Some time later, I rejoined the children as they were preparing to write their report, having first placed the camera to record our interaction. During this episode, we discussed who the report was to be written for—"people who don't know," Jasmin suggested—and what information these readers would need to know if they wished to replicate the experiment. This discussion led to the joint construction of a genre structure appropriate for their writing and a rehearsal of potential content. Just before this was completed, however, we were interrupted by the class teacher's request to the class to "clear up" and by an invitation to Jasmin and Alex to tell the assembled class about what they had done and learned. The final episode took place the next morning, as the two children worked together on their written reports. Here is the first draft of Jasmin's report.

Question. Can light bend???

1   *Materials*: One cardbord box, a glass jar filled with water (to make exprimint more clearly put food coloring in water,) sheet of white paper that can fit inside the cardbord box, scissors, ruler, pen and a very bright flashlight.

2   *What we did*: First we drawed two nawrow slots two cm. apart each other on one side of the cardbord box. Then we cut the slots, put the sheet inside the cardbord box make sure it fits just right. Then we put the glass of water inside the cardbord box, make sure the jar of water is right beside the slots. In a very, very, very dark room (place), shine the flashlight through the two slots.

3   *Observations*: You might find out that you can only see two slots on the other side of the cardbord box but it doesn't mean that you did it wrong, if you don't belive me, try taking the flashlight and tip the back of it up (slightly) and then tip it so that it is leveled again. Repet that again and again and you will see it cross together, if you don't see it that means your either tiping it to much or you did something

wrong. Now, say if you wearn't prety sure if it's crossing together and you want to be realy sure that it's crossed, try this, use one hand to hold the flashlight and one of your finger to cover one of the slots and then lift your finger up, now look at the other side of the cardbord box where the light will apear and do it again (lift your finger up and down) and if you would notice that when you cover the right slot the left slot will disappar and when you cover the left slot the right slot dissappars, you might wonder why, Because when you cover the right slot the right slot should dissappar, not the left, so this shows you that you may not see it cross but it mabe is.

4   *Other questions people ask*: Mr. Wells asked Alex (my partner) and me a question, "What do you think is causing the light bend?" I said it was the water but my partner said it was the glass so insded we did another exprimint. what we did was take out the jar of water and put in another jar but this time without water. we did exacly the same thing, and we tested it with our finger again, but it didn't crossover together. So we new it was the water.

5   *Coments*: I must say I have to thank [my teacher] for giving me an apertunaty to do this exprimint and learning so much things and also I have to thank Mr. Wells for helping us do this exprimint, thank you both of you. Another coment from myself, the exprimint was neat.

Jasmin

There are many interesting features in this whole episode and I shall return to some of them later. But first I want to tell the rest of the story.

REACTIONS FROM OTHER TEACHERS

My immediate reaction when I left the classroom at the end of the morning was that this learning and teaching episode had been rather successful, and so, shortly after my visit, I transcribed the whole of the recording for later analysis. Over the next year or two, I also showed excerpts from the videotape on a number of occasions when making presentations about the importance of talk for the coconstruction of knowledge and about the value of starting from hands-on practical experience as a basis for moving towards "theoretical knowing" (Wells, 1999). Reactions were generally favorable, although on each occasion there was a minority of teachers who felt that I had insisted too strongly on my own agenda in pushing such young children to try to explain, rather than simply letting them enjoy, the interesting phenomenon of bending light. These reactions gave me some food for thought, but not enough to make me seriously doubt the value of attempting to engage with students in ways that encouraged them to work in their "zones of proximal development" (Vygotsky, 1978).

However, a really significant challenge came a couple of years later, when I was teaching a graduate class on discourse analysis. I wanted class members to work on describing a genuine sample of classroom interaction, and as I did not want them to feel concerned about making negative evaluations of an unknown teacher's behavior, I chose this videotape in which I was the teacher, assuring them that they could be as critical as they wished of the way in which the teacher handled the situation. As events proved, this was a fortunate decision.

For most of the course we worked on the transcript that I had already prepared, examining the relationship between student and teacher contributions to the spoken discourse. It was only toward the end that we looked again at the videotape in order to consider the nonverbal aspects of the interaction. At this point, however, it became all too apparent that, in my enthusiasm to engage the children in a more scientific mode of thinking, I had more or less ignored Alex's interest in replicating the actual crisscross phenomenon and given much more of my attention to Jasmin, who showed a greater willingness to fit in with my agenda.

As I viewed the videotape again with my graduate students, all of them experienced teachers, I could not but agree with their evaluation of my behavior and I was mortified by what I saw. Certainly, if I had been aware of it at the time, I would not have been so biased in my interaction with the two children and I wondered what could have led me to behave in this way. As I reviewed the videotape, a number of hypotheses occurred to me. Perhaps it was that Jasmin, to a much greater extent than Alex, showed an interest in attempting to explain rather than simply describe what they had done; or was it that she was much more fluent in English and therefore able to enter more fully into the highly verbal activity that I proposed? Or perhaps it was that her style of interaction was much more expressive than Alex's—more gestures and responding smiles—and this made her a more satisfying conversational partner. In order to try to discover what had led me to behave as I did, I decided to carry out a much more detailed analysis.

NONVERBAL DIMENSIONS OF INTERACTION

When carrying out my earlier research on children's language development in the days before video cameras were readily available (Wells, 1986), I had become accustomed to working only with audio recordings and with the written transcripts made from them. Working in this way, I had paid little attention to the nonverbal dimensions of interaction since, apart from intonation, these cannot be recovered from an audio recording. As a result, I had focused almost exclusively on the "propositional content" of interaction, ignoring the meanings expressed through gesture, gaze, and facial expression; that is to say, I had given much greater weight to the ideational content of the interaction than to the interpersonal and affective meanings. Prompted by the comments of my teacher colleagues, however, I decided to explore these nonverbal dimensions.

However, the problem that immediately becomes apparent when one begins to attend to nonverbal communication is that there are no accepted conventions for representing these aspects of interactional behavior. Unlike the meanings expressed by words in grammatical structures, the meanings communicated through gesture, gaze, and intonation are difficult to pin down and even more difficult to record in ways that others will be able to interpret. Where lexico-grammar refers, for the most part, to discrete categories of experience—objects, actions, and perceptible qualities—nonverbal communication varies along continuous dimensions, enacting rather than referring to the meanings to be conveyed. And since these meanings are not captured in normal written text, we tend to be much less conscious of the ways in which they affect the manner in which the interaction unfolds (Olson, 1994).

The first task, therefore, was to find a way of representing these nonverbal dimensions of meaning in a form that could be included in a printed transcript. For intonation, I adapted transcription conventions from the work of Halliday (1967) and Brazil (1981), and relatively simple schemes were invented for representing gaze and spatial orientation (see Appendix). Representing gesture proved more complicated, however, since this has been relatively little studied in the context of conversational interaction. Nevertheless, with the help of Mari Haneda, a fairly comprehensive scheme was devised, based on the work of McNeill (1992).

McNeill's (1992) descriptive scheme focuses exclusively on manual gestures that accompany speech. From the videotape of Jasmin and Alex's experiment and its sequel, however, it became apparent that there are other ways in which nonverbal behavior can communicate meaning. When the two children were preparing their apparatus, and again when they carried out their experiment under the teacher's desk, their actions were meaningful in the sense of being interpretable by an onlooker as purposefully directed to the achievement of an action goal. Later, when they described to me what they had done, they reproduced very much the same behavior, but now it was intended, not to reproduce the goal of making the beams of light cross, but to demonstrate how they had previously carried out this activity. On this basis, we recognized three forms of communicative nonverbal activity: action; demonstrative action; and gesture, with further differentiation into pointing, iconic, metaphoric, attitudinal, and emphatic forms of gesture (see Table 5.1).

All these different dimensions of nonverbal communication, together with descriptive comments, were represented in tabular form in a computer-prepared transcript. (Table 5.3 below provides an example.) This

Table 5.1. Categories of Visually Communicated Meaning

Category	Code
ACTION	A
DEMONSTRATIVE ACTION	Da
GESTURE	
Deictic	
Point to a coparticipant	Pv
Point to concrete object or location	Po
Trace the path of an object or phenomenon	Pt
Abstract point to a "concept" referred to in either concurrent or preceding speech	Pe
Iconic	
Gesture that iconically represents an object	Go
Gesture referring to element of the concurrent utterance	Ga/t
Metaphoric	
Gesture that iconically represents a "concept" in the concurrent utterance (e.g., closing the fist to represent "contraction," or a horizontal movement of one hand away from the body, palm open, to represent "it was straightforward")	Gc
Gesture that represents an abstract relationship, such as "equivalent to" or "contrasted with"	Gr
Gesture representing a mental state (e.g., touching one's temple to represent "thinking")	Gm
Gesture representing communicative action, such as "telling" or "writing"	Gw
Attitudinal	
Gesture that represents an affective state, e.g., "pleasure"	Gf
Gesture that represents an epistemic attitude with respect to the concurrent utterance, such as "uncertainty"	Gz
Emphatic: Referred to as "beat" by McNeill, this typically up-down gesture marks emphasis or "indexes the word or phrase it accompanies as being significant, not for its own semantic content, but for its discourse-pragmatic content" (1992, p. 15)	E

Source: Reprinted from *Linguistics and Education, 10,* G. Wells, Modes of Meaning in a Science Activity, pp. 307–334, Copyright 2000, with permission from Elsevier Science.

coding procedure was applied to all the episodes narrated above and an analysis was then carried out to explore the patterns of interaction between the three participants and to compare the ways in which I, as teacher, related to the two children. (For a more detailed analysis, see Wells, 2000.)

INTERPRETING THE RESULTS OF THE ANALYSIS

Several interesting results emerged from this analysis. First, by attending to the spatial orientation of the three participants to each other and to the shoe box and its contents, I realized that Jasmin consistently took the lead. Whether by accident or design, when the two children were describing to me how they had conducted their experiment, she took up a position along the length of the shoe box so that she, rather than Alex, was able to manipulate the flashlight and to demonstrate exactly how they had produced the crisscross effect. When Alex tried to play a more active role, Jasmin maintained her control of the flashlight, and Alex was left on the periphery with little to do other than cover the box with an exercise book in order to make the interior dark enough for the crisscrossing beams to be clearly visible. Later, when we were discussing how they might write up their report, Jasmin again took up a more dominant position, standing facing me, while Alex was seated on my left side—again, relatively speaking, on the periphery.

Jasmin and Alex also differed in their gestures. Proportionately, Alex's gestures were predominantly associated with the experiment itself, repeating the actions involved or pointing to the path followed by the beams of light. Jasmin's, by contrast, were more interpersonally oriented; as well as producing action gestures related to the experiment, almost a third of her gestures were concerned with demonstrating and pointing to exactly what they had done, while another quarter expressed her feelings about her own involvement in the experiment or metaphorically communicated how she imagined readers of their report might feel (see Table 5.2). My gestures, on the other hand, tended to be more didactic: pointing to the slits cut in one end of the box and the bars of light on the opposite end in order to direct the children's attention to the relationship between them and, in the writing conference, emphatic gestures ("beats") to underline the issues that I thought were important to consider.

But the greatest difference between the two children was in the direction of their gaze when speaking. Except when everyone's attention was directed to the shoe box, Jasmin almost always made eye contact when she was the speaker, and she also looked at the person who was speaking; the result

Table 5.2. Distribution of Gestures by Category and Participant

Category	Jasmin	Alex	Teacher	Total
Action	16	14	2	32 (19.8%)
Point (to object or aspect of situation)	11	6	23	40 (24.7%)
Demonstration	10	2	0	12 (7.4%)
Gesture: Iconic	5	9	6	20 (12.3%)
Gesture: Metaphoric (incl. abstract point)	6	3	5	14 (8.6%)
Gesture: Attitudinal	12	1	2	15 (9.3%)
Emphasis	8	2	19	29 (17.9%)
Total	68 (42.0%)	37 (22.8%)	57 (35.2%)	162 (100%)

Source: Reprinted from *Linguistics and Education, 10,* G. Wells, Modes of Meaning in a Science Activity, pp. 307–334, Copyright 2000, with permission from Elsevier Science.

was that mutual gaze was established between us on many occasions during the interaction. Alex, on the other hand, rarely looked at his addressee, and although he did occasionally look at whoever was speaking, he seemed deliberately to avoid establishing mutual gaze, particularly with me.

During the actual interaction around the bending light experiment, I had not paid attention to these differences between the children, although, at a level below conscious awareness, I now realize I must have been responding to them. In the moment—insofar as I can reconstruct my thoughts at this distance in time—my teacherly self responded to Jasmin's enthusiasm and interest as we attempted to coconstruct an explanation of what the two children had observed, and I simply hoped that Alex, too, would be drawn into fuller participation. I certainly made one or two efforts to include him by asking for his opinion, but I did not insist on his answering at length, particularly when Jasmin answered simultaneously. On the other hand, I also noticed his willingness to be distracted by other children's attempts to show the objects they had been making, and this only reinforced my impression that he was somewhat less mature than Jasmin and either less interested in, or perhaps less capable of, participating in my attempt to raise the activity from simply replicating an experiment to constructing a theoretical explanation.

Looking back with the benefit of hindsight and of what I have learned by systematically studying the nonverbal dimensions of our interaction, I realize now how mistaken I was. However, my mistake was not, I believe, in attempting to "up the ante," as Bruner (1983) describes parents' attempts to draw their children into more intellectually demanding forms of activity. Helping students of whatever age or stage of development to tackle tasks that they are interested in but unable to manage alone is, in my view, the very essence of teaching. Jasmin obviously enjoyed and benefited from my attempts to scaffold this more challenging activity. However, I now realize that Alex did too—but not in behavior that I then recognized and valued. My mistake, then, was in expecting him to conform to my culturally bound definition of an interested and attentive student and in failing to pick up the meanings he was communicating in ways that, with my preference for verbal participation, I simply did not notice. In the next section, I shall describe Alex's mode of participation as I now understand it.

AN ALTERNATIVE INTERPRETATION OF ALEX'S BEHAVIOR

The first thing that struck me when I began to analyze the videotape systematically was the difference between the gaze behavior of the two children, which I have summarized above. Whereas Jasmin frequently established mutual gaze, Alex seemed deliberately to avoid doing so. This definitely surprised me, and even after repeated viewings of the tape, I still find it somewhat disconcerting.

In most language communities with which I am familiar, it is normal for interlocutors to make eye contact periodically during interaction. Indeed, according to standard accounts of how face-to-face interaction is able to proceed smoothly, such gaze behavior is considered to be crucial (Sacks, Schegloff, & Jefferson, 1974). English speakers use gaze to indicate when they are reaching the end of their turn and often also to select the next speaker. They also look at their addressee(s) from time to time while they are speaking in order to monitor comprehension and to ascertain their reactions. To English speakers like myself, therefore, the absence of such gaze behavior seems odd or even impolite, and it is likely to be interpreted as a lack of interest in participating in the interaction.

Not all cultures share the same expectations about appropriate interactional behavior, however (Cazden, 1988). In particular, in cultures where differential status is marked, it is a sign of respect to look down when speaking to someone of higher status, such as a teacher. Although both Alex and Jasmin are Chinese Canadians born in Canada, Jasmin's parents have more dealings outside the Chinese community than do Alex's; in that sense, Alex is perhaps more culturally Chinese than Jasmin. That being so, it may well be that, in avoiding eye contact with me, he was following his home culture's prescriptions for deferential behavior. Another possible explanation is that he was simply shy; lacking Jasmin's outgoing confidence with adults, he perhaps felt awkward in interacting with a complete stranger who simply assumed that he would be willing to enter into conversation. In either case, his gaze behavior should not have triggered such an inappropriate response on my part, and I shall endeavor to be more sensitive to patterns of behavior that differ from my culturally based expectations in my future encounters with students, whatever their cultural background.

A second aspect of Alex's behavior that I was not aware of until I viewed the whole videotape, including the episodes in which Jasmin and Alex chose, set up, and carried out their experiment, was the extent to which they had established a relationship of unequal status, in which Alex allowed Jasmin to make most of the decisions and to direct their joint activity. When I joined them, therefore, I was unwittingly drawn into their role relationship and, for the reasons given above, I was also too ready to collude in it. Close examination of the two children's spatial positioning in relation to the apparatus and to me provides ample evidence of Jasmin's assumption of a controlling role, both in the manipulation of the experimental apparatus and in her tendency to speak for both of them, frequently talking over Alex so that his contributions went unnoticed. Again, had I been more sensitive to Alex's relative disenfranchisement, I would have made a greater effort to ensure more equal participation.

But the greatest surprise was to discover how fully Alex remained involved in the whole activity, despite being excluded from full participation. As our interaction proceeded in real time, I did not notice how he was shadowing the talk between Jasmin and myself with gestures that showed he fully grasped the significance of the finger test and how he later used a tracing gesture to explain an understanding that he could not put into words. Clearly, he was not as uninvolved as his lack of speech, his willingness to be distracted by the interventions of his peers, and his apparently aimless stirring of the water in the jar during our writing conference had led me to suppose. The difference was that his preferred mode of participation was largely nonverbal, whereas Jasmin's was the verbal mode that I unthinkingly took for granted.

THE MUTUAL CONSTRUCTION
OF DIFFERENTIAL PARTICIPATION

However, just as important as the discovery of my own inappropriate way of privileging Jasmin at Alex's expense was the enhanced understanding I gained, from systematically attending to the fine detail of the nonverbal behavior, of the complex, multidimensional, and mutually constructed nature of face-to-face interaction in *any* situation. As a result of being able to re-view our interaction from a critically reflective perspective, I came to see that Alex's apparently less engaged participation in the scientific activity of explaining the phenomenon of bending light was not simply the result of his individual attributes or of my own ineptitude, but was jointly constructed by all three participants through the totality of our communicative actions and our responses to each other's actions in ways of which we were probably all to a large extent unaware.

This can be very clearly seen in a short sequence that occurred during the writing conference when, having decided upon the intended audience for their report, the two children begin to consider the form that the report should take (see Table 5.3). In this table, speaking turns are broken, where appropriate, into tone units (roughly corresponding to "idea units"); these are numbered in the leftmost column. The second column identifies the speaker and columns 4–6 show gaze, gesture, and spatial orientation, respectively. Here is how I have come to understand the interaction between the three participants (Wells, 2000).

As teacher, I am clearly involved here in scaffolding the construction of a genre appropriate to the chosen audience. However, my initial prompt, although intended for both children, is more directed to Jasmin than to Alex; because she is standing opposite me while Alex is sitting on my left, it is to Jasmin that I look while posing the question, and there is a brief period of mutual gaze between us. Not surprisingly, therefore, it is Jasmin who offers the first contribution. Rather than directly responding to my question, though, she proposes that the report should start with the "question" that they were trying to answer in 3.11 (numbers refer to tone units). In answering in this way, Jasmin shows that she sees herself as a coconstructor of the plan for the report, thereby confirming my evaluation of her as an interested and engaged student. Her no doubt unconscious movement to push her hair behind her ear as she answers suggests a certain degree of nervous tension in this challenging situation.

Alex is obviously keen to contribute too. His proposal (3.13, 3.15) connects with Jasmin's by presupposing that they are together constructing an ordered sequence of elements: first the question, then what they did. Unlike Jasmin, however, Alex does not make eye contact with either member of his audience while he speaks; instead he fiddles with the flashlight. As a result, when he pauses part way through his utterance, Jasmin is able to begin a comparable proposal, actually completing hers at the same time as he does; significantly, she also looks at me as she speaks. When I accept the proposal, therefore, it is to Jasmin that I respond; although I had been looking at Alex while he spoke, the combination of Jasmin's directed gaze

Table 5.3. The Mutual Construction of Alex's Peripheral Role

Tone Unit	Spkr	Text (with Intonation)	Gesture	Gaze	Spatial Orient.	Comments
3.10	T	So. /what is it you want to \tell them?		T<J	A / T X J	T removes glasses on "what" and holds them across chest in right hand. J looks at cap of jar, picks it up, and puts it down again. J pushes hair behind left ear.
3.11	J	Tell them- er first we've got to write the \/ question		J<>T		
3.12	T	\Yep		T<>J		
3.13	A	Then we've got to put-	A	A<X / T<A		A continues to manipulate f-light; he does not look up when he speaks.
3.14	J	-and then- .		J>T<A		
3.15	A	-we've got to write about . . \/what we did		A<X / T<A		A looks at f-light, and then briefly up at J as she takes over.
3.16	J	- write about- x <did>		T>J		T turns head to look at J at end of A's utterance.
3.17	T	/Yes				
3.18	J	and um . the */materials we used	?	J<>T		J brings both hands, palms in, against lower body on "materials."
3.19	A	then .. how- why <it does>		A<X		A doesn't look at others, and his speech is ignored. He looks briefly at T at end of utterance.
3.20	T	OK so what */\first d'you think, the /materials you used or what you \did?	E	A<T / T<>J		T makes vague gesture with left hand open and vertical.
3.21	A	What we \did		A<X		
3.22	J	The materials		J<A		
3.23	A, J	(laugh)		A<>J / T<A		
3.24	T	*\/OK, so why- why d'you think . why d'you think . \"what we did"? (to A)	Pv	T<A		T points toward J, leans forward, and turns head to look at A.
3.25	A	I think . <reading materials> (=?reading the book to identify their question and the materials to be used)	A	A<X		J leans over and turns off f-light that A is holding.
3.26	T	\OK ..		T<A		A continues to fiddle with f-light.
3.27		Why d'you think materials \first? (to J)		T< >J		T sits up and looks up at J.

Source: Reprinted from *Linguistics and Education*, 10, G. Wells, Modes of Meaning in a Science Activity, pp. 307–334, Copyright 2000, with permission from Elsevier Science.

and her more forceful manner, together with Alex's lack of eye contact, apparently lead me to treat Jasmin as the principal interlocutor. Alex gives the impression of accepting this hijacking of his contribution, since he looks up briefly to Jasmin at the end of her utterance and then down again at the flashlight, giving no indication of surprise or dissatisfaction.

But he has not given up. As Jasmin confidently continues with a further proposal (3.18), Alex takes the opportunity provided by her voiced hesitation to attempt to get back into the discussion (3.19). However, because of his own hesitation and his lack of eye contact, he is ignored by me, the teacher; I speak over him as I ask Jasmin which of the two proposed stages should come first (3.20). Despite this, Alex still persists. Together with Jasmin, he responds to my question, giving a different answer from hers. They both laugh at this disagreement and at this point Alex does at last make eye contact; but it is with Jasmin not with me, the teacher.

Nevertheless, I have noted Alex's answer and I look at him, asking him to justify his proposal. Once again, however, Alex does not make eye contact as he speaks, and his answer is hard to hear (3.25); he does not offer the requested justification but seems to have changed his mind and to be supporting Jasmin's preference for starting by describing the materials they used. I make an accepting move that invites him to say more ("OK" said with fall-rise intonation), but Alex does not continue. Perhaps he is disconcerted by Jasmin's assertion of dominance when she stretches over to switch off the flashlight that he is holding while he speaks. In any case, after a few seconds of silence during which Alex, with downcast eyes, continues to fiddle with the flashlight, I turn to Jasmin and ask her to justify her proposal. She responds, fluently and at length, with dramatic gestures that underline the mental and affective states imputed to the imagined readers of the report. Quite evidently, she is more than willing to speak for both of them, taking on the role as if by right and with my apparent encouragement.

In what follows, this pattern is repeated. Alex does not opt out of the discussion, but his contributions are spoken softly, often simultaneously with those of Jasmin, and he consistently looks down at the apparatus rather than at his interlocutors as he speaks. Jasmin, on the other hand, speaks confidently, and with strong gestures; she engages in frequent mutual gaze with me and on several occasions overrides Alex's attempts to enter the discussion. Because of the two children's different modes of participation, and because Jasmin's contributions better fit my scaffolding agenda, I collude with her in her assumption of the role of spokesperson. The result is that, although Alex is equally engaged in the activity, his less assertive manner allows his contributions to be ignored by the other two participants; what is more, he appears to be quite content to accept this less central role.

LEARNING FROM OUR MISTAKES

Judith Newman (1987) tells us that, as teachers, we should be open to being surprised; we should also be willing to investigate the mismatch between our assumptions and what actually occurred that gave rise to the surprise. In this chapter I have described how my surprise came, not in the original learning and teaching situation, but several years later when I used the videotape I had made as the basis for a course on the study of classroom interaction. Furthermore, it was not until my students pointed it out that I became aware of my biased behavior, as this was captured on the videotape. It was not a pleasant surprise; but, in prompting me to make a systematic study of the recorded interaction, it confirmed the value of Newman's advice.

The main benefit was my discovery of the critical role of nonverbal behavior in face-to-face interaction. I had always been aware of this, in the sense that I had accepted the information about nonverbal behavior encountered in my reading. But until I was faced with the problem of accounting for my differential treatment of Alex and Jasmin, I had not made this information part of my understanding; that is to say, it had remained as "inert knowledge," having no impact on my actions in relevant situations. Now, this has changed.

As a researcher, I have acquired a strong interest in the nonverbal dimensions of conversational meaning making, and having developed a scheme for describing these dimensions, I am planning to study other episodes of classroom interaction from this perspective. Although these forms of communicative behavior normally take place below the level of conscious awareness, it has become clear to me that that does not mean they are unimportant. Indeed, it is just because we are not normally aware of them that they can on occasion severely disrupt communication (Hall, 1959) or, as in the present case, lead to the relative disenfranchisement of a less powerful participant. As I gain a greater understanding of how meanings are communicated by gaze, gesture, and spatial orientation, I shall want to share this understanding with others so that they may, if they choose, examine their own behavior from this point of view.

More importantly, as a teacher, I have learned how my "logocentrism" has blinded me to other modes of meaning making that, when attended to, can make a difference in how I view students' interests and abilities and enable me to be more effective in coconstructing meaning with them in our zones of proximal development. I say *our* ZPDs, because I firmly believe that we can learn from our students (as I did here) as much as they can learn from us. In fact, I am convinced that learning and teaching in the classroom is most effective for all participants when we learn with and from each other.

And finally, as a teacher-researcher, I have once again experienced the value of inquiring into my own practice, using the analysis of data collected (in this case on videotape) to bring it more into line with my vision and, at the same time, to develop a more theoretical understanding of how my behavior impacts on my attempts to enact that vision in practice. As always, too, I have benefited from working in a community of inquiry with colleagues who share my commitment to the value of carrying out action research as a means of improving the practice of education.

PART II

Inquiries in the Intermediate and Senior Grades

Seeing Shades of Gray: Developing a Knowledge-Building Community Through Science

Karen Hume

THERE ARE APPROXIMATELY 22 feet of chalkboard running across the front and down the side of my classroom. At my choice, there is no chalk. Instead of teacher notes and math equations, the board is frequently covered with a hundred or more yellow, fluorescent pink, and neon green Post-it notes, written by my class of 24 Grade 6/7 students, and arranged by them beneath questions that have been recorded on manilla tagboard and magnetized to the top of the board.

When students aren't posting their notes, they are engaged in a wide variety of related activities: reading the notes that are already posted; standing at the board and discussing the notes with others; or writing notes at their desks, based on reading, conversation, and experimentation, and then returning to post them to "the wall." That's what we call our knowledge-building wall, and its development is the central activity in most of our inquiries.

CREATING THE KNOWLEDGE WALL

Before joining the DICEP research group, my work with students had been directed toward inquiries that resulted in tangible products (e.g., models, maps, written reports, enormous schoolwide productions) in the belief that my students' interest in products would provide them with a meaningful purpose for knowledge building. However, I was finding that, time and again, student interest in production was resulting in a focus on the skills and techniques that would simply make the product *appear* sophisticated and appealing. This might not have been a significant problem were it not for the fact that such a focus often meant that my students actively resisted any suggestion that knowledge construction be a part of our work. The final products were, embarrassingly often, almost "content free" (see also Kowal, Chapter 7).

At the time that I first read the exciting work of Carl Bereiter and Marlene Scardamalia (1994), I was actively seeking a new way to view classroom activity. I wanted to focus on the growth of knowledge and understanding, and I believed that this could only be achieved through some form of community development that stressed both cognitive and affective collaboration among students and teacher. Not surprisingly, I was tremendously inspired by their vision of a classroom being more like a research community:

> Recently, people have begun to attend more to the social processes of research teams and laboratories, which have a character and a power quite different from that of a mere aggregation of individual researchers. . . . By focusing on the individual student's abilities and dispositions, educators have failed to grasp the social structure and dynamics that are required for progressive knowledge building. . . .
>
> When we speak of schools as knowledge-building communities, we mean schools in which people are engaged in producing knowledge objects that . . . lend themselves to being discussed, tested, and so forth without particular reference to the mental states of those involved and in which students see their main job as producing and improving such objects. Restructuring schools as knowledge-building communities means, to our minds, getting the community's efforts directed toward social processes aimed at improving these objects. . . (Bereiter and Scardamalia, 1994, pp. 269–270)

This conception clearly requires some significant changes in our enactment of educational activities in our classrooms. There must be far greater emphasis on written discourse—in a form which can be accessed and acted upon by all. Oral discourse is so often controlled by the teacher, and even when not, it is limited in time, selective in involvement, and closed to further examination because there is no record of it. Bereiter and Scardamalia (Scardamalia, Bereiter, & Lamon, 1994) have dealt with this problem through the creation of a technological infrastructure called CSILE (Computer Supported Intentional Learning Environment). CSILE provides users with a visual environment for knowledge building as they contribute ideas, argue points, and ask questions, all within the framework of a written, interactive database.

When I read Bereiter and Scardamalia's work, a couple of years before the research reported in this chapter, I was teaching in a new and very well equipped school. CSILE should have been a natural activity for us. However, I never made use of computers for knowledge building, but developed the knowledge wall concept during that year instead. There were several reasons for this. To understand what a knowledge-building community might look like in an elementary school classroom, and how it is created and then sustained, was and is my overall goal and the focus of all of my classroom research. However, I believe that any innovation that requires hardware in its implementation is doomed, if not to failure, at least to limited use. This is partly because of economics and partly because many teachers have difficulty in integrating computer use into their day, either because of fear of the technology or because of unavailability of the equipment, which is often housed in a separate, and tightly scheduled, computer lab.

On the other hand, like Bereiter and Scardamalia, I believe it is an enormous advantage to community development when students can see before them the results of their work; when they can, at a glance, track a conversation; when they can cluster in front of an idea and talk about it. Discourse, according to sociocultural theory, is at the heart of all teaching and learning, in large part because it is contextually embedded in all activity (see Chapter 10). Written discourse is particularly powerful (Bakhtin, 1986) because it both represents current understanding and, simultaneously, can be reworked to allow for greater intersubjectivity— the ability of all participants to recognize each other's understanding and intentions and to work toward ensuring that mutual understanding is maintained. It seems to me that the more visible and ever present the discourse, the greater the benefit to students. The engineers at PARC, the Xerox research lab, have a room full of networked computers, similar to the CSILE design, but as each engineer works individually at a computer, his or her ideas are automatically added to a huge projection screen that fills one end of the room so that others can, on a moment-by-moment basis, see the progress in written discourse. That was what I wanted—without the computers. So I created the "knowledge wall."

INTRODUCING MY STUDENTS

Let us imagine that you have come to visit us on an October morning, just one month into our school year and one week into our inquiry on light and color. I haven't been here much longer than you; although I've been a teacher for 12 years, I'm new to this school. It's a great school—a positive, caring, and very professional staff working with, for the most part, an enthusiastic and energetic group of kids.

My class is one of five gifted classes in a school that houses all of the gifted students for the area, in addition to a regular student body spanning junior kindergarten through Grade 8. There are many more boys than girls in my class—17 to 7—a statistic that is distressingly typical for the gifted. However, there is almost none of the interpersonal tension that you might expect of this age group with this gender split. On the contrary, I think you would notice quite quickly that there is tremendous harmony in the room. This is due, in part, I believe, to the fact that the kids have been together for a while—a third of them since their identification as gifted in Grade 3—and in part to the fact that I actively promote the continued community building that supports the intentional learning that is valued in our classroom. I am with my students all day long, except for French and music.

INQUIRING INTO LIGHT, COLOR, AND KNOWLEDGE BUILDING

Much of our year's curriculum had been discussed and developed collaboratively during September, but this first inquiry is one that I have chosen. (See Wells, 1995 and 1999, for a discussion of the importance of inquiry in the classroom.) I had wanted a science topic because the use of hands-on materials tends to engage kids, because problems can often be resolved through experimentation rather than by retreat to the authority of an outside expert, and because of both of these conditions, students are often keenly aware that they are engaged in knowledge creation.

While I hoped that my students would learn more about light and color as a result of our work, my personal focus was very much directed toward three knowledge-building goals:

- Help students come to view knowledge as an improvable object rather than a fixed and predetermined entity
- Engage in collective progress toward class negotiated goals
- Begin, as a class, to examine the details of knowledge building

Specifically, what sorts of questions are most generative? What kinds of contributions are most productive? What characteristics of knowledge building seem particular to science?

Although I began with only the vaguest of ideas of how to work with these goals, their existence provided me with three touchstones that were helpful as I made on-the-spot decisions about how I would respond to my students and what I would emphasize during the course of our work together. Additionally, as I gradually shared the details of these goals with my students and we talked together about our experiences, I found that they became increasingly reflective and articulate about their own thought processes. As one student, Lloyd, put it:

> Other years we focused on getting things done, but now we take things one step further, by processing how we do things while getting them done.

Lloyd's comment is significant. Since discourse is a collective construction, it is important that goals be made explicit and that the relationship between the goals and how they are to be achieved become a topic of discussion, so that the goals can be shared to the greatest degree possible. Otherwise, as is the case in a focus on product development, there is the danger, especially in hands-on work, that alternative goals will become the priority.

Beginning Our Work

We began the inquiry with a few days of whole class activity. Students recorded what they knew and what they wondered about light. Their initial knowledge was, predictably, based on the content of our school board's mandatory Grade 4 light and color unit. They could rhyme off the order of the colors in the visible spectrum, quote the figure for the speed of light, determine which colors artists consider primary, which secondary, and how to mix them. The things they wondered about were a lot more interesting, and more complicated, particularly in the form in which they were asked, for example, "*Why* does light travel faster than sound?" and "How come light makes heat and darkness is cold?"

In an attempt to work from my students' interests, I have often tried to build inquiries out of this initial round of questions. Without exception, I have found that this is an impossibility. I don't know what to do with questions like those above, and neither do my students. When someone asks me, "Can we live without light?" all I can think of to say is "No." While some of my difficulty may be attributed to the fact that I don't have a background in science, much more lies in the phrasing of the questions, many of which force a focus on print research or, at best, on the standard science textbook experiments.

So, facing this dilemma and not knowing what to do about it, I stalled. I put out a table of supplies—flashlights, prisms, a holograph kaleidoscope, a Fresnel lens, mirrors, and magnifying glasses. Students didn't even remove their backpacks and coats before they started exploring; this interest continued unabated for several days. We also did a few days of small group and whole class work with diffraction gratings to look at the visible spectrum and with mirrors to examine the path of light in reflections.

While there was some fleeting interest, I noticed that the knowledge my students gained was procedural rather than substantive, and that this bored them. This was not surprising. For inquiries to be meaningful, they must have implications for action beyond the classroom (Wells, 1997; see also Chapter 10). While it was important that my students learn to use diagrams as well as text to show their thinking and that they be able to refer back to a detailed written record in order to note subtle differences in their experimental observations, these skills were viewed as school skills—meaningless without a relevant context in which they could be put to meaningful use.

Sharing the Responsibility for Progress

The next day I addressed the issue head on:

> I think you need to take ownership and responsibility for the way you are feeling about things at any given time. Dylan Thomas, I think, said it best. He said, "Somebody's boring me. I think it's me." . . . Within a classroom situation, the only possible way for you to be bored is for you to expect to be entertained, and feel that you are not getting the response you are looking for in your desire to be entertained. So here's my request. If somebody's boring you, look to yourself. Decide for yourself what it is that you need to understand about light that you are not currently understanding, and make use of the resources that we have available—hands-on, print, and people, and our personal knowledge—to try to deepen your understanding of the area of light that you're finding difficult to understand.

In making this speech, I was attempting quite deliberately to communicate that I expected our inquiry to be jointly negotiated and that I would assume neither full responsibility nor full blame for its success or failure.

I was trying to ensure that all students were given a "way in" to the inquiry, an invitation to engage with whatever problems and features of light and color were most salient for them.

I asked that we summarize what we had learned in our first three days of work on light, which we were easily able to do, and then reiterated that our work could take any direction, especially now that we had a common base from which to work. I emphasized that questions were most useful when you could actually do something with them in the attempt to build understanding, and then I asked my class to tell me the questions they'd really like to address while I recorded them on a whiteboard.

There isn't room to include all of the 28 questions that were called out over the course of a half hour, but just a representative few will show quite clearly the substantial difference in the quality of questions from this session, compared to those offered just five days earlier:

What is the difference between a colored filter and a tinted lens?

If you bounce light off a mirror and put a prism up to it, would the color spectrum reverse?

Can light be trapped or slowed down enough to become an object you can touch?

Is it possible for light to take up space?

Most of our new questions were more open to experimentation, more focused, and yet broader in scope with more possible connections and applications. This "commitment to frame questions and propositions in ways that allow evidence to be brought to bear on them" (Bereiter, 1994, p. 7) is critical to knowledge building, not just because it helps to teach the frames of reference of the particular discipline (i.e., what is considered evidence), but also because it allows for a variety of possible actions to be taken by my students rather than reliance on predetermined, fixed, and authoritative information.

There was such a marked difference in the quality of these questions that I asked my students to explain it. Joel said that it's because the class is "very much more interested." I asked why. David responded:

We can get a lot more interesting puzzles because now that we know more and are learning more, we've started to see like shades of grey and more questions that we wouldn't have thought about before because we didn't know enough to think about them.

This speaks to the importance of a round of whole class and small group activity *before* attempting to work with student generated questions (see also Van Tassell, Chapter 3). The common base that we had built in our few days of whole class and small group work not only provided us with a number of shared understandings and a language for discussing them, but also primed the pump for new questions.

In my call to action—"Decide for yourself what it is that you need to understand about light that you are not currently understanding"—I stressed individual responsibility for progress and individual ownership of the process. If each student doesn't have something on the wall that matters to him or her, collective progress suffers, with a few students assuming responsibility for all the work. I believe it is only when individual responsibility is combined with collective responsibility and involvement that collaborative knowledge building can be successful. Certainly, for this class, in the course of listening to each other call out their questions, the individual responsibility that they were willing to assume was clearly transformed into a collective sense of pleasure, the beginnings of commitment to this "something" that we have created and are doing as a class, not something that is being imposed on us by a teacher.

This was evident in the crackle of energy, the high good humor that filled the room. Kids laughed and cheered each other's contributions. Interestingly, the more difficult the question, the more inspired and enthusiastic they seemed to be. Warren Bennis, an author in the field of organizational leadership, notes that this is a common characteristic of the "Great Groups" that he has analyzed: "Curiosity fuels every Great Group. The members don't simply solve problems. They are engaged in a process of discovery that is its own reward" (Bennis & Biederman, 1997, p. 17).

At the end of our inquiry, David speaks to this in his claim that

> the unresolvable topics in advanced physics, having to do with hyperspace, electrons, and properties of light . . . advanced our knowledge the most . . . (because) you have to use hypothetical examples. This is good because you have to conduct thought experiments. Anything is questionable, so it makes for a fun and informative discussion within a small group.

Bereiter (1994) sees this willingness to live for a time in a state of uncertainty and cognitive dissonance as one of four commitments that are essential to progressive discourse in science. He also acknowledges that it is likely the most difficult of the four to achieve, an observation very much supported by my teaching experiences! Nevertheless, I've found that as long as there is a collective willingness to question all assumptions and evidence in the effort to make progress, various individuals are able to fall short of the ideal without endangering the collective's work.

One of the challenges of knowledge building is coming to grips with the fact that the members of the larger knowledge-building community (the community of scientists or geographers or historians . . .) of which you are just a small part have addressed and perhaps resolved the very questions that you are trying to address. For some teachers and students, the frustration of this can be off-putting. There is a sense, at times, that you are reinventing the wheel, wasting time "discovering" something that you could more efficiently look up in a book. Here we come face to face with often unquestioned beliefs about the nature of knowledge. If knowledge is equivalent to information, we'd be well advised to look it up in books or on the World Wide Web. But if *knowledge* is the "object of the activity of knowing" and *knowing* is "the intentional activity of individuals who, as members of a community, make use of, and produce, representations in the collaborative attempt to better understand and transform their shared world", then, as Wells argues, "knowledge is always specific—strategically constructed in, and an inherent part of, the particular, current activity" (1999, pp. 76–77).

My students are, to my surprise and delight, remarkably comfortable with this perspective on knowledge. They seem interested in what they are able to work out for themselves, not whether it has been already determined by someone else. At the same time, they are very much aware of the larger knowledge-building community within which their work is taking place— as evidenced by several comments that were made about how solving a particular problem would qualify us for the Nobel Prize!

Choosing Questions

Once our questions had been recorded, I invited students to take responsibility for the ones they would like to address and I introduced the knowledge wall:

> You'll put your ideas up on the wall to invite other people to come and add their ideas or further questions they have because they might not understand something you've written or they might have a disagreement with something you've written. And at the end of all this I'd like you to take responsibility for explaining the class' current level of understanding at that point of our response to that question. Okay?

Most students signed up for several questions, often ones that were different from the ones they had volunteered during our question-generating session. The groupings of students were quite varied, suggesting that students signed up on the basis of interest, not friendship.

In the remainder of this chapter I will track the development of understanding that took place in response to just one of the 28 questions and will explain why I think this particular bit of data is an excellent example of knowledge building in my classroom.

DEVELOPING A QUESTION

When students were originally asked to individually record what they knew and what they wondered, three students—Deb, Jared, and Chad—expressed an interest in knowing why our eyes are different colors. Deb repeats the question in the whole class session, asking, "Do people with blue eyes see better than albinos and people with green eyes?" The word *albino* is a trigger for this class, having some unusual connection with an albino-eyed plastic rat that was, it seems, a favorite pet through much of the previous year. Not surprisingly therefore, there is a buzz of undertone comment following Deb's question. Only two of these comments can be heard even reasonably clearly on the tape:

ERIC: Do albinos see *?
PAUL: They have no color cones . color cones

I am working quickly—and probably subconsciously trying to minimize the albino connection—so my recording on the whiteboard is slightly different from Deb's initial question. I write, "Do people with blue eyes see better than people with other color eyes?"

Deb, as we shall see, reintroduces the albino question once the wall is begun, and she makes a number of contributions, but she does not sign to take responsibility for the question. Neither do Chad or Jared. Chad's interests have moved on to other areas; he plays no role in this section of the wall. Jared, too, focuses on other aspects of light, contributing to the wall very near the end when questions of experimental design come to the fore. (Interestingly, there are several sections of the wall where Jared contributed at the point of discussion of experimental design.) In the end, it is Nicolas and Eric who take responsibility for the question.

On the very first day of its development, this question is one of five that has responses posted to it. Nicolas and Eric start us off, with reference to a printed source that is likely seen by them as a quick and clear-cut answer. Their initial posting and the five that followed it are as follows:

> Irises have no effect on sight. "The color of our eyes has nothing to do with how well they see." (*The Eye and Seeing* by Steve Parker). (Nicolas, Eric, Oct. 2, 1:17 p.m.)

> I think this is true because it is what I always believed. (Matt C.)

> Then why do people have different colored eyes and how come albinos have some trouble seeing? (Deb, 1:18 p.m.)

> Where did you find your info on albinos? (Eric, 1:20 p.m.)

> My dad told me one day when I saw a girl with pink eyes! (Deb, 1:21)

> How does your dad know? (Albert 1:30)

Matt has agreed, on the basis that it fits within his own framework of understanding: "It is what I always believed." Deb, however, disputes the authoritatively worded claim, citing compelling evidence of her own—the words of her father (a doctor) when she asks him about a girl she has seen on the street. That Eric replies with a question, rather than simply a repetition of the quoted source, suggests that he recognizes the possibility that the source may be incorrect, and/or that he is willing to engage in the discussion, rather than simply closing down the issue.

This willingness to talk about it is important, both to our community and to the knowledge building. It is part of an overall climate of acceptance in the classroom, a climate that is obvious on the wall in 57 different instances of support—either for an idea, or for the right of the individual to take a stand. It is also obvious in the 24 coded instances of invitation to others to contribute to a topic or to refute an idea. Both support and invitation, I would argue, demonstrate not simply an awareness of the community, but an emphasis on its importance to the work.

The overall climate of acceptance is also apparent through its absence or, more correctly, its opposite. In response to Albert's question, "How does your dad know?" Deb replies that he is a doctor. Nikki, who is one of three students new to our class this year, isn't persuaded by the medical degree. She asks for more:

NIKKI: Does your dad have any proof?
DEB: Yes! Years of scientific research.
NIKKI: I mean, does he have any SOLID proof?
DEB: Eyes! They do those funny eye tests on albinos and "ordinary" people.
NIKKI: Only eye doctors do stuff like that.
DEB: So do scientists.

In this little interchange, Nikki has performed a very important function for our community. She has drawn a distinction between tacit, informal knowledge and scientific evidence and proof. By this she has raised the bar for her classmates, encouraging them to draw on evidence that would be acceptable to a community of scientists. However, Nikki has also rocked the affective boat. She is a new kid, and her discourse practices are different from those of the other girls. Her postings contain none of the tentativeness that, in the early days, were the hallmark of the others' responses. She doesn't say, "What do you think?" or "I guess this is true, but it may not be." To the others she seems perhaps too cheerfully certain and too unconcerned about hurting people's feelings. Several students react on the wall:

I think Deb is right! (Amber)

Deb rules because Nikki is wrong. (Unsigned)

I agree with Deb as well. (Amy)

To Nikki's credit, she doesn't back down: "How critical! I wasn't even making a point. I was asking a question." Over the course of this inquiry, Nikki learns the implicit discourse rules of her new community and she makes some adaptations. To the credit of the other students, girls and boys, she is quickly recognized for her skills in furthering the knowledge of the group. Eventually, others adopt some of Nikki's structures, such as requesting proof for informal knowledge.

Our Question Heats Up

Although Deb keeps the issue of albinos alive for a while longer, the initially posted question really generates interest on the second day of the inquiry when Mandi, who had been absent the day before, returns and adds her name as the third person who is keen to take responsibility for the question. Knowledge building is tedious, perhaps impossible, if there is only one perspective offered and it is accepted without disagreement. Mandi ensures that we have multiple perspectives and competing viewpoints in her posting of a claim that is contrary to that of her partners, Eric and Nicolas:

> Yes, people with blue eyes see better than people with other color eyes. A way to prove this is all four of the people in our class that wear glasses don't have blue eyes. (Mandi)

From this moment on, there is intense commitment to this topic, with 21 of the 24 students contributing their ideas, their arguments, and their questions, many of them several times. With a total of 71 postings over the life of the inquiry, this question received not only the most attention, but also the most heated debate. Engagement with the issue was, at first, completely affective, both individually:

> It doesn't matter what color your eyes are! My eyes are green and I can see better than my sister (who has brown eyes), but I can also see better than my mom and her eyes are the same color as mine. Color does *not* matter. (Amber)

> Sometimes my eyes are blue (They change color depending on what I am wearing) and I wear glasses. (Amy)

and collectively:

> No way! (From the brown eyed people)

Notice that Mandi's posting, while not popular, is not ridiculed. Nevertheless, Mandi is completely taken aback by the reaction. She believes that she has simply stated the obvious and is surprised that it is taken personally. She posts her feelings on the wall:

> I'm sorry if I offended anyone with glasses. All I'm saying is the majority of people with glasses don't have blue eyes. (Mandi)

Mandi's willingness, first to present an alternative viewpoint and then to talk openly about the emotional response it creates, is representative of most members of our class. The independence of thought required to present something that is in opposition to a shared view has been critical to the development of knowledge since long before Copernicus argued that the Earth revolved around the Sun, not vice versa as Ptolemy had taught

and the Church had believed. Peer pressure, so typical of many intermediate classes, is death to such intellectual independence. But in a climate
of acceptance such as we enjoy in our class, students help each other learn
to criticize ideas, not people, as in these comments made by Heather and
Nicolas during a whole class discussion:

> Some people take the questions and comments personally, like blue
> eyes versus green eyes. These aren't personal questions. At the
> same time, people shouldn't boast about having blue eyes. It's not
> fair. (Heather)

> I agree. Someone was going around saying "I have blue eyes!"
> (Nicolas)

I believe that providing space for this sort of discussion is one of the
most important actions that I can take as a teacher. Metacognitive reflection, on the knowledge-building process and on the affective development
of our classroom community, helps students build their competence, both
cognitively and affectively. It also encourages joint ownership of our work.
Perhaps most important, it emphasizes that I consider the talk important
and intimately connected to action in our classroom, whether that action
is part of "doing science" or of developing interpersonal relationships. (For
the role of talk in affective development of a classroom community through
class meetings, see Donoahue, Chapter 2, and Davis, Chapter 4.)

Engaging Cognitively

Questions that encourage an affective response help to engage students,
but if progress in understanding is to be made, students need to quickly
move beyond an "is too, is not" kind of argument to a point where engagement is cognitive, with evidence appropriate to the discipline being brought
to bear on the issue. As a first step, students must figure out what they need
to understand.

For this question, as well as for many others in this inquiry, my students' first resort when they disagreed with something but couldn't say
why was to demand proof. This usually wasn't successful, as Cadie
discovers:

> CADIE: Yeah right, Mandi. Where is your source?
> MANDI: My proof is our class. Four people in our class have or
>   have had glasses and none of them have blue eyes.

The limitations of demands for proof are quickly apparent and are made explicit by several people during a class discussion:

ALBERT: I think people should stop nagging at little errors. Put up responses that are logical.

JOEL: There are still too many people saying "What's your proof?"

IAN: I agree. People are saying "What's your proof?" for the sake of argument, not for information. Our object is to learn, not to outsmart someone.

Joel makes use of theoretical knowledge, stating on the wall that Mandi is wrong; that "Genetics makes you have different eyes." David builds on Joel's statement, introducing the term hereditary pigmentation:

Eye color has no effect on vision; it is only a matter of hereditary pigmentation. Glasses have nothing to do with this either. They are used by people whose retina is too close or too far away from the pupil. (David)

Managing the Wall

I have several responsibilities during our inquiry, most of which are directed toward the achievement of my three stated knowledge-building goals. I make contributions to the knowledge wall, assist groups in finding resources, pull everyone together for whole class progress reviews and some selected light activities, videotape small groups each day as they work on their questions, structure the opportunities for the discussion and resolution of conflict, and—a full time job—keep ongoing track of the growth of the wall.

Immediately after Joel and David's postings, I plead for us to summarize the writing that is under each question. The wall is getting so crowded that I'm having great difficulty tracking the introduction of new comments. I've discussed this with the class and someone has suggested that we number the Post-it notes—the number of the entry in the top left corner, and the connection to another number in the top right, as in "This is Post-it #6 to the topic, and I'm responding to Post-it #1." We have done so for the last couple of days, and it has definitely been easier, but now the sheer number of notes is creating a space problem that can't be solved. Nevertheless, I meet with vehement resistance to my suggestion that we summarize, until I reassure them that we are not ending the inquiry, but rather are providing ourselves with a fresh start at knowledge building. We can remove all the notes and continue our building based on each question's summary. I'm told by my students that *summary* is the wrong word, that *progress update* would be better. No argument there!

Clearing the wall, which started as an organizational need, becomes important to my goal of viewing knowledge as an improvable object. Writing a progress update forces close attention to all aspects of the developing argument because students have a responsibility to faithfully report what has happened in the knowledge building so far. It also, as Paul argues, levels the playing field:

> A lot of people look at the ones with all the Post-it notes because they're interesting. We should go to all and not just look at the ones with lots.

The progress update for the eye color question is brief: "After much debate, nearly everyone agrees that color has nothing to do with how you see. GENETICS IS EVERYTHING!" You might want to think of "Genetics is everything!" as a schoolyard chant for that is how it is used for a while. It doesn't appear on the wall very frequently, but it is uttered many, many times and in a very playful tone whenever students discuss this question, or any other they cannot resolve! The reason it doesn't appear on the wall is that students have finally figured out what they need to understand. Before arguing *why* people with blue eyes do or do not see better than others, they need to determine *if* this is in fact the case.

Once it is established that this is what everyone really needs to know, making eye tests and administering them to each other is a logical next step. It is also a reassuring one. When you are grappling with questions that draw almost exclusively on theoretical knowing—questions like, Are there any conditions under which the speed of light can be altered?—it is a great relief to have a question to which you can confidently direct your already considerable skills in instrumental and procedural knowing.

While there were times when the creation and administration of many different eye tests under wide-ranging conditions gave me pause, I trusted that the number and variety of tests would help my students to really understand why science has the rules for evidence that it does. I trusted the science, and more important, I trusted my students. As I worked to understand their knowledge-building efforts, I came to have great respect for their intelligence, thoughtfulness, and tenacity, and great admiration for their collective desire to know.

Sure enough, Nikki starts us off by introducing the question of statistical significance and of tester error when she refutes Andrew and John's eye test:

A test like that proves nothing since that was definitely not enough people in the test to prove that the majority of blue/green eyes sees better than others. Besides, Andrew wrote the test, right? Of course he knew what it said! (Nikki)

Andrew concedes that he doesn't have enough people in his sample, and he tests some more. Ultimately, he acknowledges, much to John's chagrin, that his sample size just isn't large enough.

Jared thinks that one million would be a fair sample size. Someone else says seven billion. This argument is one of a few that students bring from the wall into our class discussions. Eventually I am appealed to in an effort to settle the sample size question, and once asked, I take advantage of the opportunity, offering a spontaneous minilesson about sample size, followed by a couple of weeks of focus on this in a math unit about probability. This is one of the ways in which I think I can be of most help to my students. I can offer help that is specifically related to the task at hand, but that goes beyond the task, demonstrating connections to other aspects of life. By reassuring myself that I have lots of time and many opportunities, and by staying aware of those opportunities when they arrive, I find that I can be "contingently responsive" in helping my students to achieve their, and my, goals.

WRAPPING IT UP

Almost one month into the inquiry, the blue-eyes question is still of considerable fascination to a great many people, but with the hands-on activity losing its usefulness, there's an increasing sense of students trying to wrap up where they stand on the question, offering some tentative responses. *Tentative* is the operative word. My students are aware that since they can't, at least to their satisfaction, answer the question "*Do* blue-eyed people see better than people with other colors of eyes?" any discussion of *why* is going to be necessarily tentative and uncertain. Nevertheless, they are prepared to try. At this point it is interesting that there is a resurgence of concern for the affective, with many students qualifying their responses with reminders that they are not saying that blue eyes are best.

Various alternatives are offered, all connected with the findings from other questions on the wall. One anonymous student, for example, claims that eyesight is based on the amount of light coming into your eyes and that there's no basis for believing that blue-eyed people let more light into their eyes than people with any other color of eyes.

Concluding the Inquiry

It had originally been my intention that we create a publication of our understanding that could be shared with parents and perhaps a few scientists, inviting their response and continuing through another round of knowledge building based on that response. Unplanned events, as well as the natural rhythms of classroom life, conspired against this happening.

However, we left the inquiry with no sense of failure or incompletion. We had achieved our goals. We enjoyed the development of knowledge for its own sake, as something that we could examine, something that we created, that we truly knew. This can, admittedly, cause quite a dilemma for a teacher. The desire to put the bow on the package by tying up all the loose ends—administering the unit test, requiring the notebook full of neatly produced notes—can be quite irresistible. That I was able to resist it is due to two reasons: (1) I was as tired and ready to move on as everyone else; and (2) I could not do that to my kids. I could not give them a message, however well intentioned, that said in effect, "Now that you have labored over these questions, let me tell you the facts. Here are the answers to your questions. Take notes."

Bereiter and Scardamalia say that one characteristic of knowledge building is an interrelatedness of ideas over time and in new contexts. Andrew's final statement tells me that the question was still alive, and that it will continue to live on:

> How do we know genetics is everything? I don't wear glasses and I have very good eyesight, but my mother and grandparents wear glasses. My dad is the only one who doesn't so how (I know I said this also) are genetics everything? I think I'm going to look into this. (Andrew)

THE PLACE OF THIS INQUIRY
IN OUR CLASSROOM COMMUNITY

Our class has continued to explore the characteristics and the processes involved in knowledge building, both through history (an inquiry into the Black Death and one into the sinking of the Titanic) and in coresearch work about the role of discussion in our classroom (see Chapter 9).

In each of our inquiries, we make extensive use of the whole class discussions and the community development and maintenance activities that were discussed in this chapter. In some inquiries, we use a knowledge-building wall; in others, we have been experimenting with small group "inkshedding" techniques (Newman, 1991) and with class newsletters. We've looked at what happens to the knowledge when the sources are taken predominantly from the visual medium (as in our Titanic inquiry) rather than print. In all situations we engage frequently in both oral and written metacognitive reflection, and we frequently look back at our reflections to see how our ideas have changed over time. In taking these actions, we find ourselves quite naturally living out the cycle of action research practiced by all members of our research group (Wells, Chapter 1). That this cycle comes naturally is a tribute to its value, for both teacher and students, in the day-to-day life of the classroom. We enjoy sharing what we discover, contributing our voices to the progressive discourse that is essential to the transformation of our schools into exhilarating, intentional learning environments; in other words, into knowledge-building communities.

CHAPTER 7

Knowledge Building:
Learning About Native Issues
Outside In and Inside Out

Maria Kowal

Good afternoon, your honors. My group and I are representing the government of Province West. We feel strongly that the land that the Wishga'a are claiming to be theirs, although they FEEL that it is theirs, truly isn't. During this presentation, we'll, we will talk about economic issues, human rights issues and other land claim issues. I will now pass the stand on to the next speaker, who will be talking about economic issues.

—Keith

[Reading an entry from a "historical" Wishga'a journal] "Today some strange looking foreigners arrived in a large boat with many large instruments aboard. They raised a flag and used the land like they owned it. They seem to be ignoring us." We have been here since time immemorial. Our great-grandfathers passed the land down to our grandfathers and so on. The band and I would like to know why you even THINK the land my father gave to me is yours. I did not sign a treaty, nor did the others in the band, saying that you could have the land. And in the years that have passed, we have taken care of the land.

—Jon

So in conclusion, I have to say that to me it is somewhat ridiculous that the government would even think that the land belongs to them. Our tradition has been broken, our bands have been sepa-

rated, and our land has been taken. . . . Having our own government is a necessity because many problems have been inflicted
on us. We believe that if we govern ourselves, we could give help
that we are not getting right now. We are prepared to sign a treaty
saying that we wouldn't evacuate nonnatives from our land. We
KNOW the land is ours and will ALWAYS be.

—Frank

THE QUOTES ABOVE are from students' oral submissions to
a teacher panel of Supreme Court judges, the final stage before judgment is handed down in our classroom simulation of the determination
of Native land claims. They are the culmination of a miniunit conducted
during seven 50-minute periods over three days in my Grade 7 English
language classroom. The activity was designed to introduce the students
to some of the issues surrounding Native land claims in Canada, a prescribed social studies theme for this grade level. Native studies in the past
have focused heavily on Native culture and traditions prior to European
contact. A criticism of this approach is that it can reinforce historical ste-
reotypes regarding Canada's First Nations and that present-day Native
issues and their historical background remain poorly understood. For this
year in my social studies program, I had set myself the pedagogical goal
of addressing some of these concerns, the land claims topic being one of
the means I used in realizing it. The unit also provided me, as a teacher-
researcher, an opportunity to gain a clearer understanding of the teach-
ing/learning process when simulations and role play are used in the history classroom.

This chapter describes the activities planned to enable the students to
begin to develop an appreciation of the issues at stake. Middle-class, urban
13-year-olds, they began as outsiders to the issues. As they assume sides
(federal government or First Nations) in our simulated appeal before the
Supreme Court of Canada, they begin to build understanding based not
only on a strengthening knowledge of the facts with which they have been
presented, but also on human empathy—siding, sometimes passionately,
with the human and civil rights of those groups they have chosen to represent. They are given the chance to begin to come to grips with the issues
from the inside out. Similarly, my investigation of each component activity of the simulation provided me with an insider's understanding of how
each stage progressed. Teacher planning stages were audiotaped, the students' classes were videotaped, and then students were invited to view
themselves on video and comment on their reactions to the activities and
the learning that occurred.

THE VISION

In planning my social studies program I seek out opportunities that will actively involve my students in their learning and may help them to see some relevance in the skills and issues we learn about for their own lives. During this school year, for instance, we participated in a project to create a CD-ROM for future students' use, in which my students had an opportunity to conduct a survey of local parkland, using the equipment and techniques of professional surveyors and geographers. We also went on an overnight field trip to a local fort to learn about and experience nineteenth-century garrison life during the War of 1812. In another unit of study, students worked in groups using the Internet and various news media to research and teach their peers about many important examples of humans and their interactions with their environment, such as earthquakes, tornadoes, and fragile environments.

As a teacher-researcher and member of DICEP, I wanted to explore teaching/learning processes during such activities, particularly student interactions and my role in facilitating the students' learning. I also wanted the students to recognize these activities as valid learning experiences, not just "time off real work," as many students described them when surveyed at the beginning of the year. From my research during the year, I realized I needed to investigate a specific teaching/learning experience in detail in order to gain a better understanding of how far my goals of creating successful and relevant learner-centered activities were reconstructed by the students as they carried out the activities.

In preparing to teach the Native Studies element of our social studies course, I met with our board's Native Studies teacher advisor and had frequent discussions with a colleague from the junior division (Grades 4–6) who had experience in curriculum-writing in the area of Native Studies. I wanted to find out what resources were available to help me go beyond the traditional approaches to teaching Native issues in order to expose the students to the complexity of the issues and to help them see the issues through the eyes of the First Nations people themselves. Our curriculum (Toronto Board of Education, 1995) stated that the social studies course should enable students to do the following:

- Outline different ways people are and have been involved in democratic process and change (10.9)
- Analyze relationships among bias, prejudice, stereotyping, discrimination and persecution (11.7)
- Analyze the struggle for basic human rights (11.8)

- Describe how groups have struggled to gain power in Canadian society (13.9)

Teaching materials were available on Native land claims issues in the Canadian context, a theme that appeared to me to be an excellent vehicle for exploring these curricular objectives. The preparation of arguments for and against granting Native peoples ownership of disputed areas of land would be one obvious approach to adopt and could be readily built into a role-play simulation that required the students to act as representatives of the conflicting sides before a mock Supreme Court of Canada.

I had used simulations in the past, and I recognized their potential as means of creating learning experiences that required students to assume an active role in their learning. However, I had been left with mixed feelings upon their completion regarding the overall quality of the students' learning. The final product was often disappointing for me, and I had the feeling that I had not played an active enough teacher role during the classes leading up to the final presentation. I had ideas about how to structure a unit to avoid some of the areas of weakness I had encountered on prior occasions, and I anticipated being able to benefit from the support and resources offered by DICEP to record each stage of the unit from inception to finish. By the end of the unit, I was hoping to have a better understanding of how each stage helped or hindered my students in coming to understand how Native land claims have been dealt with in the Canadian context. From this research, I hoped I would have more confidence in planning and using simulations with my students in future years.

In planning the unit, I talked with other members of DICEP about possible ways of structuring the research and decided to try to involve my students as coinvestigators. Through coinvestigation they might develop an awareness of themselves as learners, providing insights for them as well as for me. Coinvestigation might also serve as a means of helping the students become aware of the "real work" going on during a "time-off" activity. Gordon Wells and Mari Haneda agreed to assist with the videotaping and to be participant-observers through all stages of the unit. We decided to introduce the idea of coinvestigation to the students in launching the unit, to talk briefly about our experiences as researchers, and then to invite the students to participate in the analysis of some of the data. Gordon would prepare a video montage of key episodes from the unit, and as the students later watched the videotape of themselves at work, they would be asked to comment on the episodes in terms of what they thought was happening.

THE THEORY AND CONTEXT GUIDING MY PRACTICE

Pedagogically, I wanted the students to become aware of the complexity of the issues they were dealing with, as Duckworth (1987) does in her discussions with primary students. I did not want my students to adopt a form of "collective guilt" and feel that the "right" solution was to automatically give back to the First Nations what had been "taken" from them when European explorers first arrived in Western Canada; nor did I want them, alternatively, to reject the "return" of native lands as not worth considering. In fact, I wanted the students to develop some empathy for both of the sides involved. As Giroux (1991) in his theory of "border pedagogy" suggests, empathy is one of the tools that postmodern society can use in handling its diversity successfully.

From a teacher-researcher perspective, there were two issues that I wanted to explore. First, how do we as teachers enable our students to develop empathy for another group when their experiences are perhaps far removed from the group they are trying to understand? Role-play is often suggested as a way to encourage our students to develop empathy for others (Hume & Wells, 1999), but how successful is this approach? Students are after all experiencing the events through their own eyes and can only try to imagine the other person's view. Or is this effort in itself enough to begin what will become a lifelong process of trying to understand many sides of an issue before coming to a final decision about how to respond? Second, how would each of the component parts of the simulation, including group discussion and writing about the issues, help the students not simply to know the facts about the issues but also to understand them?

The end of the school year was rapidly approaching, with its awards assemblies and other additions to the regular schedule. As the students' homeroom teacher, responsible for math, social studies, and language, I could use time from my language arts and social studies classes to complete the unit in a relatively short period of time, but in that case I wanted to include a specific language objective in the unit. I intended to focus on aspects of formal rhetoric, the devices that well-honed public speakers such as lawyers, politicians, and teachers use to present their arguments clearly and convincingly.

To increase my teacher's contribution to this simulation, I planned to use two periods to present the students with a video and a text, both of which were rich in information, about the decades-long struggle between the Nisga'a band and the government of British Columbia, which, coincidentally, was again making news, for the Supreme Court of Canada had agreed that week to hear an appeal on behalf of the Nisga'a. The short timeline ruled out the possibility of the students conducting independent research for this unit, even though the newspapers and newscasts were running stories about the issue and the information would have been quite accessible to them.

However, I did not view this transmission approach as a problem. The students had successfully conducted independent research in many other parts of the program throughout the year, so I had covered that area of the students' learning. In fact, I know that a part of my teacher psyche was actually quite happy with the tidiness of the unit: no trips to the library to arrange and no chasing down students who had been unable to locate relevant information. In two periods, I would provide the students with all the information they needed to begin building their cases.

PUTTING VISION INTO PRACTICE: WHAT THE DATA SHOW

The data presented here are from key stages of the unit and offer three perspectives on the teaching/learning process: what was said in the classroom; my reflections and interpretations of what was happening; and student reflections from the follow-up discussions, in which they said what they thought was happening and commented on the effectiveness of the strategies used.

When I was first presented with a sample of the data—the series of video clips from each of the stages prior to the court hearing, which Gordon had also shown to the students—I was reminded of Lave and Wenger's (1991) theory of the process of "legitimate peripheral participation" at work. To me, it was quite striking and exciting to see how the students began the unit with very little knowledge of land claims issues and the Canadian justice system and how, through the activities, they began to be drawn into a deeper and more engaged understanding of the facts and processes involved.

Stage 1. Introduction to the History

The first periods were taken up with showing the video and reading a text about Frank Calder, the Nisga'a chief, and his people's struggle to have their case heard fairly by the Canadian justice system. I had planned this section quite clearly for myself. I would start by finding out what the students already knew about the land claims issue—nothing, as it turned out—and what they knew about the Supreme Court, which was limited. They were outsiders to the issues, unaware that there even were any, without any knowledge of the facts that would enable them to discuss the issues, and probably not seeing any reason to bother about discussing them.

At this stage in the unit, I saw my role as their teacher to be that of helping the students begin to grasp and understand some of the issues and to help them see why these issues, such as fair access to the judicial system, were of relevance to all Canadians, not just to a First Nations band out West. I wanted to bring my students closer to the subject matter, to bring them into the inner circle where they would be able to participate in discussing the issues. The video and text about the Nisga'a struggle were my vehicles for achieving this objective. As both were quite dense and information rich, making considerable use of technical vocabulary, I used strategies that I thought would help the students understand the legal, historical, and philosophical arguments being made.

At various stages throughout the video, I stopped it to ask specific questions about what was being said. The discussion was teacher directed and consciously contained many Initiation–Response–Follow-up sequences. It was a definite strategy on my part to draw students' attention to the subtlety of the points being made. Although such a strategy is associated with conduit metaphors of communication (Wells, Chapter 1), I still saw myself as working within the majority of the students' ZPD, assisting them to understand something more fully than if they had been left to view it without discussion. Similarly, I also had a definite plan for the reading of the text. A synopsis of Frank Calder's submission to the Supreme Court of Canada, it contained much technical vocabulary and made some significant, yet quite subtle, points that I wanted the students to understand fully. My students had a wide range of reading skills: Some would be capable of independently understanding the text, some would need assistance to understand the subtleties, and some would find the text at their frustration level, including three ESL students. Therefore, I decided to let them read the text independently and then to have various students read the text aloud so that we could discuss what was being said. It was my intention to provide as many students as possible with an opportunity to read the text, and to build in opportunities for the stronger readers to explain it to the rest of the class so that, even though this was a whole group lesson, all students would be actively engaged and learning. I would try during this activity to open the discussion up in order to allow more students to participate and encourage more progressive discourse, in which one student could build on the comments of a previous student.

Yet, as we worked through the text, I was only too aware of the stifling heat of our June classroom, and the slow rate at which we were progressing. In theory, it had seemed fine; in practice, it was beginning to seem like a big mistake. The students were subsequently asked to comment on this part of the unit, and I was really not looking forward to hearing their comments about my teaching effectiveness at this stage. However, the feedback was more positive than I had expected. For instance, reading the text aloud and answering specific questions had, according to the students, helped them to gain a better understanding of the points being made and seemed, in general, to have been a useful, if somewhat dull, activity.

> GORDON: What was the point of that (part) do you think?
>
> JANE: To understand it . so if anybody was stuck we read it aloud and discussed it
>
> GORDON: Was it worthwhile spending the time on it?
>
> KEITH: Well, yeah . yeah . yeah . because, well, when you read it by yourself you might think you understand it, but you don't really, but unless like you discuss it then you- then you . . .
>
> RICHARD: Never would know (if you had understood it)
>
> KEITH : Yeah . if you don't understand a part of it or get what's going on, when you like discuss it in a group you sort of get an understanding of what's going on . . .
>
> JANE: If you discuss it then you understand it more because you're actually talking, you're like reading it in your mind
>
> GORDON: That's interesting, you say you understand it because you're talking?
>
> JANE: Well, the more you talk about it the more you understand it . If you're reading it only to yourself, like in your mind, you don't like understand it
>
> KEITH: It's like studying for a test . it's- . it's- it's better to study like write down what you're studying on a separate piece of paper because then it gets stuck in your mind better . . This way, like discussing it out loud it just sticks in your mind better . it makes it easier to understand (the teacher) . . . asking questions helps you to understand

What these data suggest is that the students, no doubt familiar with such teaching episodes from years of exposure to them, understand and can clearly articulate the purpose of such teacher-fronted discussion. On an important metacognitive level (Hume, Chapter 6), they know what is going on, which perhaps in turn increases for them the usefulness of the strategy. They can clearly articulate how this structured discussion assists them in the knowledge-building process. In fact, their comments, unbeknown to them, are a restating of parts of Vygotskian social cultural theory! In order to complete the simulation successfully, however, knowing the facts wasn't enough. It required an understanding of the facts and the application of them to the legal cases to be constructed. And the students would have to use their understanding to persuade the judges of the superiority of their case.

Stage 2. Making the Facts Their Own

After this lesson, I divided the students into heterogeneous groups and introduced the simulation—a land claim dispute between two fictitious sides: the Wishga'a First Nations band and Province West. The students would have two and a half lessons, working in groups, to put together their cases and rehearse them. Drawing on past experience, I decided to provide a structure for the students to work with. Their first task was to work individually to list points for each side to support the respective claims to ownership of the land, based on the information that had been introduced in previous lessons. After this, they were invited to share their thoughts and choose which side they wished to represent at our court hearing. The element of choice at this stage was important. The brainstorming they had completed individually would help them to decide as a group which side they felt they could support more strongly, and I did not want them to be forced to make an argument they did not really believe in. The students were being drawn closer to the center of the issues: they were beginning to develop a personal affinity with the subject matter and were being asked to reinterpret the facts and arguments they had heard to support a position that they wanted to support. In fact, one of the groups contained two students who had developed strong affinities for opposing sides. It was clear that neither student was willing to let the other make the call as to which side they would be representing, and even when the group had decided democratically through a vote to take the government's position, one student was still unable to go along with the decision of the group. We decided that, given the importance of assuming personal closeness with the issues, this student should be allowed to switch groups.

Because of my disappointment with the overall quality of students' final presentations in previous simulations, this time I intended to intervene and provide the students with more structure to follow during the group work sessions, a scaffold to help them organize their ideas. I drew connections for the students between this activity and other successful oral presentations and written work they had done during the year. I encouraged them to structure their submissions as follows: to assign each member of the group with a specific point to make, in which she or he would begin the presentation by stating the issue concerned and then listing supporting details to make a case, before offering some kind of concluding statement to push the point home. Overall, there should also be someone

to introduce the group and the issues they would be covering and someone to summarize the points made and to rebut the points made by the
lawyers for the opposing side. We talked briefly about rhetorical devices
that had been used by participants in the courtroom scenes in the video—
repetition, personal stories, and pleas to the judges' emotions—devices
which the students might use to make their own arguments more convinc-
ing. We also talked about some of the characteristics of the register they
would need to use in order to "sound" like lawyers. I was aware that my
lofty language goals of teaching rhetoric had been reduced to about five
minutes of classroom discussion, but that was all the time we had available to us. I also suggested to the groups that, in order to make their points
as strongly as possible, all members should contribute to the drafting of
each person's contribution. I envisaged them identifying a point to be made,
discussing and delving into the issue, and then working together to help
an individual member write down the main points.

However, as I circulated from group to group, I found that things weren't
going quite as I had planned. I was not convinced that the students really
understood the simulation and the issues involved. So, I began the next lesson by reviewing the simulation with the students, using analogies to offer
them another way in. For instance, if they were a non-Native businessperson
with children in the local school, how might they feel if the land were given
to a Native band with rights to self-government? How might their lives be
changed? What fears might they have?

The students now had two periods to put their case together and then
rehearse it. I had seen the group work primarily as a chance for the students to talk about and explore the issues in more depth, and to write down
their points in preparation for their submissions. However, the task required much more of the students than I had anticipated and, as is always
the case, my goals were reinterpreted by the students as they proceeded
to carry out the activity (Brooks & Donato, 1994). At one stage in my teaching career I would have found this unsettling (Kowal & Swain, 1994); at
this stage I expected it, but trusted that what occurred as the group members worked together to construct their cases would be what was necessary for them to complete the activity successfully.

Both of the groups that were videotaped spent a considerable amount
of time discussing procedural issues: who would go first, what each person's
role would be. Both groups decided, apparently independently of each other,
to call witnesses to support their case. This led to even more procedural
discussion in both groups about how this would be done.

When the students did discuss the points to be included, the talk did
not proceed in the manner I had imagined. I had envisaged the students
brainstorming each of the points to get as much supporting evidence for

the person making the point as possible. This student would ideally take notes and then reorganize them into a well-constructed argument in defense of the whole group's case. For me, then, the opportunity to talk was to provide a vehicle for creating deeper understanding of the issues. However, although the students had understood the purpose of the earlier mentioned teacher-led discussions, they did not seem to have the same metacognitive understanding of the potential of the group discussion. They went straight into final copy mode; when a student made a point, it was written down verbatim, and there appeared to be little further discussion of the ideas. A similar characteristic has also been observed in research on writing: students rarely view writing as a tool for developing thought (e.g., Bereiter & Scardamalia, 1987; Wells, 1999). On those occasions when the students did start to talk about the issues in more depth, with or without stimulus from one of the adults in the room, the subtlety and breadth of the points raised in these discussions were still not fully incorporated into their final presentations. I do not think that the students failed to understand the points; but perhaps they still needed an adult to help them get some of the ideas captured fully on paper or, alternatively, once they had been discussed, perhaps the "wonder" of the learning had passed and so was not included in the final presentation. Frank mentioned in the follow-up discussion that, for him, the learning occurred as they were talking about the ideas. The writing down of the ideas was not as important for him.

One area that the students did successfully discuss and work into their presentations was style. I had felt disappointed that we had only been able to talk briefly about specific devices, but it appeared that using the correct register and some basic rhetorical devices was inherent in the task. "We wanted to sound like a professional. We were doing that court thing and we wanted to win" (Keith). The editing that Keith completed as the group worked on his part of the presentation shows this quite clearly. Here is the first draft of his introduction cited at the beginning of this chapter:

> I'm Keith Jones. My group and I are representing Province West. We feel strongly that the land that the Whis'ga [sic] are claiming to be theirs, although they feel that it is theirs, isn't. During this presentation, we will talk about economic issues, human rights issues, and land claim issues. I will now pass the stand to Nell who will talk about the economic issues. Thank you.

Frank remembered the effectiveness of talking with emotion as a point is being made and was concerned that this element should be present as his group presented the case for the Native bands. His concluding comments, also included at the beginning of this chapter, were delivered in animated style.

Similarly, before the hearing took place, the students wanted to discuss how to set up the classroom so that it was like a real courtroom. In my opinion this "getting into role" was also evidence of the students identifying more and more with the roles they had assumed.

The novel decision to call a witness, used by both sides, was another sign of the students making the issues their own, by assuming the persona of one of the individuals involved in the disputed land struggle. The government group called to the stand a businessman, who talked about his investment in the disputed area and his fears for the future under First Nations rule. Jon, the witness for the First Nations group, read from a mock journal that had been passed down through his family, which was cited at the beginning of this chapter. The voice was imitated directly from documents which had been read aloud during the video the students had heard, although the final version which Jon presented was much shorter than the versions the students came up with in their discussion of the point.

At the beginning of the second period of group work, I suggested to the students that they should leave time to rehearse their presentation before the "real thing" later that day. The impending performance before the two teachers who had agreed to play the role of Supreme Court judges was an impetus to both groups to pull things together. They really needed to understand the issues clearly and be coherent in their presentations. Here again there was further evidence of the students making the issues their own, and now that the procedural issues had been dealt with, there was some evidence of their using the opportunity to talk as a means of increasing everyone's understanding of the issues. For instance, some students began to draw their own analogies to explain their points more clearly to the other members of the group.

Stage 3. The Final Presentations

When I watched the video of the final presentations, I had to recognize how much the students had accomplished in two and a half periods. As the excerpts presented show, there was a definite attempt to use a courtroom register, and the students achieved this quite well, even if their Grade 7 voices did surface at times. They had taken their understanding of how a courtroom worked and called witnesses to the stand, requiring them to swear an oath of truth. The final speakers for each side did offer counter arguments, albeit brief, to rebut what the other side had said and did summarize the points made by all the members of the group. But, at the time of the simulated Court Hearing, I was still a little disappointed at the brevity of some of their presentations. There was a lack, in some cases, of supporting points to really develop what they were saying, and I remember noting to myself that I would need to look again at how the unit was structured to see if I had missed something. In the event, listening to the students' comments from the follow-up discussions helped me to begin to understand how I might be able to improve the unit.

Stage 4. Student Comments About the Unit

In the follow-up discussions, the students were asked how they felt about the approach we had used in this unit. Their comments suggested that I had been able to realize my pedagogical aims of enabling them to develop empathy with the sides involved and to see the complexity of the issues being explored.

> GORDON: I was just wondering how the project helped you to have a better understanding of the issues
> JANE: Well we actually sort of felt what it was like . instead of just reading about it, we actually like DID it
> KEITH: Yeah, and like we felt like all the frustration and the feelings that the people would have felt, I guess
> FRANK: Well I've always been on the Natives' side, I've always thought that they should get their land back, but now I've seen like, a bit more of the views of the government
> TINA: Yeah, I saw both sides I guess.

However, in terms of the usefulness of each part of the unit, the reactions were more varied. I was confronted with an interesting disparity between the two groups, which provided me with a key to improving the structure of the unit. The general reaction from the group representing the government was that each stage was helpful in enabling the students to understand the issues.

> GORDON: Which part would you say was the most useful?
> KEITH: I think they were all equally important because, because before- before we get to do, we have to find out what to do and we can't just find out what to do and not do it . . and so I think they're equally important

A similar question to the group representing the First Nations position elicited a very different point of view, summarized in the following comment from Frank:

Um, the video (was the most important part) . . . with the simulation you just repeated everything you- we said the whole past few days . . with the video you learned it for the first time

As I considered this statement, I remembered that members of this group, although identifying strongly with the First Nations position, had not used the group work time as intensely as the group representing the government and I was beginning to understand what might have prompted Frank's comments. For the First Nations group, the arguments had been all but written out for them, because the video and text had described the issues from a Native perspective. Keith's group, on the other hand, had needed to respond to the arguments that had been presented in the materials. Their task was more interesting because it required them to construct a new argument to counter the one already presented.

MY INCREASED UNDERSTANDING
OF THIS TEACHING/LEARNING EXPERIENCE

So here I stand with my insider's perspective on this teaching/learning situation. What knowledge have I reconstructed from my experiences and the information from the observations to increase my understanding, and how might it transform my future practice? Well, previous experiences had encouraged me to be as proactive as I could in setting up the learning situation, providing information for the students, and trying, at each stage of the unit, to give them a plan or a scaffold to help them through the task they had to complete. For me, this was an issue of teacher responsibility, and I was comfortable with the action I took—although I could probably have stepped back at some stages and will fine-tune my approach in this respect in any future simulation.

I succeeded in realizing many of my pedagogical objectives. Was role-play an effective means of border-crossing, promoting empathy and understanding of others' perspectives of an issue? Yes. The simulation was also an effective vehicle for helping the students understand the issues involved and the grayness surrounding right and wrong and for encouraging them to use a particular register in the presentations. In addition, it served well as an introduction to the Canadian legal system, even showing how the justice system has sometimes been discriminatory and prejudiced.

What insights have I gained from my research, in the classroom and from my reading, about knowledge building in this context? I have taken the students' comments cited in the previous section as a starting point, and using Wells's construct of the "spiral of knowing" (1999; Chapter 10)

as a framework for analyzing the events of this unit, I have been able to gain an increased understanding of some of the dynamics of this teaching/ learning situation. Central to this analysis are Wells's four segments: experience, information, knowledge building, and understanding. In brief, Wells suggests that understanding is achieved when learners have the opportunity to transform experience and information through knowledge-building activities, in particular through opportunities for progressive discourse.

Reviewing my data from the unit, the information (video, text) and experience (e.g., student analogies used during the group work and the witnesses' testimony) segments are well represented. The final presentations demonstrate good, albeit briefly stated, understanding of some of the issues raised. Overall, the simulation provided some opportunity for knowledge building, but could have been planned to allow for more—as the students' comments suggest. Ironically, given my own reservations, the teacher-fronted discussions of the video and the text appear, according to the students, to have been useful knowledge-building activities. In the students' opinions, what the unit lacked was an opportunity for them to find and incorporate their own information for their presentations. What this information would have been might well have differed for each of the groups. For Frank's group, it might have included independent research to find additional information about the First Nation struggle regarding land claims. Keith, when asked how the unit could have been improved, said that he would have liked time to go and complete research about how the legal system works in order to make his group's presentation more authentic.

Although, in planning the unit, I had been pleased that it required no independent research, I realize in retrospect that independent research is not something we do because it's a skill to be covered, but because it is often an integral and motivating part of the learning process and, as such, should have been included in this unit. Because much of the information, particularly for the Native group, was known to all the students, there was perhaps less motivation to take this information and use it to persuade the other group, since everyone had heard the issues already. Keith identified weaknesses in the presentation that his group put together, too, but was not given the opportunity to do anything about them. In truth, as I now see, I wanted the students to perform for me so that I could evaluate how well they understood the issues I had put before them. My goals limited the opportunities for the students to follow through on points of significance and interest to them. In fact, without an opportunity for independent research, the whole unit for the group representing the First Nations position was really based on the conduit metaphor of education, and so a potentially important opportunity for knowledge building had been omitted from the planning. Time had been an issue for me, but in any future simulation work, the research element could easily be incorporated, without using up more class time, by giving the students a week to conduct the research in their own time before coming back to the group to discuss the issues.

During my initial analysis of the data, I thought that if the students had come to the discussion with independently researched information to share with the group, this might also have deepened the level of group discussion and overall understanding of the issues. However, with further reflection on my own experience and the reading of a colleague's work (Hume, Chapter 9), I think this is too simplistic a statement to make. If I think back to the independent research teaching unit that regularly constitutes a part of my geography program, then I know that those students who have already had many opportunities to conduct independent research in previous years are very good information finders. However, in Wells's terms, their overall expertise in transforming information into understanding is not so well developed. In short, I am not convinced that if the students came to the discussion with more information to share, the ensuing discourse would automatically be more progressive, thereby enhancing the knowledge-building experience. As Hume's (Chapter 9) and McGlynn-Stewart's (Chapter 8) research shows, students do not automatically understand the value of talk in knowledge building. Yet Hume's success in her coresearch of classroom talk suggests that increasing students' awareness of the learning process might be an additional, important factor in making the group work more of a transformational experience for the students, rather than simply a "knowledge telling" one (Bereiter & Scardamalia, 1987).

At the beginning of the research, we explained to the students that we were going to involve them as coinvestigators in the research. In retrospect, I see that, although the discussions with the students that we held toward the end of the unit were insightful for me as the teacher, the students were a little puzzled by the activity. When asked, they could not think of any way in which the viewing of the video clips had been useful to them beyond being "weird" to see themselves at work. For the students to have been real coinvestigators, they should have been more actively involved as researchers during the unit. Given the shortness of the time period, it would have been difficult to achieve such an objective within this particular unit. However, I am beginning to think that, conducted over a longer period of time, the coinvestigation of independent research as a transformational knowledge-building practice could be a valuable topic for future action research, both for me as a teacher and for my students as conscious knowledge builders.

CHAPTER 8

The Leadership Lab: Creativity, Compassion, Community

Monica McGlynn-Stewart

THE DEVELOPMENT of the Leadership Lab that I describe in this chapter was not my first involvement in action research. As a classroom teacher and as a member of DICEP, I had carried out projects on a variety of topics. For example, earlier in my career, I investigated the use of written and oral language in the learning and teaching of geometry in a primary classroom (McGlynn-Stewart, 1996), perceptions of fairness and ownership in a language arts unit in a junior classroom and, most recently, how we in DICEP function as a community of inquiry (McGlynn-Stewart, 1998). So when the opportunity arose a few years ago to continue my work with high school age students, I jumped at the chance. As principal of a new independent high school, I consciously brought the principles of DICEP and of good elementary practice to my new position. I believe that students need to be respected and given appropriate challenges at every age, and that the most effective learning communities are communities of inquiry.

Our goal in creating a new independent charitable high school in our large urban setting was to develop a creative, vibrant, and compassionate community of leaders. This was the focus of the whole school, but more particularly of a unique course we developed called the Leadership Lab. We wanted the community to be one of inquiry, both in the way that the students approached the theme of leadership, and in the way that we as teachers facilitated the course. This is the story of how we consciously used the inquiry principles of the action research cycle—*plan, act, reflect, change* —to lead to both understanding and change within this innovative course (Dick, 1997). In the interest of clarity, I have grouped the elements of planning, acting, reflecting, and changing in a way that may seem as if we only engaged in each stage once. Of course, the cycle was ongoing throughout the year.

Because my coteacher and I use a broad definition of leadership for the school and course—one that integrates the school with the wider world our students are about to enter—we looked to organizational development literature for inspiration and guidance. We were very taken with Peter Senge's (1990) notion of the "learning organization." We were excited by the idea that we could create a structure in which not only did the students learn, but the whole school could encourage systems thinking and shared leadership and could turn dissonance into opportunities for adaptation and growth.

We also found the work of Chris Argyris (1990, 1991; Argyris & Schön, 1974) very useful, both for our own development as teachers and for curriculum considerations. His Harvard Business Review article (May/June 1991), "Teaching Smart People How to Learn," helped us to understand the difficulty successful people (students and teachers alike) have when faced with the challenge of reflecting critically on their own learning.

One of the most important aspects of inquiry learning and teaching, and key to the action research cycle, is reflection. Donald Schön's (1987) work reinforced for us our belief that we all learn best through reflection on our practice.

THE SCHOOL VISION

In our first year of operation, as principal, I had the honor and duty to oversee the incarnation of the vision of leadership that we set out in our school calendar:

> Those who emerge as leaders in their fields share many traits above and beyond a broad knowledge. Whether they are politicians or business people, artists, scientists or community activists, they are people who have the ability to think creatively, to plan and to establish goals. They are self-confident and able to motivate others as well as themselves. They look upon life as a series of challenges, not as an accumulation of obstacles. They are risk takers, who are willing to fly in the face of tradition without ignoring the lessons it has to teach. And they have a drive that is balanced by compassion.

No small task, as can be imagined! From this belief grew a unique experiment in high school education—a high school that is private, yet charges no tuition, and a charity that focuses on economically challenged and/or marginalized bright young people and seeks to develop their leadership potential.

We are a small school, at present 10 staff, part and full time, and 28 students ranging in age from 15 to 19. Our first students came from public and private schools, and from the city and surrounding areas. One girl moved from another city to attend, and another commutes one and a half to two hours to attend. All students are academically able, with some designated as gifted, and all were deemed to have academic and leadership potential, even if recent school performance was not exemplary. Our goal was to target lower socioeconomic level students who might not otherwise have a chance to attend a small specialized school. We also wanted a wide racial and ethnic mix.

As it turned out, our socioeconomic mix was more diverse than our racial and ethnic mix. We had a combination of wards of the state, new immigrants, and students from working, middle, and upper-middle classes. We also had several languages represented. The school is located in a downtown area on major transportation routes in a converted turn-of-the-century bank.

The school seeks to pair academic rigor with a well-rounded and socially conscious approach to education. In addition to the traditional high school curriculum of arts, sciences, languages, and technology, we have added a new concept—the *Leadership Lab*. For two hours a week, plus three to five hours of community work, our entire student body engages in leadership development activities.

During the Leadership Lab, we attempt to integrate creative projects, physically active programs, and volunteer service components of the curriculum, as well as using experiential learning techniques to explore leadership skills, issues, theory, and history. In addition, we regularly bring in local leaders from diverse fields to share their perspectives on leadership and their paths to their present positions.

In this chapter I will explore the development of this course in its first year, from concept to practice, by examining the teachers' and students' plans, reflections, and ongoing restructuring.

THE PLANNING STAGE

We wanted the students, and their parents, to be involved in the first stage of the action research cycle—the planning stage. The focus of the school is leadership, so we began the orientation weeks for the whole school with an exercise that called upon all of us to collectively take a leading role in the formation of school policy, programs, and atmosphere. For this we used an organizational development tool called *Open Space Technology* (Owen, 1992).

This technique involves stating the givens, or nonnegotiables, of the organization, and then opening the floor for the participants to propose ideas, concerns, issues, or questions for discussion. The proposals are tacked to the wall and given a time and location for discussion. Everyone then chooses to join the discussions that are meaningful to him or her. The person who makes a proposal becomes the champion of it and guides the discussion and planning group.

Parents, teachers, and volunteers participated equally with the students in making proposals and guiding discussions during our schoolwide orientation. Some of our nonnegotiables, items that were not up for discussion, were these: We had traditional school hours; class attendance was mandatory; discriminatory language or actions would not be tolerated; and we would follow all laws and government regulations regarding school operation. The following are some examples of the 21 proposals from the group:

Need for more technology
Learning and service outside the school
Freedom of expression
Dispute mediation
Dress code
Grading
Counseling
Creativity

At the end of the discussions, which took place over two and a half days, the group leaders submitted a summary of their discussions and of the steps that would be needed to take the issues further. These summaries and plans were collected in a book of proceedings as a record of our collaborative beginning and as a springboard for action.

THE LEADERSHIP LAB

We were committed to following through on these proposals throughout the school, but planned to focus on them more particularly in the Leadership Lab. In addition to the students' and parents' ideas and plans for the school and the Lab, we of course had done a lot of planning ourselves. We developed an overview of the Lab that reflected the overall aims of the school and that was, we hoped, sufficiently open-ended and flexible to meet the individual needs of our students.

We proposed that the Leadership Lab pursue five areas of study:

1. *Leadership theory*—study theories of leadership and great leaders (individual research project on a leader of the student's choice)
2. *Human relations*—interpersonal skills, group dynamics, and team-work (participation in leadership lab experiential activities and discussions)
3. *Develop self-awareness*—complete a series of assessments to gain a deeper understanding of self (complete assessments such as the EQ-I, Meyers-Briggs, True Colors)
4. *Volunteer in community projects and internships* (regular volunteer work and debrief experiences in Lab class)
5. *Participate in a mentoring partnership*—meet with a mentor on a regular basis (prepare for and debrief experiences in Lab class)

These five components were to be explored, experienced, and discussed in a yearlong lab class that met for two hours every week. Each student was to keep a journal to reflect on his or her learning.

In retrospect, my cofaciliator of the Leadership Lab and I realized that our outline was overly ambitious and somewhat vague for our high school students. However, as we had hoped, they were not shy about giving us feedback on the course.

A TIME TO ACT

When we had completed the first leg of the first cycle of action research—planning—we were ready for the second leg—action. We dove into the course, attacking all five areas of study at once. We had guest speakers, completed assessments, experienced role play and other drama activities related to leadership, explored readings on leadership theory, and helped the students arrange their volunteer work and mentoring relationships. However, with feedback from the students, we soon realized that we faced a number of challenges.

Many of the students were having trouble in seeing the Lab as "real" school. They had difficulty in giving it the same value as their more traditional academic courses. Although they were quite interested in the course in theory, when it came to completing their assignments, they argued that they did not want to take time away from their "real" schoolwork.

We had anticipated this reaction to some degree, and had tried to give the course the same weight and credibility as academic courses by making it a mandatory part of the schedule. However, because we didn't give marks in the same way as in other courses, and because the classes and assignments were very different from anything that most had experienced before, some students still viewed the course as secondary to their more traditional courses.

Nevertheless, we were initially mystified by the variety and vehemence of student response to the course that we received both orally and in their journals. Responses ranged from very positive to downright hostile. Here is an early journal entry from a girl in her graduating year:

> I really enjoy leadership lab. I like writing journal entries every week as I find it makes me think thoroughly about things and events. The lab itself is always interesting as well. There is always something different on the agenda. The guest speakers are a good idea as they really bring reality and a down-to-earth look at work, jobs, futures, careers, etc.

And here is a Grade 11 boy reflecting on an evaluation after first term:

> I feel strongly that I have greatly improved my social skills in this course. I have gained confidence in speaking to groups of people. I would like to continue with our current work as I find it productive and useful.

In contrast, there were some very strong negative feelings about the course. This is from the journal of an older student who was repeating his final year:

> Sorry I know that this isn't what you want to hear, but I haven't really gained anything from the leadership lab and feel that it has been a waste of time. I would like to finish the year with pretty good grades and finally graduate out of high school.

And this from one of our youngest students:

> I feel that the course is irrelevant, at times, and that a lot of the information we receive is vague.

Our challenge was to be responsive to the students' desire to excel at their traditional subjects while encouraging them to embrace this new method of learning.

A Variety of Student Responses

We discussed the great disparity of responses to the course with the students early on and they had some very interesting theories. A few pointed out that we had a great range of experiences and maturity levels within the group. Those who had come from other alternative schools or were home schooled seemed to have little to no adjustment period. Those who had come from very traditional schools and homes found the program mind-boggling. The students also came with very different agendas. Although they were all good students, some wanted to focus solely on their academic courses and were not interested in anything that diverted them from that focus.

Other students pointed out that although they appreciated the course in theory, they did not have the time or energy to fully participate at this time in their lives. Here is a candid reflection from a senior girl after second term:

> I think that if these leadership exercises fell at a different time in my life I may have gotten more out of them. As it is, I am so exhausted with the demands of this school in conjunction with my family life that I find that I really need some time to spend alone and with my friends.

Still others acknowledged that their own lack of participation led to their dissatisfaction with the Lab:

> During this term I have not participated enough in Leadership Lab discussions nor in the process of writing journals, which I think is pretty bad! Therefore, I have not gained much from the Leadership Course.

Although we were willing to adapt and change, we had to accept that for some of our students, the demands of adjusting to a new and academically challenging school left them little energy or desire to embrace the Leadership Lab fully.

BALANCING STRUCTURE AND OPENNESS

Another challenge we faced was balancing structure and open-endedness. For some students, the course offered too much choice and not enough direction. The students were asked to arrange or at least initiate their own volunteer work and mentors based on their interests and passions. We were very willing to help with logistics and suggestions, but we wanted the students to take the initiative. The experiential activities and discussions in class had no right or wrong answer, and some students wanted marks rather than anecdotal comments on their journals and oral reports in order to gauge their performance.

Other students relished the freedom to work within a relatively loose framework. We wanted to give space for the students to make the course their own without letting them get lost in what some saw as vagueness. Some students definitely wanted to be spoon-fed—to be told what to do and say in order to please the teachers. This we tried to discourage while meeting their need for more security.

The final challenge we identified was a big one. It was to be clear in our own minds about what we expected from ourselves and how flexible we were willing to be in the face of some humbling student feedback. We challenged ourselves to be open and take risks with new approaches, just as we were asking the students to do.

REFLECTING ON THE CHALLENGES

We had made our plans, we had put them into action, we had gathered feedback, and now it was time to reflect on the challenges we had identified. Armed with our own observations, records of the students' comments in class and outside of class, and their journal entries and class evaluations, we reevaluated every aspect of the course.

As we planned changes based on our data, we continually went back to the leadership philosophy and goals of the course and the school. Were we promoting creativity, self-confidence, risk taking, and compassion? Since there were two of us cofacilitating the Lab, we were able to compare our observations and interpretations after class, as well as often asking the students for feedback. We challenged each other's assumptions (e.g., are the students lazy or tired or badly behaved or was the lesson just plain inappropriate?). We encouraged each other to continue our professional reading and consulted other teachers and group facilitators that we knew. I often brought my dilemmas to DICEP and was always rewarded with a fresh perspective on a problem.

A TIME TO CHANGE

As a result of this reflection, we decided on three fundamental areas of change: the content of Lab sessions; the physical setting and student groupings; and the nature of student work we expected.

We began the Leadership Lab in September with the EQ-I, an assessment of emotional intelligence. We knew, of course, that it is not a good idea to start any new group with anything resembling a test if you are trying to develop a relaxed and nonthreatening atmosphere. However, it was the only time the assessors could come, and anyway, our students appeared so confident that we didn't think it would be a problem. While we were waiting for the results to come back, we facilitated a series of role play and drama games to explore self-concept, perceptions, emotions, and communication.

We soon realized that we should have held back on these "risky" activities until we knew our students better and had established more trust. As we learned through doing these activities, we had a very self-conscious group without strong interpersonal skills. Their EQ-I test results were very low. It took us a great deal of time and effort to help the students deal with what they perceived to be a failure.

After the first six weeks, we pulled back to the type of nonthreatening activities with which we should have started the year. We discussed articles and videos of interesting leaders, as well as bringing in guest speakers who embodied different leadership styles and approaches. We began to focus more on the volunteer projects in which the students were engaged, and to draw concepts from their "real-world" experiences.

In time we did regain most of the students' trust and confidence and were able to reintroduce some more personally challenging experiential learning activities. We had many positive comments from the students on the changes we made to the content of classes, particularly on the increased focus on guest speakers and the volunteer program. One girl had been particularly negative during our opening sessions. This is her comment after first term:

> I definitely enjoy the Leadership Lab more now than I did at the beginning of the year. I have enjoyed the guest speakers that we've had (or at least most of them) and appreciate the insight they have given me relating to the different aspect of life they partake in. I've enjoyed the volunteer activities I've participated in. I've met lots of interesting people and done lots of exciting things.

Changes in Student Groupings

At the beginning of the year, the whole school met in a circle once a week. We thought that this would be a great way to develop community and to encourage democratic discussions. There were problems with this format from the first day. The students were not listening respectfully to each other and many were either showing off or tuning out. When we asked the students what was going on (after all our class management tricks had failed), they told us that they felt that the circle, in addition to the type of personal material we were discussing, was too "touchy-feely," too much like group therapy. A couple of students felt so uncomfortable that they wanted to sit outside the circle. There were others, of course, who felt so comfortable that they wanted to lie down in the middle of the circle!

This response told us that the large group circle needed to change. Our next strategy was to circulate among small group discussions spread around the ground floor. Because many of the students had come from teacher-directed educational environments, they had trouble staying on task, or even seeing the point of an exercise, if a teacher wasn't right there to monitor and evaluate. We tried in vain to explain our "innovative" ideas about student grouping, so we decided to illustrate our point.

One day when the students came into the Lab, instead of a circle, there were rows of chairs with my cofacilitator at the blackboard at the front. The students came in uncharacteristically calmly and quietly, took a seat and got ready to take notes. As we proceeded to engage the students in a lively discussion of their opinions about concepts of leadership, they were craning their necks to see the various speakers. They got the point. They agreed that a traditional class arrangement was not appropriate for the content of our class.

As we were mulling over what to try next, I was approached by a self-chosen student delegation who came bearing written proposals for changes in the course. One of the changes they requested was that the group be split in two and that each half would meet every second week. I wasn't thrilled with this idea because I wanted to keep the community together, and it would mean less time with each group to cover our planned curriculum.

However, I felt it was more important to reward the leadership and responsibility the students had displayed in making their case. We enacted their proposal the next week with excellent results. The students were calmer, participated more, listened respectfully to their peers, and were generally more positive. It is difficult to say whether this improvement was the result of the smaller group, of the less frequent meetings, or because we had honored their request and rewarded their initiative.

The final change we made to student groupings, also in response to student requests, was to increase the frequency of the one-on-one "check-in" interviews that I had been conducting occasionally with the students, and to incorporate them into class time.

Changes in Student Work

The work expected from the students at the beginning of the year included oral participation in class, monthly oral presentations on project work, weekly journal entries, and enthusiastic participation in class events and out-of-class volunteer and mentor activities.

As I have already outlined, class discussions were quite disastrous at the beginning, and presentations were weak. Journal writing met with a lot of opposition, and the students were not giving us the information and reflection on their activities that we requested. Furthermore, some students found our early classroom activities childish or embarrassing.

In response to student requests, they were given the option of doing more oral presentations in lieu of weekly journal entries. When we discussed the journal issue with the students, we realized that many had never written in a journal before and were unclear about what to do. We did two things to remedy the meager journal offerings. First, we offered a workshop on journal writing, including examples of the type of writing and reflections one could include, and second, we created forms to cover all of the detailed information we required such as volunteer hours and self-evaluations. We later realized that we had overdone the forms, and the students who had been asking for a more direct way to deliver information to us were now complaining of the avalanche of paper. As one girl pleaded:

> PLEASE . . . Less paperwork!!! We get so much homework that a shift to less would help us balance our lives a bit more.

Our movement away from threatening activities such as the drama games, and our movement toward smaller groups, significantly improved the problem with lackluster oral presentations and oral participation in class.

THE ACTION RESEARCH CYCLE

In the first year, we planned, we acted, we reflected, and we made changes. We had gone through the action research cycle many times, but we were not finished learning or teaching. As we prepared for the second year, we had the opportunity to involve our returning students in the early stages of planning. It was important to us that we not only follow the action research cycle to better understand and to improve our practice as teachers, but that we include our students in the process, and not just as data.

From the beginning of the year, we tried to make our thought process regarding the course transparent to the students. Before we made changes, we explained our values, theories, and assumptions as well as the evidence we had used to come to our conclusions. We explained why we thought each change was appropriate, but we emphasized that it was the students' needs, opinions, and reactions that were key to the process and content of the course, and that no change was final.

By the end of the year, the process of change in the Leadership Lab had become one of the things that the students commented on most frequently. The students reported that they appreciated our willingness "to be open to discussion and change," and that in response to student feedback we were ". . . easy to approach, understanding and compassionate."

Using the action research cycle as a guide to understanding and change helped us to sort through the often confusing and overwhelming time of starting a new school and an experimental, experiential course. It helped us to organize our questions and observations, and gave us a framework for systematically reflecting on our course. When we made changes, we felt confident that they were well grounded, but not carved in stone. We wanted to be examples of the kind of leaders we were studying, and to create an atmosphere in which leadership potential was nurtured.

IN RETROSPECT

Perhaps because it was so ambitious, I learned more from this action research project than any other, and I learned most from reflecting on what wasn't working. I learned that high school students, in contrast to my early elementary students, were greatly concerned, and at times consumed, by worries about their future. They felt great pressure to achieve high marks to ensure university entrance and were anxious about the adult world that lay ahead. Those with unclear ideas about their future careers were not interested in theoretical issues of leadership. They wanted concrete information about the job market and assurances that there was a place for them in it. Those who were more confident in their studies and had a clearer idea of their future plans seemed more open to and interested in our theoretical explorations.

Learning style was another factor that I didn't sufficiently consider. I knew from my elementary teaching that students learn in different ways, and that not all types of learning experiences are equally appropriate for all students. In spite of this, I didn't give enough opportunities to those learners who needed concrete, hands-on activities. In retrospect, we should have started the year with visits to the businesses, studios, or schools of our guest speakers, and generally spent more time out in the community interacting with "leaders." We should have encouraged and expanded the kinds of projects that the students chose as their volunteer projects, such as decorating and maintaining the school, and hosting new and visiting students.

The cool, confident exterior of the students fooled me into believing that they were more confident than they were. I didn't anticipate how nervous they would be when asked to initiate contact with volunteer agencies or set up meetings with adult mentors. If I had realized this, I would have made more of an effort to have had the mentors and staff from the volunteer sector come to the school to meet the students on their own turf.

In short, I should have used more of my elementary classroom knowledge, experience, and training than I did. I believe that the philosophy and many aspects of the practice of good elementary teaching are central to creating a successful community of inquiry in our Leadership Lab course, and indeed in any school course. In my former role as elementary classroom teacher and in this role as principal and cofacilitator of a high school lab, I know the importance of students finding their work meaningful. And the most meaningful work, of course, is work that arises from one's own questions.

I also know, and should have paid more heed to, the importance of accepting and respecting the knowledge and experience that students bring to the classroom, and of introducing new experiences at a pace and in a manner that suits their needs. Furthermore, I should have acted more fully on my knowledge that it is essential to get to know one's students as individuals, and to establish a safe atmosphere, before expecting them to take risks. I believe that all of these factors are relevant to good teaching for all students and in all curriculum areas.

Although the Leadership Lab was far from ideal in its first year, I believe it was a viable community of inquiry. We established a culture where questions were invited, valued, and explored. Both the content and the process of the course were driven by the students' and teachers' questions and reflections. We supported the students as they pursued their questions and gave them many options for systematically and collaboratively researching and presenting their findings. The course grew from student questions, and was strengthened by the findings of both students and teachers. We, as teachers, were openly inquiring into our own practice, and we included the students in our questions, data collection, analysis, and conclusions.

What we in DICEP have come to value and pursue in our educational communities of inquiry has much in common with an increasingly pervasive school of thought in organizational development literature. In Peter Senge's (1990) vision of the "learning organization," knowledge and leadership is shared. Inspiration for innovation and change is sought throughout the organization in ways that belie the traditional hierarchy. It seeks to promote high creativity and learning through allowing employees to self-organize and collaboratively investigate projects of interest.

Through the concept of "double loop learning," Chris Argyris (1991) points out that traditional problem solving is not enough to create a dynamic and productive organization. He recognizes that effective learning is not just intellectual, but encompasses the whole person, including emotions and values. He believes that a successful organization will be one filled with questioners who critically reflect on their role in, and contributions to, the organization as a whole. That is, an organization of people learning how to learn.

There are significant links between sociocultural theory and collaborative action research and the organizational development theories I drew upon for my inquiry. Sociocultural theory is rooted, of course, in social and cultural activities. In his paper, "A Sociocultural Approach to Mind: Some Theoretical Considerations," James Wertsch (1985) identifies general themes in the work of Vygotsky. A significant theme is "the claim that higher mental functioning in the individual has its origins in social activity" (p. 141). Vygotsky, upon whose work sociocultural theory was founded, believed that individuals need to be given the opportunity to act on ideas and problems with others in order to construct individual understanding. Senge and Argyris, too, place high value on joint activity as essential to a problem-solving process.

The first two of Senge's five disciplines in his groundbreaking *The Fifth Discipline* (1990) deal with organizational learning through joint activity. The first, "team learning," exhorts organizations to allow their employees to work in teams in which individuals suspend their assumptions to create a flow of meaning. The second, "building shared vision," promises that if the group can create a picture of the future together about which they are excited, each individual will then be motivated to contribute to that vision. The social activity of working together creates meaning and understanding that the individual can then act upon.

Argyris (1991) exposes the folly of businesses that base their hopes for success on leaders who rely on individually mastering a set of skills or body of knowledge and who have little tolerance for questions with multiple answers. These leaders engage in what Argyris calls "single loop learning" — a very limited type of problem solving that does not critically examine the situation as a whole. The ideal is double loop learning, in which individuals in the organization work together to question fundamental assumptions and together create "valid knowledge" upon which effective solutions can be based.

Much of the work of DICEP is based on an examination of language in learning and teaching. Vygotsky identified the essential role played by technical and psychological tools, chief of which is language (Wertsch, 1985). He believed that the mediating role played by language is of supreme importance in the development of higher mental functions. Senge and Argyris also place prime importance on authentic dialogue as a tool for organizational learning. Senge believes that high levels of creativity are fostered when groups are encouraged to build on one another's ideas, and adapt and change, outside of the traditional hierarchy of power and influence. Argyris argues that it is through joint critical reflection, and joint examination of questions with multiple answers, that an organization can transform itself into a productive culture of learners.

Through the use of collaborative action research, we in DICEP attempt to analyze our learning and teaching, with the dual goal of understanding it and changing it for the better. We attempt to understand the multifaceted nature of teaching and learning, and the ways in which all the component parts fit together to create the whole. This "systems thinking" is, for Senge, the key to organizational excellence. In order to be effective, an organization must consistently examine the whole system, rather than just fix isolated problems. In order to adapt and change productively, Senge argues, it must be attuned to its patterns of operations. Argyris takes a similar research stance. His key to effectiveness is to create a culture where everyone is in the habit of "asking tough questions, collecting valid data, analyzing it carefully, and consistently testing the inferences drawn from the data" (1991, p. 106).

As I searched the organizational literature to ensure that the principles of the Leadership Lab were consistent with current innovative business practice, I was delighted to find that there was a great compatibility between DICEP's notion of a community of inquiry and progressive thought on inspired organizations. Our hope is that teaching according to the principles of a community of inquiry will enable our students to take their place as leaders in the most creative and dynamic organizations. If this student's reflection is any indication, I think that we are on our way:

> I want to say that I was very skeptical about this school in the beginning. I trusted the traditional laws of regular schools. Now I love the fact that we all respect each other's views or opinions about everything. It reminds me more of a meeting place for people to come and discuss everyday problems. I noticed every student is able to debate or state his or her opinion about something. If all institutions had the same technique of relaxing people and opening

their minds, the world would be a much warmer and accepting place. We're here to help each other in any possible way we can. It is a fact that we cannot solve each other's problems, but we can assure each other that there is always someone you can depend on. We are responsible not only for ourselves, but for making the world a better place.

CHAPTER 9

Coresearching with Students: Exploring the Value of Class Discussions

Karen Hume

IN SEPTEMBER, Andrew was very quiet. He was, and is, unfailingly kind and polite. He is clearly intelligent and reflective, evident not just because he's a member of my class of 24 Grade 6/7 gifted children, but because, like his classmates, he virtually sparkles with intelligence and humor much of the time. In September, however, Andrew was passionate and energetic only when he was telling me how much he hated, absolutely *hated*, all of the talking we were doing in class.

I encourage my students to tell me how things are for them in the classroom, and I try to pay attention when they do. It is important to me that we become a close-knit community of learners, inquiring into the workings of the world and our own actions with both zest and courage (Wells, Chapter 1). In my work as a member of the DICEP research group, I have become familiar with the exhilaration, the pure rush of adrenalin that overtakes me, when I feel myself creating new knowledge and taking new actions in my work, based on a close examination of collected data and stimulating conversations with like-minded colleagues. I want my kids to feel that same pleasure, to be aware of their intelligence, of their power to create (Donoahue, Chapter 2). It's hardly surprising, therefore, that much of my work with my students centers around the development of a knowledge-building community within the classroom (Hume, Chapter 6).

Knowledge building is a term that's meant to suggest a particular stance in my classroom: a focus by all participants on knowledge as an object that is both constructed and continually improved through the multiple perspectives and competing viewpoints that we bring to a question. As various perspectives are raised, students marshal evidence to support their views and to contribute to the building of our collective understanding. Knowledge building, therefore, like almost all classroom activity, relies on oral and written discourse. Andrew's second-day criticism—"The only thing I don't really like is how you kind of let the class talk so much and so long, making [it] kind of boring for the people who don't really like to share thoughts, like me"—was therefore both worrisome and at the same time inconsequential. I was worried because I knew we were in the very early days of a year full of talk. I was at the same time completely unconcerned. I couldn't even conceive of learning without talk, and after all, Andrew was the only one who had expressed a concern. The couple of others who had written about talk in response to my second-day generic question—"How's it going?"—expressed a view that was much more in line with my own feelings. "I love the little 'talks' we have in the middle of the classroom," Deb wrote. And Amanda said, "I really like the way we have full class conversations. It makes school much more enjoyable no matter what we are talking about." I hoped that Andrew's concern was simply "his problem," perhaps representative of his learning style or personality, but certainly something that he would need and want to overcome in view of the sheer mass of fascinating conversations that our class would be enjoying! I wrote a "Hang in there; let's wait and see how it goes" response to Andrew, and hoped for the best.

A week later, I received this letter from Andrew:

> It's going okay. I'm still very annoyed with all our talks. . . . I feel kind of like we're not getting a lot of work done and we're learning nothing but math, music, French, gym, and how to talk, not things that I think are really productive. Please try to fit some others things in other than talking. I can't stress that enough. I'm really serious about it. That's it.

I met with him and asked him to say more. Visibly distressed and in a rush of speech, Andrew reported that he's not very good at talking, that he's shy, that he doesn't like to talk, and that you don't learn anything from talk. My rejoinder that I thought he was very good indeed at talking, that he had important things to say and made good sense in saying them, just seemed to upset him further.

We were at a crossroads. I was unhappy that Andrew was so unhappy, and I believed that his passionately felt concerns needed to be taken seriously, but I was unwilling to stop or even significantly lessen the whole class talk. The best solution seemed to be to ask Andrew if he would be willing to coresearch the issue with me, to look together at the question of the role of talk in our classroom. Could we try together to determine if, when, and how talk might make a difference to our learning?

I imagine I was a picture of calm, confident assurance for the fraction of a minute that it took Andrew to give me a firm, clear "Yes," but inside I was in turmoil. I had always wanted to coresearch with students, to involve them well beyond the level of video camera operator and general gofer, but I had never done it. It made good sense, given my philosophy, to make action research one of the structures for engaging students in both knowledge construction and community development, but it had taken me years to learn to focus on data and draw useful information from it. Who was I to even suggest that I could help Andrew, or any other student, acquire those skills? And what were my motives for proposing this research? I know that learning occurs in the talk. Was I just going to go through the motions with Andrew, burying him in a mountain of transcripts and baffling him with my pronouncements from the research literature until he eventually admitted defeat and claimed to know it too?

Weeks passed while, with Andrew's ready agreement ringing in my mind, I continued to panic. Should we try to define learning? Should I be providing some sort of instruction in discourse analysis? And above all, what could I possibly do to make this true coresearch as opposed to an academic exercise for an unsuspecting student? I searched the literature for models, ideals, reassurance. Wells (1994) provided encouragement, but I couldn't find anyone who had actually tried it. Even the limited literature on participatory research (e.g., Maguire, 1987; Whyte, 1991) discussed only cases of adults in work situations, usually where the researcher was someone from outside the organization. I began to wish for that outsider status. If you really made a mess of things your professional career might suffer, but you wouldn't have to live with your mistakes day in and day out!

Finally, concern about disappointing Andrew overwhelmed my uncertainty about how to proceed. I asked Andrew if he would like to get started, and if he would like to involve anyone else. The answer was "Yes" to both questions so, at his request, I told our class about Andrew's concern and asked if anyone else would like to join us in researching the question. Four boys immediately offered—Joel, David, and Eddie from Grade 6, and Paul from Grade 7. (The all-male composition of the group shouldn't be seen as unusual since 17 of my 24 students are male.)

This chapter is an account of the work of our coresearch group over its first year. Describing the complexity of a single moment in time is impossible. Discussing that complexity across even the three meetings that I've chosen for analysis means dealing with four hundred utterances, six participants, and the historical and social context of my classroom. And so, not because it is ideal, but because it is at least manageable, in this chapter I pull our meetings apart, considering in turn each of three aspects—knowledge construction, participation, and action—before attempting to put them back together again in a tentative, preliminary explanation of how and why it all works.

THE SETTING

We meet in our empty portable classroom after everyone has eaten their lunch and the others have gone outside to play. Although small, the room is well organized for our way of working. Student desks are in six clusters of four around the outside of the room, with a couple of tables and a big open space in the center for our Class Council meetings and our whole class conversations.

We think our classroom is both attractive and interesting. Since I was new to the school, as well as new to teaching gifted children, we all met for a day in August to get to know each other and to set up our room. I should correct that: I got to know the kids and they, me. Most of them have known each other, and have been in a class together, for anywhere from one to four years. Still, it was a new experience for everyone to have a say in setting up a room, and the results reflect our wide-ranging interests. We have lots of books, a few science toys, a blue glass head, a miniature greenhouse, half a dozen plush monkeys and apes hanging from a rope ladder, and posters of the Chicago Bulls basketball team, Dungeons and Dragons, and "Everything I wanted to know about life I learned from Star Trek."

THE DATA

We come to the meetings prepared, having read, and usually made notes on, both the previous meeting's transcript (all coresearch meetings are audiotaped) and on a transcript of whole class talk (selected sessions are videotaped, with selection based on either a "feeling" that something interesting may happen, or simply on the availability of time to set up the recording equipment!).

It was my decision to use transcripts as a data source, a decision consistent with my belief that the complexity of talk can only be analyzed through faithful review of a full transcript. My research partners don't question the use of transcripts, but express a flash of concern about my workload. Eddie thinks that if one of us were to learn shorthand or if we were to hire a secretary, the transcription burden could be lifted from my shoulders, but we decide that until that day I'm the one who is the "amazing typer" as Joel puts it, so I type and photocopy the transcripts that the group has decided to analyze, and deliver them faithfully a couple of days before the meeting.

Previous experiences of showing transcripts of their talk to adolescents and preadolescents had me convinced that I would have to suffer through hours of obsessive counting of the number of comments made by each speaker and recountings of agonies of embarrassment over saying "stupid things" before we could even begin to look at the transcript as a data source. However, this wasn't an issue with this group. For the most part, their fascination with the transcripts was a fascination with how speech and actions are recorded in print.

In fact, this fascination has served a very useful purpose. It can be difficult to encourage students to question sources, to approach written information as problematic and tentative when they so often assume anything in print to be fixed and authoritative. Transcript analysis seems to be one way around this dilemma. My coresearchers point out when they think I have missed a word, shortened an interchange, or attributed a comment to the wrong speaker. They recognize that the transcribing of speech into print is an act of interpretation. As Andrew pointed out:

> I'm always really wondering what this transcript is going to look like and how you interpret things. I don't know if other people are thinking this. Maybe it's just me. I'm always thinking—Oh, two people are talking at the same time. What's that going to look like? I'm always wondering about that.

Like other researchers, we deliberate about what conventions we need to observe in order to render our transcripts as useful to our purposes as possible. We have talked about: using asterisks to indicate indecipherable words (Paul); the recording of simultaneous speech (Andrew); the need for providing contextual notes prior to the first utterance of the transcript (Andrew); the inadequacy of a transcript in providing information about people's actions—that is, how many and who had their hands raised during a particular interchange (Andrew); and the importance of retaining speech hesitancies because "we should keep what we actually said" (David). (See Wells, Chapter 5, for an interesting perspective on analyzing nonverbal communication.)

KNOWLEDGE BUILDING

I was determined from the beginning that the methodologies we used in our work should emerge from my students' close reading of the data, not be imposed by me as the "right way" to analyze a transcript. I didn't want my own biases about talk to color the way we examined the data, and I didn't want my greater expertise in analysis to establish a hierarchy of roles within our group. However, at the same time that I was adopting an attitude of "benign neglect," this was still an area of great personal concern. I knew, from experience in graduate school and teacher research groups, that if we didn't stay close to the data from the outset, our initial ideas could quickly turn into entrenched, unsupportable positions. This would be catastrophic, not only in possibly furthering beliefs about the uselessness of talk—ones that I could not accept—but in negating the significance of the requirements for evidence and support that we had in place in the knowledge-building work we had been doing in science and history.

I viewed our first meeting as a time when we would put our initial thoughts about talk on record, and felt temporarily released from this concern with data sources and evidence. Partway through that meeting, when it seems that everyone has decided that the learning potential of talk is directly related to interest in the subject, I ask, "How do you think we can use the talk to help us learn if it was a subject that, let's say, EVERYBODY in the class was interested in? How does the talk make a difference in the learning?" Andrew replies that in talking with people you gradually recognize other points of view. Paul extends Andrew's comment by offering an example from a recent science class:

> Like, when I was doing a progress report, I was saying something about molecules and how they compared to matter. Lloyd and Eren pointed out something that possibly could not be true, so I fixed it, and it's a lot better now. I'm glad I did.

Joel chimes in with a phrase that we'd consciously adopted in a couple of our September whole class conversations, and then offers his own example:

I can connect [my emphasis] with Paul because when we were doing the knowledge building for the light unit, when me and Matt were doing our thing, we had an argument over whether atoms or electrons is the thing that photons get, like, sucked into. And like Matt explained his point of view and I explained mine, through like talk, and we also drew little diagrams to help show each other what we're talking about, and then we finally resolved it.

I am amazed and tremendously relieved. Even before we have recourse to transcripts, my coresearchers are supporting their statements with evidence drawn from personal experience, and they are making connections to each other using phrases we have adopted in class. I am beginning to realize that knowledge construction in action research is like knowledge construction in any other area of study.

This perception holds true through the next two meetings as the students use their knowledge-building skills to make some fascinating discoveries about talk. For example, on six different occasions, they connect various entries in a transcript in order to see and describe a pattern. They identify: forms of talk, subject change, points of connection in knowledge building, and patterns of interaction. This pattern seeking and identification is a tremendously important behavior because it encourages the explicit connecting of new information to the preexisting pattern, thereby offering another support for the pattern or, if it doesn't fit, forcing a reexamination of the entire data set.

One example will demonstrate not only the awareness of pattern, but many of the other skills that we bring to bear in reviewing a transcript. In the October meeting, we had observed that talk often goes in circles, with people restating the comments of the last speaker and adding something that's just a little bit different. Joel asks to start the November session, obviously excited about something he has discovered in that October meeting transcript:

I think this is the first one that mentions it is 23 (utterance number) and it's Paul saying. . . . I underlined it—"Like people would just basically say exactly what everyone else was saying, and add like a tad of their own opinion." And then I put, "look at conversation 26" and it says, "If you just keep going and connecting to what's above it is eventually going to peter out. Either that or it will just start to repeat something that's been said, and then it will go in circles." And then Paul says the same.

In addition to identifying the pattern and trying to explain it to us, Joel has done three important things. He has directed us to the specific spot in the transcript where we will find the evidence, a behavior that is to be repeated, by Joel and others, eleven more times in this transcript and the next. He has described the strategies that he used in reviewing the transcript. And he has demonstrated a willingness and an ability to observe and reflect on his own group's actions.

I want to encourage the strategy of going beyond the data to make reasonable inferences and predictions, so I ask:

> Why do we do that? I mean that's a really common thing for people to do. Conversations don't tend to be everybody making these totally unique contributions. We often kind of restate things in our own words. Why do you think people do that?

Various ideas are offered, then Eddie says, "I think it might depend on making it so they can understand it more by repeating it themselves. Like when you say something, it's easier to understand it than when you like read it or something." This is a great opportunity for me to situate our questions within the larger research community and I attempt to grab it:

> There's this huge area, this body of research that learning really occurs through talk and that you actually have to engage in the talk for learning to take place.

My young colleagues—appropriately, I think—disregard this premature attempt to broaden the context of our work to include published researchers. Their interest seems to be that the knowledge they are creating is new to their group. As Bereiter (1994) reminds us, this is more important in knowledge construction than that it be new to the world.

David takes a turn to tell us his strategies and tentative conclusions:

> What I did is I just looked through it (the transcript) and then I made observations, so I wrote notes. One of them, one note, was "Mindless repetition with just a little addition of opinion makes talk go in circles." I think that is caused by people who say something that someone else has already said so they just change it a bit. Also, disinterested people, when they hear something they know or can connect with, they jump out and say it and argue it, even though it has already been said and argued. They want to join the conversation, so they repeat the only things they know about the subject so they can join the conversation.

My students are behaving as apprentice researchers. They make connections to their experiences and to each other in support of their developing theories. They identify themes and patterns across data. They honor the researcher behavior of staying close to the data, citing specifics in support of their claims. They demonstrate an ability to reflect on and critique data, even words they themselves have said ("I also disagreed with myself a couple of times," says Eddie), when evidence fails to support their earlier claims.

Perhaps most important, there is considerable talk in all meetings of the strategies we have used in our analysis. This is beneficial not only because it makes it apparent that the kids are choosing and using strategies but because, in making a strategy explicit, it is open to use and modification by others. In sharing our ideas, and our particular areas of strength and expertise, we demonstrate a dedication to collective, rather than individual, progress.

With regard to my own participation, I am delighted to discover that my most frequent contributions to knowledge building are suggestions of strategies for analysis, and that these suggestions are offered only at times when they might be useful to our progress. At various points, for example, I suggest that we do the following: give an overview response and then look for evidence to support our feelings; read the transcript aloud in order to hear the language and improve our understanding; support a view by providing evidence from the transcript; and refocus on the original research question and then explore what action we can take to find out more.

My student colleagues also offer a variety of excellent strategies, including: demonstrations and explanations of how to mark transcripts in useful ways (underlining, circling, highlighting, connecting statements, writing notes in the margins); using later transcripts to understand earlier ones and vice versa; visualizing; and designing a model.

PARTICIPATION

My early concern about taking over the group has proven to be completely unfounded. As Andrew puts it, "Basically, you're just part of the group. You just talk when you want to talk." Group members are quick to voice their approval of another's ideas and equally quick to challenge. I am challenged as frequently as anyone, although perhaps a little more gently and indirectly, as in this exchange:

> ANDREW: Matt goes "I have the answer, not a test for it" and you
>   say "Okay, well wait a second"

EDDIE: Yeah, and he never comes back in

ANDREW: Yeah, and you say "Can you think of a test that will help you to determine it?" Were you asking him a question or were you just asking everyone?

KAREN: Usually when somebody does that, I'm asking them, but I'm also opening it up to everyone so that the person doesn't feel put on the spot

ANDREW: 'Cause I was wondering because you asked him like three questions- if those were just telling him that no we don't want your answer right now, or were you actually wanting to ask him those questions?

KAREN: I was actually trying to ask him those questions . I don't like to shut somebody down and just say, "No I don't want your answer" . . I was trying to get him to look at it from a different way, but at the same time I knew that in such a short span of time it's often hard for people to switch gears like that and look at things differently, so I was also kind of asking them for the class

ANDREW: So Matt probably didn't have his hand up after that, right?

KAREN: No, he didn't

I would challenge anyone to identify the preceding dialogue as that of 11-year-olds with their teacher. It is truly a conversation of researchers who are genuinely trying to understand the reasons for, and the implications of, a particular action. The goal is clear—to understand more about the talk in our classroom—and all are engaged with this goal. Status in the classroom is not an issue; ideas are protected or challenged, not personalities or roles.

I had been concerned about status after our first meeting. I was afraid that I had taken my nondirective injunction to myself too far and had basically divorced myself from the process, inadvertently creating perceptions of my place in the group as that of the observant, and possibly judgmental, teacher. In my journal I wrote, "It's only going to be CO-research if I get with it and behave as a participant, not an observer!" What changed over the course of our meetings—just my perception, or something in the way I was behaving?

To answer this question, I tried first to define my criteria for a successful coresearch experience. I decided, soon after the first meeting, that the work could be considered successful only if it were codeveloped, cogenerative, and of equally committed participation. If it really is to be a CO-research group, I reasoned, my kids should be assuming as much ownership of the group and our work as I do, and should be as involved as I in the direction that the project would take. Not only would this be a standard expectation of any group of adult coresearchers, and therefore a reasonable expectation for us, but I have also always considered it a criterion of effective knowledge-building work and effective inquiry in any area. Work that is meaningful is work that is both cognitively and affectively engaging. It is driven by the participants, beginning with the asking of "real" questions and continuing through a commitment to staying with them until some personally satisfying understandings are achieved.

Working from the belief that question–response–follow-up is the standard form of classroom teacher-student interaction, whereas multiple perspectives and connecting responses are necessary for knowledge construction and inquiry, I examined the patterns of interaction across three transcripts. In the first, I clearly set up an expectation that each student will be heard from in response to my questions. I invite a student to "start us off," leading the next student to preface his remarks with "Okay, well I'll go now." Although the kids quickly move into a conversation in which they begin to make connections to each other's comments, I maintain control of the dialogue, going so far at the end as to invite each to make a "final comment," and thanking each speaker in turn. It is only in reviewing the transcript and realizing that my students are engaging in knowledge construction behaviors in spite of my clumsiness that I am able to relax and trust that subsequent conversations can be fruitful without being stage-managed by me!

In our November and December meetings, I am still the one who asks the majority of questions (a teacher behavior), but the questions result in a multiplicity of responses, most of which connect to each other rather than to the original question, and many of which lead into interesting issues that are then explored by the group. For example, in our December meeting, we examine a lengthy transcript excerpt that leads us into a discussion of how classroom conversations might be handled so that people have the opportunity to make the statements that will be critical to progress, and why those statements, when made, are sometimes ignored by others. This harks back to an argument the boys have made from the beginning, that our classroom conversations are often difficult to follow. When they first said this, I didn't understand the problem. I anticipate well; I know my kids and their speech mannerisms and, with my responsibility to "manage" the talk, I tend to follow discussions very closely. I would have said that our conversations can be very long and frustrating because everyone wants lots of opportunity to speak, but hard to understand? No.

Now, after reviewing whole class transcripts, I agree with my coresearchers: Our talk *is* difficult to understand. Eddie explains why:

You (meaning "anyone") focus on the one thing and you kind of get caught in what you're thinking. . . . when you've got your hand up when someone else is talking, you're thinking exactly about what you want to say. So when the person's talking, it's just going in one ear and coming out the other. You're not paying attention to it at all.

As a research group, we are beginning to recognize the dilemma in this. We are thinking that an effective learning conversation looks like a big web with multiple points of entry and many connections. We are pretty sure that this is going to prove superior to the easy-to-follow, but less effective in knowledge construction, linear form of conversation that is often typical of classroom discussion. However, not only is a multifaceted conversation far more difficult to track, but it is also far more difficult for any member of that conversation to determine whether his or her contribution will be a valid one to make, and it is also going to take a lot of time, leading to "all that talking" that was part of Andrew's initial concern.

Three months into our research work, we begin to try to pinpoint the differences between the frustrating whole class talks that often consist of unrelated or tangentially related comments that take us in circles, and our satisfying and productive research group talks, which also go in circles sometimes, but still seem to lead us somewhere useful:

EDDIE: I hardly ever find anything (worth noting) in the class transcripts
KAREN: How come?
EDDIE: I don't know . . it's just, um, harder for me to find stuff to say
ANDREW: I don't think they talk as focused on the subject

Near the end of the meeting we pick up the thread again as Paul and others respond to a question about my role in the group:

You're asking questions and we're answering, but it's on a different level because our answers—you start with one question like "How is talk effective in learning?"—and someone answers, and that leads to another question and so on and so on, until we stand where we are right now. So it's kind of like student and teacher; on a different level though. Our answers are usually making up other questions, unless we start going in circles.

Eddie adds that asking questions of the answers takes everyone into "more and more depth, (so) we come to have a better understanding of it (the question) than when we started." He makes the link, as he did back in October, that a resource is key:

> The transcripts are a means of like practicing, of seeing if our testing—if our theories are actually correct on the transcripts, 'cause if what we say works in the transcripts and it works in a couple of transcripts . . . then I think we can pretty much say it's a pretty sound theory, whereas if we have a good theory but when we try to back it up it doesn't work, then we have another, we can say "Well, that didn't work, but at least we tried."

Both the content of the discourse and its dialogic form highlight the progressive nature of our work together. In Eddie's comment above, there are echoes of David, Joel, Andrew, Paul, and myself. Ideas surge and resurge through the pages of the transcripts, initiated by one member, but then picked up and modified by another and another until it feels wrong to attribute any idea to a single speaker, and instead, we can conclude that this is something we have constructed together.

That is not to say that participation in the group is equal. Construction of a frequency table shows me that it clearly is not, but all that really says is that frequency of contribution is not a very useful indicator when you are engaged in the construction of knowledge. In any group, even one dedicated to collective progress, there must be a recognition that different members will likely make different kinds of contributions based on their interests and areas of expertise. While I think it's too constricting to suggest that we play roles in a group, perhaps something can be learned from examining the kinds of contributions made by individual members.

ACTION

A defining characteristic of action research is that it consists of cycles of inquiry where understanding informs practice, and the new practice leads to new understanding (Wells, 1994). I noticed that comments in our classroom coresearch meetings became increasingly focused on suggestions for action. These action suggestions are of five basic types (the number of suggestions is in parentheses):

1. *Class activity* (12). *Examples*: Talk about subjects or do units of interest to most and observe for level of involvement; split into small

groups so people have a chance to say what they want and to argue; let the class read photocopies of transcripts; have teacher explain concepts to the class more thoroughly.

2. *Presentation by our research group* (10). *Examples*: Make a video; present to small groups; put questions in video for people to answer; modify video based on rest of class response and contributions.

3. *Experimentation* (7). *Examples*: Transcribe more tapes so we have a large body of data from which to work; produce a false conversation based on false premises and see what happens; videotape class during topic of interest and observe for fidgeting, eye contact, body language.

4. *Our group's meetings* (3). *Examples*: Change subject when the talk stops being useful; go back to our original questions when we start to go in circles; look at more transcripts.

5. *Transcript preparation* (2). *Examples*: Provide contextual information at beginning of transcript; learn shorthand

Andrew makes far more suggestions than anyone else, twice as many as the next most frequent person (David), and four times as many as any of the rest of us. His suggestions cohere around a central issue. He wants more individual ownership, more say over where a conversation is going, more opportunity for everyone to say what they would like to say and not be disappointed by having someone else say it before them. Andrew believes this can happen if conversations are held in small groups rather than large, so he proposes that both classroom conversations and our ultimate research group presentation be conducted in small groups before any work is done with the whole class (see also Davis, Chapter 4). He uses an instance from the end of September science transcript, where the conversation is limited to a few people, to support this view. Interestingly, this is one of the few instances of referral to a transcript for support of a recommended action. Initially surprising, it seems less so when we realize that action research decisions are based on the researcher's theory, which is in turn related to a buildup of evidence and a development of ideas over time, rather than to specific isolated events. This is certainly true for Andrew, whose ideas are so internally consistent that I believe he is working from a theoretical framework.

The same is true of David, although David adopts a more strongly experimental approach, consistent with his approach to all subjects. David's language is a language of research: "We could watch what people do and how they get involved." "Let's look at our work as multiple drafts, modifying after each response from others." As with Andrew, there is tremendous internal consistency in David's responses, suggesting that he is also working from theory rather than simply responding to specific events.

Joel, Eddie, Paul, and I have made far fewer action suggestions so far, making it difficult to discuss our frameworks, or the kinds of contributions we offer, with any degree of certainty. I should note, however, that there are suggestions of actions to be taken that will further our research, and there are also actions that we take that demonstrate our commitment to the group and our ownership of the process. In this latter category, all members have played an active role. It still amazes me that everyone meets willingly at lunch time, with advance work done and in hand. If only that were the case for all action research groups! It impresses me that our language is that of a collective. Any one of us might say, "We need to meet soon."

Finally, it thrills me that involvement in the research is, at the group's initiative, seeping beyond the boundaries of our group and our meetings. From the time in November when Eddie came to our meeting with his copy of the transcript marked "Eddie and Company" and nonchalantly informed us that he and his mom "read it together, and I think she might have wrote down some of the stuff that is in here," through Andrew's mom confessing that she'd read a meeting transcript because Andrew asked her to, but then couldn't put it down, to the two-hour presentation that we gave to a hundred student teachers, the interest of others in our work has been most gratifying.

But, while we enjoy the approval of others, and we feel an awareness of our "own intelligence, our power to create" that I had hoped for at the beginning of the year, as a teacher-researcher I am left with the big question: Why? Why is this coresearch activity working so well? And perhaps more important, What will this work mean to anyone else in the world, or even to these students in the months and years ahead?

I initially viewed the activity of coresearch as likely to be important for the achievement of two of my classroom goals: building community by stressing the involvement of all in defining and solving classroom problems, and engaging my students in the activities of theorizing and evidence seeking that would reinforce and justify our use of these skills in other subject areas. As a teacher I expected new learnings about my students by engaging in this process, but not new learnings about talk or the strategies of action research and knowledge construction. However, I believe there have already been some significant learnings about how coresearch about a classroom issue can contribute to the development of any classroom knowledge-building activity.

INTERIM CONCLUSIONS

Prior to this experience with my coresearchers, I had viewed knowledge building as a particularly effective way to acquaint students with the discourse practices and knowledge requirements of the various disciplines. That was why I originally panicked and felt that perhaps I should teach the standards of action research before we could begin to examine transcripts. And because my prior knowledge-building experiences had been in two distinctly different disciplines, each with its own particular set of discourse and evidentiary requirements, I had assumed that knowledge building around an action research issue would be unique; that there would be no cross-pollination of ideas or processes from other subject areas or other experiences in my students' lives.

What I have found is that my early attitude of benign neglect, born of not knowing how to set up or manage the actions of our group, combined with the fact that this was a new experience for all members, has allowed us a virtually unfettered experience of knowledge building, in some ways quite unlike our earlier experiences in history and science. Our coresearch group has created useful research processes that are resulting in our making substantial progress in addressing the issues with which we are concerned. These processes have not been created in a vacuum. Instead, my students have done what I always hope students will do. They have taken the knowledge construction skills that we developed in other areas of the curriculum, and they have appropriated these for use in our action research work, transforming and re-creating them as necessary for the new situation. For the first time, I see the potential of knowledge building as an act of creative transformation of practice rather than strictly one of socialization into our cultural heritage. The power of knowledge building that I alluded to earlier is that it fulfills both functions extremely well, and often simultaneously.

One of the difficulties of knowledge building in the classroom is that of finding the questions that students really want to answer. So often we think we've found them, as do our students, but they end up not having the mass appeal, the generativity, or the longevity that we had hoped. Action research questions are different. They are about who we are, how we live together, and how we learn. Addressing these questions is deeply satisfying because we are the only ones who can address them. We can create knowledge that is genuinely new, particular to us, and of great fascination. At the same time, we can take action and in the process change both ourselves and our environment. We can see ourselves grow. Eddie spoke for the whole group when he commented on the presentation we made to a university group of preservice teachers:

The people in our coresearch group definitely think that it's a good thing. Joel said that the coresearch group has improved the friendships of all the people in it, and it has helped us understand the classroom without disrupting it. David added to that by noting that since the coresearch group started, all of our speech patterns have improved. He also noted that we've made a lot of headway in the topic of learning through talk. Paul said that the coresearch group has helped him pay more attention during class discussions and that he no longer fidgets with things in his desk during our class discussions. Andrew said that it is worthwhile, and that we're learning a lot of things about talk we never would have noticed without the group. And me? I think it's just an all round good thing.

In coresearching the value of class discussions, my student colleagues and I have learned a great deal that will allow us to take action and become different. We have recognized the difficulty of tracking and maintaining conversations that encourage multiple points of entry and a wide variety of perspectives, while at the same time we've seen evidence of learning and stronger individual interest in the topic when we have such conversations. We've decided that some problems that occur in class conversations aren't always a result of "not listening"—as teachers tend to tell students—but rather that it's easy to get lost in the talk if you don't have lots of opportunity to "say" in order to learn and in order to feel part of the interactional dynamics of the classroom (see Wells, Chapter 10).

Our interim conclusions provide us with wonderful opportunities to take action. When students become involved in knowledge building around action research issues they have opportunity, likely for the first time, to experience the connection between knowledge and development, both individual and collective. I think this cannot help but change their understanding of the nature of knowledge, helping them to recognize it as an object that can be continually improved through their active participation. When groups of students have this collaborative experience, the possibility exists for the creation of vital knowledge-building communities which may, through their example, transform the way we think about teaching, learning, and school.

Since the first word and the initiating event of our group belonged to Andrew, it seems appropriate that he also be given the last. In his presentation to the preservice teachers, Andrew claims,

We found out that we were not at all opposed to talking, so it was an interesting group. After a few sessions we talked about *how* we learn through talk and what constructive talk is. It was quite interesting and fun to do. I think this is a really great thing to do and you can do many interesting things and experiments to make talk much easier to understand as well as more learning with it too!

When asked if other kids should have the opportunity to engage in action research, and whether they would enjoy it if they did, Andrew didn't need any time to think about his reply:

Yes! Our group is about having a point of view, supported by evidence and your own thoughts, whatever they may be. If another group in another class wanted to start a successful coresearch group, I think it would be quite easy as long as they have a wide range of ideas and thoughts, aren't shy to speak up, and have an issue or topic in their class that they really want to know more about.

PART III

Taking a Larger View

CHAPTER 10

The Case for Dialogic Inquiry

Gordon Wells

As a RESEARCH group, the members of DICEP consider the development of a theoretical framework to be an essential part of carrying out action research. In the effort to understand as well as to improve one's practice, theory both grows out of practice and helps in making sense of it; it also suggests the kinds of improvement that might be attempted and provides a rationale for explaining the reasons for these changes to others. At the same time, theorizing is never finalized, since it is conducted in a dialogue with others; it is also only valuable when it shapes and is shaped by action.

This has been the case with the theory presented here. Of course, it is only one person's way of putting the key ideas together, but the framework itself has been developed over many years of dialogue: with the other members of DICEP, with colleagues around the world, and with authors— many no longer living—who have contributed to its development. However, since for some readers, the ideas presented here may be unfamiliar, I shall attempt, where possible, to make them more meaningful by illustrating them with reference to the inquiries reported in the preceding chapters.

THE GOALS OF EDUCATION

Everywhere there is currently much talk about a crisis in public education and a need for major reform. At the same time, there is a widespread lack of agreement about what form education should take in the century ahead and about the kind of changes that most need to be made. On the one hand, policy makers and educational planners emphasize the need to improve standards and accountability. They talk about improving the "delivery" of a standardized curriculum, of "outcomes," and of nationwide forms of assessment that will ensure that these outcomes are achieved. On the other hand, the message of academic researchers is more concerned with students achieving "depth of understanding." Instead of outcomes, they emphasize "process," and the importance of "inquiry," "construction," and "collaboration." Between these two perspectives on education lies the arena of day-by-day classroom practice. This is the disputed territory inhabited by practicing teachers. Although often sympathetic to the philosophy underlying the latter perspective, they are nevertheless forced by their conditions of employment to act in conformity with the former.

The reasons for this mismatch are in large part historical and are to be found in the social, economic, and intellectual changes that have taken place during the twentieth century and, more important, in the ways in which those with different responsibilities for public education have responded to them. Certainly, the last hundred years have seen a massive increase in the scope of public education and in the expectations about what it should achieve. Whereas, a century ago, a minimum functional competence in reading, writing, and arithmetic was considered an adequate target, current demands for complex forms of information handling in the workplace have substantially raised the requirements for print, mathematical, and computer literacy (Resnick, 1987), and for a basic familiarity with key concepts in the natural and human sciences. In addition, whereas in the past only a small proportion of school graduates was expected to achieve a college or university qualification, this is now the target for the majority, with a high school diploma being the minimum requirement. With the resulting vast increase in the scale of responsibility for educational provision, it is not surprising that policy makers and administrators should be preoccupied with universal outcomes, with the maintenance and improvement of standards, and with accountability to parents and tax payers for the services they provide.

In itself, this macrolevel concern with standards, equity, and accountability is admirable. However, the form in which this concern is being realized in practice is much less acceptable. Education cannot be reduced to a utilitarian preparation for the workplace, however technologically sophisticated the skills that are being trained. Nor can the activity of learning and teaching be managed as if it were a sequence of operations on a production line, with uniformly adaptable, knowledgeable workers as the intended outcome.

Education is only secondarily about the preparation of the workforce. Its primary concern is with the maintenance and improvement of society in all its manifestations and with enabling individual students both to contribute to society and to achieve their human potential. As many of the great pioneers of public schooling realized, the health of a democratic society and, hence, the well-being of its members, depends on the committed and informed participation of its citizens in making decisions about public affairs and in putting those decisions into effect. From this perspective, therefore, just as important as the acquisition of productive skills for the marketplace is the development of a critical understanding of the relationships between socially valued ends and the means for achieving them, and of the disposition to use both skills and understanding in ways that contribute to the common good as well as to the satisfaction of individual or sectional interests.

A commitment to these transformative goals of education clearly has implications for the manner in which learning and teaching are carried out, day by day, in schools and classrooms. It seems evident to us that, in order to be able to participate effectively as adults in a democratic society, students must engage in activities in school that induct them into the values and practices that should characterize such a society, as well as equipping them with the knowledge and skills necessary for productive participation. On the one hand, this means that, from the beginning, students need to be given the opportunity to develop personal initiative and responsibility, adaptable problem-posing and -solving skills, and the ability to work collaboratively with others (Dewey, 1916). And on the other, it means that classrooms and schools must themselves become more democratic, more critical of the ways in which knowledge is created and used, and more willing to listen respectfully to students' opinions and suggestions.

This focus on understanding—that is to say, knowing oriented to effective and responsible action—is also the thrust of most of those educational reforms that have been influenced by recent developments in research and theorizing about how people learn. As will be explained in more detail in the rest of this chapter, this work has shifted the emphasis toward students achieving personal understanding of information rather than simply being able to recall it on demand, and to coconstruction rather than transmission as the means by which this understanding is achieved. In addition, rather than assuming that all classrooms and their members are essentially equivalent and that, therefore, one curriculum fits all, it is now being recognized that classroom communities are each unique, always situated in particular times and places and made up of diverse participants—teachers as well as students—with individual identities, interests, and motivations. It is thus clear that there can be no universal blueprint for successful learning and teaching. Each classroom must find its own way of working, taking into account both what each member brings by way of past experience at home, at school, and in the wider community—their values, interests, and aspirations—as well as the outcomes that they are required to achieve.

From this perspective, it is also recognized that the evaluation of what students have learned cannot be adequately achieved by standardized assessment, using decontextualized multiple-choice or short-answer tests (Gipps, 1999). More valid as a measure of the progress that has been made is an evaluation of the student's ability to bring his or her knowledge and skills to bear in solving new problems that are of some personal significance, and an assessment of the strategies that he or she uses in the process. That is to say, in order to know how well students, teachers, and schools are achieving their objectives, it is necessary to find ways of carrying out authentic assessment.

Clearly, the differences just sketched between these two broad perspectives are due in large part to the different responsibilities of those who adopt them with respect to the education of the student population. But it also stems from the different conceptions of knowledge and of coming to know that are presupposed by these two perspectives and from the role that language and other meaning-making systems are believed to play in the construction, use, and dissemination of knowledge. The changes that have taken place in these areas constitute another important aspect of the context of our work that needs to be considered.

CHANGING VIEWS OF KNOWLEDGE AND COMING TO KNOW

As well as an increasing demand for more knowledgeable graduates from public education, the last hundred years have also seen important changes in the way in which knowledge itself is understood (Case, 1996). At the beginning of the century, most people thought of *knowledge* as "true belief," that is to say, as the sum total of those facts and theories that had been empirically verified and could therefore be taken to be correct. Such beliefs, it was supposed, could in consequence be treated as objective, independent of particular knowers and of the cultural conditions under which they were established. Certainly, this view of knowledge has sustained the advances made in the natural sciences and in the technological application of their findings in industry, most notably in the rapid rise in the last two decades of computerized communication and information processing. It has also had a significant influence on the way in which large organizations are managed.

Not surprisingly, this positivist view of knowledge has also been influential in education, both in shaping the content of the curriculum and in prescribing the practices of instruction and assessment. According to this perspective, the major function of education is to ensure that students acquire the knowledge that is considered most useful and important, and teaching is conceived of in terms of organizing what is to be learned into appropriately sized and sequenced chunks and arranging optimal methods of delivery and opportunities for practice and memorization.

However, while it is obviously important that students should be helped to take possession of the accumulated knowledge that is valued in the society in which they are growing up, this cannot be achieved by simple transfer. In other words, knowledge cannot be handed over as if it were the intellectual equivalent of a bag of groceries to be delivered, or a message to be transmitted and received over the Internet.

To see the inappropriateness of the "transmissionary" conception of communication, it is only necessary to compare reports of the same event in different newspapers. What is considered salient varies from one to another and, unless the copywriters are quoting verbatim from an identical source, the beliefs, opinions, and motives attributed to the principal participants are often markedly different. More important, each newspaper has its own slant on what is considered to be significant. At the same time, a similar variability is also to be found in the readers of any one of these papers. We each have our own interests and current concerns, along with varying amounts of relevant past experience; these influence how we make sense of what we read and how we determine its significance for future action (Kress, 1997). Thus, reading involves an active transaction with, and interpretation of, new information, and because of our unique life trajectories, we each construct different versions of what we read.

The same diversity is equally true of learning. Just as important as what is common to groups of individual students in terms of their biological human inheritance is the diversity that characterizes any class or school, particularly in large urban centers, such as the one in which DICEP is located. Not only do students differ in gender and ethnic and social background, in the language(s) that they speak at home, and in their current levels of performance on school tasks, but they also differ in the values they have learned at home and in their aspirations, interests, and experience outside the school. Given this diversity in what students bring to school and to each curricular activity in which they engage, it is clear that the administrative desire to implement a one-curriculum-fits-all model, in which knowledge is identically delivered to passive student receivers, is completely at odds with current conceptions of how learning occurs (J. G. Brooks & M. G. Brooks, 1993).

Furthermore, theories of knowledge and coming to know that fail to take student diversity into account provide little help for teachers, who not only have to respond appropriately to the different individuals for whom they are responsible but who, themselves, differ in similar ways. Teaching, like learning, involves an active coconstruction of knowledge in collaboration with particular students in a particular place and time. It also involves the teacher as an individual, who has values, beliefs, and interests, as well as preferred ways of working with students, that have been learned and modified over the course of a lifetime of personal and professional experience. Teachers, like students, bring the whole of themselves to their interactions in the classroom; whether they are aware of it or not, their manner of teaching depends not only on what they know but on who they have become.

CONSTRUCTING KNOWLEDGE IN COLLABORATION
WITH OTHERS

Current conceptions of knowing and coming to know have resulted from two major changes that have taken place during the course of this century. The first of these challenged the idea that knowledge is passively acquired as a result of being shown or told and, instead, proposed that coming to know always involves an active constructive process, in which new information must be brought into relationship with what is already known. If the new information appears to be compatible with what is known, it will be easily assimilated, although it may be reformulated to some degree in the process. If, on the other hand, it is in conflict with what is known, either the new will be rejected or existing knowledge will have to be transformed in order to accommodate the new. In either case, however, what is known by any individual is the outcome of a continuing constructive process that depends on opportunities to encounter and make sense of challenging new experiences.

"Constructivism," as this way of thinking about coming to know is called, owes a great deal to the work of Piaget (1970) who, on the basis of numerous detailed observations and experiments with children, proposed an account of intellectual development that emphasized the learner's active, exploratory transactions with the environment. In his view, the successive stages to be observed in children's development resulted from major constructive transformations of their ways of making sense of their experience that depended both on the maturation of innate structures and on the occurrence of experiences that gave rise to cognitive conflict. In the 1960s, Piaget's theory became the basis for early education programs that emphasized "discovery learning" and a supportive rather than a directive form of teaching. Although the majority of educators would no longer give so much weight to independent discovery as the key to learning, Piaget's conception of the learner as actively constructing his or her own knowledge on the basis of what he or she brings to encounters with new information and experience has taken a firm hold and is presupposed in almost all recent work on learning and development. As is generally agreed, "knowledge is not passively received either through the senses or by way of communication; rather, knowledge is actively built up by the cognizing subject" (Glasersfeld, 1995).

The second change occurred, at least in part, in reaction to the first. Piaget's concern was with what is universal in human intellectual development. What he paid less attention to was the cultural context within which development occurs (Cole & Wertsch, 1996). For Vygotsky, by contrast, this was at the heart of his account of learning and development, and significantly, in much of his writing he used his criticisms of Piaget's ideas as the basis for the development of his own. However, although Vygotsky was writing in the 1920s and 1930s, in the postrevolutionary period in Russia, it is only since the 1980s that his ideas have begun to become known in translation; since then, his sociocultural theory has stimulated increasing interest among educators and has inspired a number of important attempts to realize his vision in practice (Gal'perin, 1969; Holzman, 1995; Moll, 1990; Wells & Claxton, in press).

In contrast to Piaget, Vygotsky placed strong emphasis on the importance of culture and social interaction in accounting for individual development. According to Vygotsky (1978, 1987), the relationship between the individual and the culture of which he or she is a member is one of interdependence; in their development, each shapes and is shaped by the other. Of course, to some extent at least, Piaget also recognized the importance for the child's intellectual development of knowledge obtained through social interaction with others; however, he considered this interaction to be simply a source of information, rather than essential to the very process of development. By contrast, Vygotsky argued that, although based in our biological inheritance, the capacities for acting, thinking, feeling, and communicating that make us human are crucially dependent on cultural practices and artifacts and on interaction with others, through which they are appropriated and mastered in the course of goal-oriented joint activity. We become who we are, he argued, through engaging in culturally valued activities with the aid of other participants and of the mediating artifacts which the culture makes available. In these particular, "situated" events, both activities and artifacts are transformed, as are our own resources for thinking and doing, as, acting together, we adapt, extend, and modify both intellectual and material resources in order to solve the problems encountered. Most of the preceding chapters illustrate this situated characteristic of learning (see also Wells, 1999).

The significance of Vygotsky's theory for conceptualizing the relationship between knowledge, coming to know, and educational practice is far-reaching. First is the emphasis that he placed on the role of artifacts in mediating activity. These include not only material tools (such as knives, wheels, and more recently, combustion engines and computers), but also symbolic meaning-making systems, such as language, mathematics, and various modes of visual representation, as well as the representational artifacts that are created through their use, such as maps, historical accounts, scientific theories, and works of art of all kinds. Such artifacts also include the institutions, such as education and law, multinational corporations, sports clubs, and religious societies that provide the organizational frameworks within which a culture's activities are organized (Engeström, 1990).

Traditionally, in education, attention has been given mainly to representational artifacts, such as textbooks and works of reference. Because such artifacts are so integrally involved in intellectual activity of many kinds, they are often treated as if they were actually repositories of knowledge that can be mastered simply by reading and memorizing them. Nevertheless, such a belief is mistaken. Artifacts of all kinds, both material and symbolic, certainly encode the knowledge that went into their production and can, in that sense, make it available to other people. However, in order genuinely to master the cultural knowledge associated with these artifacts, novices must actively participate in the activities in which the knowledge is used, construct their own understanding of it, and be assisted and guided by others in learning how to do so (Lave & Wenger, 1991; Rogoff, 1994).

It was to explain the characteristics of this assisted performance that Vygotsky developed the concept of the *zone of proximal development* (ZPD) (Vygotsky, 1987). This is the second feature of his theory that is important for education. Taking issue with the use of intelligence tests to categorize and place children with what would now be called severe learning difficulties, he argued that it is not the child's independent performance that should be the basis for making educational decisions but the extent to which he or she can benefit from appropriate teaching. This window between what a learner can manage to do alone and what he or she can achieve with help is what Vygotsky meant by the zone of proximal development. It is this zone that should be the target for all teaching for, as he argued, it is only "instruction which moves ahead of development, and leads it" that is helpful to the learner (1987, p. 211). The significance of this principle has been explored in many DICEP inquiries, in particular in this volume by Van Tassell (Chapter 3), Davis (Chapter 4), and Kowal (Chapter 7).

Vygotsky died before he could develop this key insight further but, in more recent work, it has been extended in a number of ways. First, it has become clear that the ZPD is not a fixed attribute of the learner; instead, it is specific to the task in which he or she is engaged and it is created in the interaction among the learner, the available cultural resources, and the ones who are providing assistance. Second, it is not only teachers who can perform this function; peers can also provide assistance to each other and so can artifacts produced by those who are not present in the situation, such as books, illustrations, and information accessed via the Internet. However, it is important to emphasize that such artifacts only assist learning and performance for those learners who already have the skills and disposition to actively engage with them. Third—and perhaps most important—learning in the ZPD is not confined to students; teachers too can learn in the same way, both from colleagues and from the students that they teach. In fact, working in the ZPD should be a learning experience for all participants, although, obviously, what each learns depends on the different concerns and prior knowledge that they bring to the situation (Wells, 1999).

The importance of recognizing and valuing diversity is a further implication that follows from his theory. Vygotsky stressed the need to adopt a historical approach in attempting to understand development. This is important on at least three levels. First, both what is considered necessary for students to learn and the levels of performance they are expected to reach at each stage are cultural constructs that change over time; these expectations also differ from one culture to another as a result of the historical differences between them in the ways in which they have interacted with their immediate environments (Diamond, 1998). Second, individuals too have different life trajectories; not only is each person born into a particular culture at a particular point in its history, but the specific sequence of experiences that shapes who she or he becomes also differs from one individual to another, even within the same culture. This means that, even when involved in the same activity, participants inevitably understand it somewhat differently from each other and have different contributions to make to it; they may even have quite different goals in view as well as different ideas about how to attain them.

Finally, since learning takes place through participation in particular, situated activities, we also need to consider the microhistory of these activities. As has just been suggested, the way in which an activity unfolds depends upon the specific participants involved, their potential contributions, and the extent to which the actualization of this potential is enabled by the interpersonal relationships between participants and the mediating artifacts at hand.

These principles are obviously important when organizing learning and teaching activities, for they contradict the belief that the curriculum can be planned and delivered in a predetermined manner and emphasize, instead, the extent to which the action and interaction through which learning occurs are emergent in the situation and dependent on the uptake of "teachable moments," as they arise. This was clearly illustrated in the example of the autopsy of the chrysalis in Chapter 1 and in Hume's coresearch in Chapter 9. Similarly, from a research perspective, these principles underscore the need to attend to the way in which meanings and understandings are progressively constructed over time as events and ideas are revisited, extended, and reflected on in the discourse of groups and the whole class together. As will have been noted, every one of the preceding chapters emphasizes this developmental perspective.

KNOWING IN ACTION AND REFLECTION

Taking into account these insights from the work of Piaget, Vygotsky, and those who have extended their work, we arrive at a very different understanding of knowledge from the one that prevailed at the beginning of this century. Knowledge is not fixed, autonomous, and independent, as proponents of the "knowledge transmission" conception of education seem to believe. But neither is it contained as sentencelike propositional objects in individual minds, to be retrieved and processed on demand, as is suggested by those who take the computer as their metaphor for intellectual activity. Rather, knowledge is constructed and reconstructed between participants in specific situations, using the cultural resources at their disposal, as they work toward the collaborative achievement of goals that emerge in the course of their activity.

Put rather differently, then, knowledge is only truly known when it is being used by particular individuals in the course of solving specific problems; and then it is open to modification and development as it is reconstructed to meet the actual demands of the situation. In other words, to place the emphasis on the acquisition of "general knowledge" independent of occasions of its meaningful use is to reverse the way in which, over many millennia, it has been constructed and appropriated in and for situated action. Even the theoretical knowledge that we rate so highly is only of value when it is used in solving problems, and then the solutions achieved nearly always have implications for practical action in real-life situations.

Thus it is on *knowing in action undertaken jointly with others* that the emphasis needs to be placed, and on opportunities for reflecting on what has been learned in the process. It is in this situated knowing, involving both action and reflection, that the knowledge of more expert others comes to make personal sense and is most readily incorporated into one's own personal model of the world. This is what we understand Vygotsky to have intended when he emphasized the importance of working in the zone of proximal development. For what students come to know and to be able to do depends on the type and range of activities that they are asked to engage in, on the challenges that these activities present, on the artifacts available to mediate their activities, and on the assistance they receive in meeting these challenges, both from teachers and peers and from more distant experts beyond the classroom.

Considering now the implications of this view of knowledge, several things seem clear. First, in designing curriculum, it is not decontextualized knowledge that should be given pride of place. Rather, it should be problems and questions that are likely to be of significance to students as they try to understand and act effectively and responsibly in the world that they inherit from previous generations. As we are becoming more fully aware, progress is by no means inevitable, and our current way of life presages potential disasters as well as possible improvements. Which of these come to pass will depend very much on the decisions taken by the citizens of tomorrow, and these decisions, in turn, will depend upon the education that tomorrow's citizens receive today. Certainly, the knowledge that has been developed in the past is likely to be important to our students in this quest for understanding and responsible action. But it is important to them, not as an inert body of propositions and procedures detached from any personally meaningful situation, but as a compendium of resources—a tool kit—to be mastered and modified in and for use in solving problems that are of significance to them.

This does not mean abandoning the conceptual frameworks provided by the established disciplines. These are also tools—or, better, tool kits—that have been built up over generations as means for tackling tasks in particular domains. However, no one of them has universal validity; each is the best that is currently available for solving certain types of problems, but each is also open to further revision and improvement. Furthermore, many real-life problems require the utilization of knowledge from several quite different domains and therefore also of different modes of knowing (Donald, 1991).

The second implication is that, in learning and coming to know, students should not be thought of as solitary individuals, each working independently of—and often in competition with—others. Our achievements are never exclusively our own since they are always made possible by our being able to take over and use resources created by others; without these cultural resources we should not be able to function at all. This is true of the greatest thinkers as well as of students in school. As Newton remarked, he only succeeded because he stood upon the shoulders of giants. In fact, collaboration has always been the most powerful approach to problem solving, and it is equally effective as the basis for learning. Thus, while it is important for each individual to gain the level of autonomy and self-direction necessary for responsible decision making and action, it is equally important to emphasize mutual interdependence and the value of collaboration.

Third, placing the emphasis on knowing rather than on knowledge also has the advantage of drawing attention to the different modes of knowing that are involved in solving the wide range of problems that are encountered in daily life (Gardner, 1983; Wells, 1999). Currently, our society accords greatest value to theoretical knowing and to the ability to deal in generalizations and abstractions that can be manipulated independently of the particular objects, events, and relationships to which they refer. It is this sort of knowing that is emphasized in high school and universities and that provides entry to high status professional occupations. However, it is important to recognize that this mode of knowing can only be built upon prior experiences of tackling problems arising in the course of specific, practical activities and that, furthermore, its ultimate value is in advancing understanding and enabling more effective action in the future.

A further implication is that there can be no scale on which the achievements of either individuals or cultures can be measured or compared in absolute terms. All modes of knowing have arisen to mediate the activities of cultural groups in the particular ecological environments in which they find themselves. The particular modes that have developed in different cultures over the course of recorded history can be seen to have been influenced both by the affordances and constraints of the local environment and the problems it posed for survival, on the worldview and values of the culture, and on the impact of outside influences as a result of conquest or colonization. The current hegemony of Western technical-rational knowing itself owes much to a particular historical sequence of chance events and should not, therefore, be thought of as having universal superiority (Diamond, 1998). Indeed, there are many problems facing the world today for which it does not provide useful solutions.

For this reason, as Van Tassell (Chapter 3) and Kowal (Chapter 7) make clear, it is important in planning curricular units to emphasize the interdependence of the different modes of knowing, recognizing that as different modes are best suited to different tasks, all are equally necessary for the activity as a whole.

The last and perhaps most important point to make is that knowing in any mode is not a purely cognitive process. All modes of knowing are embedded in action, and since they are mediated by material tools of various kinds, they involve the body as well as the mind. Recognition of this might help us to abandon the prevalent conception of the mind as a container of disembodied ideas and to see it instead as a way of talking about "mindful" or purposeful and informed knowing in action. Nor is knowing a purely individual activity. It not only depends on the mastery of mediational means appropriated from other members of the culture, but it also almost always occurs in the course of activity undertaken with others and only has significance in relation to such activity. Finally, knowing is not a cold activity without affect. On the contrary, not only is it accompanied by feelings of effort, occasional frustration, and satisfaction when goals are achieved, but the motivation to engage and persevere with a problem is rooted in commitment to values and purposes that are strongly affective in origin. In sum, knowing and coming to know involve the whole person. Furthermore, it is through their participation in activities with particular others, involving different modes of knowing and acting as well as the use of the appropriate mediational means, that individuals develop their unique identities and their potential to contribute to the wider society.

DISCOURSE AND KNOWING

It might seem self-evident in the light of the preceding discussion that language is at the heart of education. Not only does it mediate the knowing in which students engage, but it is also the chief medium of the activity of learning and teaching. Perhaps it is just because this seems self-evident that so little attention is typically given to the ways in which language is used in schools; its uses are simply taken for granted. However, in the last quarter of a century a growing body of research has begun to describe in some detail the different emphases that are given to spoken and written language at different ages and in different areas of the curriculum and to document the different functions that language serves in the various activities that constitute learning and teaching (Barnes, 1976; Britton, Burgess, Martin, McLeod, & Rosen, 1975; Galton, Simon, & Croll, 1980; Martin, 1993; Nystrand & Gamoran, 1991).

What emerges from this classroom-based research is evidence that a large proportion of educators make an implicit, although quite sharp, distinction between language, which they see as a means of communication, and the intellectual activity of individuals that generates the thoughts that are communicated. This separation frequently gives rise to what has been referred to as the "conduit" metaphor of communication (Reddy, 1979): language carries thoughts as trains carry goods, with no interaction between them. The results of this separation are that, on the one hand, work on language is largely devoted to the formal features of written language—rules of grammar, spelling, essay structure—often learned and practiced with no genuine interest in what the writing is about, and on the other hand, attention is rarely given to the implication of the fact that the processes of thinking, such as categorizing, hypothesizing, reasoning, and evaluating, are not only realized in language, in the sense of being made manifest in speech and writing, but also actually constructed and improved through its mediating means.

It is this separation between language and thinking that underlies the repeated finding that, in a majority of classrooms, there is a prevalence of what Tharp and Gallimore (1988) call the "recitation script." In such classrooms, what is given preeminence is teacher talk, the reading of textbooks for information transmission and consolidation, and multiple-choice tests or short essay answers to check that the information has been correctly received and memorized. However, as will be clear from the previous discussion of knowledge and knowing, students do not come to know simply by listening and reading, nor does spoken or written recall of information on demand provide satisfactory evidence of the extent to which there has been a real increase in understanding.

If, as I have suggested, knowing is largely carried out through discourse, we should not be looking for learning in the time *between* the input from the teacher or text and later output in answers to spoken or written questions. Rather, we should expect to find the learning occurring *in and through* participation in the activities that make up the curriculum and, in particular, through the discourse that often constitutes the greater part of these activities (Nuthall & Alton-Lee, 1995). This means that students' opportunities for learning and knowing are crucially dependent on the nature of the activities in which they engage and on the functions that language performs in these activities.

In classrooms in which the conduit metaphor of communication is implicitly accepted, most activities involve monologic uses of language, either in speech or writing, with a clear role and status distinction between teacher (or textbook author) and students. Teachers and textbooks transmit information and students demonstrate that they can reproduce it on demand. These characteristics are also apparent in the recitation script; although involving teacher and students in alternating turns, it is nevertheless typically controlled and directed by the teacher's questions (often concerning information students are supposed to "know") and the evaluations that the teacher gives to the students' responses (Mehan, 1979). This genre of classroom discourse is frequently referred to as the IRE/F (Initiation-Response-Evaluation/Follow-up) sequence and, in several studies, it has been found to be the default option, to which the teacher always returns (Cazden, 1988; Lemke, 1990).

Recognizing the limited opportunities for real interactive uses of language—and thus for mastering the mediating means of knowing—that are made available to students in discourses of this transmissionary kind, increasing efforts have been made in recent years to find alternatives. Much of the pioneering work has been carried out by leaders in the fields of language and literacy education: Barnes (1976), Britton (1970), Mercer (1995) in England; Moffett (1968), Goodman and Goodman (1990), Harste (1993), Nystrand (1997) in North America; and Christie and Martin (1997) in Australia. But another key influence has been that of Bakhtin (1981, 1986), whose emphasis on "dialogue" has recently become known in the English-speaking world.

Bakhtin was a contemporary of Vygotsky, and although there is no evidence that they collaborated, his work on discourse complements and extends Vygotsky's insights about the role of discourse in the individual's appropriation and mastery of the "higher mental functions" (Vygotsky, 1981). Two of Bakhtin's ideas are of particular importance for education and both are concerned with the essential dialogicality of discourse. The first draws attention to the principle of "responsivity." Utterances both respond to preceding utterances and are formulated in anticipation of a further response. Every utterance, therefore, is "a link in a very complexly organized chain of other utterances" (Bakhtin, 1986, p. 69).

The second involves the principle of "multi-voicedness," that is to say, the recognition that, in any utterance, there is more than one "voice" speaking. As Bakhtin observed, in learning to talk, we do not take words from the dictionary but from the utterances of other speakers. The words we use thus carry for us echoes of the previous uses to which we have heard or read them put and, initially our own use of them is a sort of "ventriloquation," as we speak through the words "borrowed" from others. In both these ways, our utterances are inevitably "filled with dialogic overtones" (Bakhtin, 1986, p. 92); our meanings are taken over from others as well as being our own constructions.

These two ideas are particularly significant for the attempts that are being made to situate knowing and coming to know in the coconstruction of meaning that takes place in discourse that is truly dialogic (Wells, 1999). In our own work, we refer to this dialogue as the discourse of knowledge building (Scardamalia & Bereiter, 1992), and as I shall explain below, we see it as an essential component of the inquiry approach to learning and teaching that is the focus of our collaborative research.

The mediating role of dialogue in knowledge building is probably most evident in face-to-face discussion, where one speaker immediately responds to another. In order to make a useful contribution, the current speaker first has to interpret the preceding contribution(s) and compare the information presented with her or his own current understanding of the issue under discussion. Then she or he has to formulate a contribution that will, in some relevant way, add to the common understanding achieved in the discourse so far, by extending, questioning, or qualifying what someone else has said. Other participants contribute similarly, turn by turn. As Bakhtin observed, such discourse is filled with dialogic overtones, for our knowing is part of a joint activity and the understanding we achieve builds on the contributions of others and invites their further response. What is more, it is frequently in this effort to make our understanding meaningful for others that we have the feeling of reaching a fuller and clearer understanding for ourselves.

Knowledge building also takes place in the written mode, where, although on a different time scale, it works in essentially the same way. When community members write, it is to make a contribution to an ongoing dialogue; they too respond to, and build on, the contributions of others and they also anticipate a further response (see Hume, Chapter 6). However, what makes writing particularly powerful as a mediator of knowing is, first, the possibility it allows for the writer to make an extended, fully worked-out contribution, and second, because of its slower rate of production, its facilitation of a more reflective and self-critical stance. In fact, the writer engages in a dual dialogue: with the audience to whom the text is addressed and with himself through dialogue with the emerging text. By the same token, reading another's text also needs to be undertaken dialogically. In order to understand it, one not only has to interpret the information it presents, but one also has to engage with it responsively, whether in a dialogue with others or in an inner dialogue with oneself. As in spoken dialogue, therefore, understanding develops through using the texts, both those of others and one's own, as generators of meaning and as "thinking devices" (Lotman, 1988) in the formulation of further responsive contributions.

The sort of discourse just described applies most obviously perhaps to the collaborative building of theoretical knowledge, but in general terms it also applies to the other modes of knowing. Whether theoretical, practical, or artistic, however, one thing is likely to be constant: *knowledge building takes place between people doing things together*, and at least part of this doing involves dialogue.

Equally important, it is through the same sort of collaborative knowledge building that each of us develops understanding of what other people have already come to know, as this is represented in texts and other knowledge objects. From this point of view, it does not really matter whether the knowledge that is constructed is totally new or only new to us. For, as Popper wrote about understanding the products of theoretical knowing:

> We can grasp a theory only by trying to reinvent it or to reconstruct it, and by trying out, with the help of our imagination, all the consequences of the theory which seem to us to be interesting and important. . . . One could say that the process of understanding and the process of the actual production or discovery [of theories] are very much alike. (Popper & Eccles, 1977, p. 461)

The same also goes for the kinds of knowledge created through the other modes of knowing: we have to engage in meaningful activities with others, using the relevant texts, tools, and practices, in order to come to understand them. It is for this reason that we place such an emphasis on inquiry as a means of learning and coming to know.

THE SPIRAL OF KNOWING

At this point it may be useful to summarize the main points that have been made above about the relationship among experience, discourse, and the enhanced understanding that, in our view, is the goal of all inquiry. This I have attempted in Figure 10.1. This figure is to be read as a spiral, with each cycle starting from personal experience. Even from an early age, individuals bring at least some relevant past experience to new situations, and this provides the basis on which new learning builds. In the current situation, new information is added from the environment, in the form of feedback from action or, symbolically, through representations produced by others in speech or writing. However, the goal of each cycle is only reached when an enhanced understanding of the matter at issue is achieved, through integrating the new information into the individual's existing model of the world. This integration occurs through knowing in action in some specific situation and almost always involves dialogic knowledge building with others.

As the term implies, knowledge building is an active process of meaning making. It can be achieved through telling stories, developing explanations, making connections, and testing conjectures, through action and / or the creation of further symbolic representations in speech or in some more permanent artifact such as a written text. This critical phase in the

Figure 10.1. The Spiral of Knowing. *Source:* Adapted from *Dialogic Inquiry*, by G. Wells, 1999, New York: Cambridge University Press. Copyright 1999 by Cambridge University Press. Reprinted with the permission of Cambridge University Press.

spiral of knowing is essentially interpersonal and collaborative and always aimed at increasing understanding. If this goal is achieved, each cycle results in an improved and more coherent base of understanding for both the group and participating individuals. That is to say, there is a transformation of their individual models of the world in terms of which to construe further experiences and interpret new information.

This spiraling process continues throughout each individual's lifetime and occurs in practical situations in the workplace and community as well as in educational institutions. It can also continue when the individual is alone, through the dialogue with self that Vygotsky (1987) referred to as "inner speech." However, what distinguishes the spiral of knowing in the classroom is—or should be—a focus on systematic inquiry and the deliberate planning of opportunities to engage in the dialogue of progressive knowledge building, in which students not only develop their understanding about particular topics but also master the modes of meaning making and genres of discourse that mediate knowing in the different disciplines.

As a result of our efforts to promote this sort of progressive dialogue, we have come to recognize the importance of having an "improvable object" as the focus of the knowledge building. This object may be a material artifact, as in the construction of functioning models made with junk materials that I witnessed in more than one DICEP classroom, or symbolic artifacts such as the recommendations as to what to do with the injured chrysalis (Chapter 1), the opposing cases made to the Supreme Court in Kowal's history class (Chapter 7), or the theory of effective class discussion being developed by Hume's students (Chapter 9). In such dialogue, contributions are made and listened to, critiqued and extended, with genuine engagement and a commitment to produce the best outcome of which the group is capable. A major focus of our current inquiries, therefore, is to discover how to generate such improvable objects in relation to the abstract topics that are specified in the official curriculum.

AN INQUIRY APPROACH TO CURRICULUM

In the social constructivist approach to education that DICEP has adopted, learning is not seen as an end in itself, nor as a separate, self-sufficient activity. Rather, it is an integral aspect of participating in a community's activities and mastering the tools and practices that enable one to do so effectively. The questions we have found ourselves needing to consider, then, are: What should be the nature of classroom activities? and To what object should they be directed?

Early in this century, Dewey offered some helpful suggestions in the context of his exposition of the curriculum for his experimental school (1900/1990, 1938). As is well known, he proposed starting with "ordinary experience," emphasizing the importance of involving students in "the formation of the purposes which direct [their] activities" (1938, p. 67) and in selecting "the kind of present experiences that live fruitfully and creatively in future experiences" (1938, p. 28). As more recent writers in this tradition have made clear, the key characteristic of investigatory activities of this kind is that they take as their object significant and often problematic features of the students' experience and environment and have as their intended outcome a growth in the students' understanding, where this is taken to mean, not simply factual knowledge, but knowledge growing out of, and oriented to, socially relevant and productive action (Cohen, McLaughlin, & Talbert, 1993).

It is not only Dewey who places inquiry at the heart of the curriculum, however. The same emphasis on firsthand investigation, both through hands-on experimentation and through the use of reference material, is found in the school-based projects of such cognitive scientists as Brown and Campione (1994), Gardner (1989), Palincsar and Magnusson (Palincsar, Magnusson, Marano, Ford, & Brown, 1998), and Scardamalia and Bereiter (Scardamalia, Bereiter, & Lamon, 1994). In each case, a major purpose of the activities in their classroom communities is to cultivate a general stance with respect to the world of experience that might be characterized as a disposition to engage in systematic inquiry about the questions or topics in which one is interested. From this perspective, then, inquiry is as much about being open to wondering and puzzlement and trying to construct and test explanations of the phenomena that evoked those feelings as it is about mastering any particular body of information although, of course, the two facets of inquiry are ultimately interdependent.

As we have discovered, the choice of experiences that provide the topics for investigation is critical. Not only must they be such as to arouse student interest, engaging feelings and values as well as cognition; but they must also be sufficiently open-ended to allow alternative possibilities for consideration. They also need to be able to provide challenges appropriate to individual students' current abilities, while at the same time encouraging them to collaborate with others in constructing shared understanding that is both practical and theoretical. The key feature of activities of this kind, we have come to believe, is that, for the students, *the goal of inquiry is making not learning*, or, as I put it above, working on an improvable object. Motivated and challenged by real questions and problems, their attention is on making answers and solutions. Under these conditions, learning is an outcome that occurs because the making requires the student *to extend his or her understanding in action*—whether the artifact constructed is a material object, a demonstration, explanation, or theoretical formulation.

However, in arguing for an approach to curriculum that is organized in terms of questions for inquiry, two further points need to be made. First, for a question to be real, the student must really care about making an answer to it. However, it does not follow that the only real questions are ones that are first asked by students. Teachers' questions or questions suggested in texts that students are reading can become equally real if they correspond to an existing interest or awaken a wondering on the part of the student. What is at issue here is the student's attitude to the question, rather than where it originated; for it to motivate genuine inquiry, the question must be taken over and "owned" by the student (Van Tassell, Chapter 3).

The second point is that inquiry does not have to start with a clearly formulated question. In fact, some of the most absorbing questions arise only after some preliminary work on the topic has been carried out, or as a by-product of trying to answer some other question (Hume, Chapter 6; Scardamalia & Bereiter, 1992). They may also occur quite spontaneously and unexpectedly in the course of reviewing work carried out to date.

Over the course of our work together, we have constructed a generalized model for planning whole class units of study according to the principles just discussed. This model of an inquiry-oriented curriculum is shown in Figure 10.2. However, I must make it clear that this model is not to be taken as a flow diagram, prescribing the steps and their sequence to be closely followed on every occasion. Rather, it attempts to identify the key components of organized inquiry and to suggest the relationships between them. In this sense, it is a tool for thinking with rather than a blueprint for action.

The model assumes that there will be an overarching *Theme* or topic within which individuals or, even better, groups of students will carry out inquiries on subtopics that they wish to investigate and that can contribute to the overall theme. One of the purposes of the *Launch* component, with which the unit starts, is to present the theme in a way that arouses interest and provides a challenge that can be taken up in a variety of ways according to students' interests and abilities. The next two components, *Research* and *Interpret,* work together. Research is concerned with generating evidence for the chosen question through empirical investigations of various kinds and from consulting relevant sources, such as maps, photographs, historical documents, as well as encyclopedias and other works of reference. Then, in the Interpret component, the evidence is evaluated in relation to the question. It is important to emphasize that these two components stand in a reciprocal relationship to each other and to the question under investigation. Evaluating the evidence helps to clarify the question and may even lead to its revision; conversely, interpreting the evidence in the light of the question will often show that more accurate or different evidence is required in order to make progress toward an answer (see Hume, Chapter 6). Clearly, then, there may be several cycles through these two components before any conclusions can be drawn.

Eventually, though, it is important to focus on the fourth component, *Present.* As many people have observed, there is no better way to discover how well one has understood something than by preparing to present or explain it to others who are interested but less well-informed. This requires attention both to the information to be drawn on and to its organization in terms of the appropriate genres, for example, description, explanation, evaluation (see Kowal, Chapter 7). At this stage, too, it may well be necessary to return to the research-interpret cycle in order to clarify details or to fill in gaps that have become apparent.

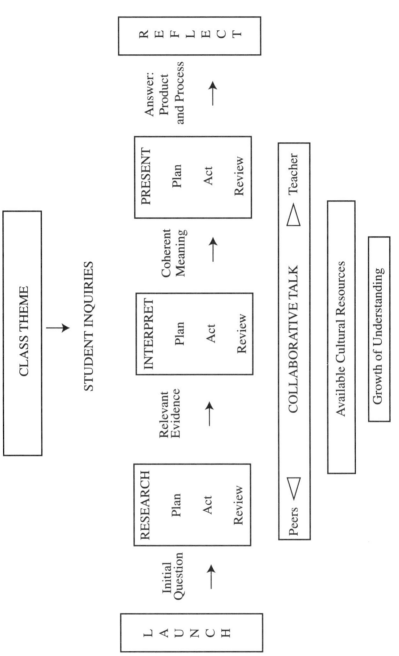

Figure 10.2. Model of an Inquiry-Oriented Curriculum. *Source:* From *Dialogic Inquiry,* by G. Wells, 1999, New York: Cambridge University Press. Copyright 1999 by Cambridge University Press. Reprinted with permission of Cambridge University Press.

The actual presentation to an audience serves two important purposes. First, it provides an occasion for the presenters to receive constructive feedback from peers as well as teacher. And second, it contributes to the developing understanding of the overall theme by the class as a whole. From this point of view, it is beneficial to invite interim presentations as the group inquiries proceed so that each can be enriched by the connections that are made among them in relation to the overall theme.

It is this sort of exploratory discussion that constitutes one aspect of the final component that we refer to as *Reflect*. As just suggested, periods for whole class reflection on progress made to date can significantly contribute to the knowledge that is constructed. But it is particularly important to engage in such reflective discussion at the end of a unit in order to make connections both within and beyond the theme, to attempt to resolve any conflicting perspectives, and to note further questions for investigation. This may also be an appropriate moment at which to consider how the knowledge constructed by the class compares to the culturally accepted version and, if there is discrepancy, to explore why this might be so. Finally, reflective discussion provides an occasion for considering the social and ecological significance of the knowledge that the class has constructed, for it is important that this be related to students' lives in the world beyond the classroom.

There is, however, a second purpose for the Reflect component, and that is to consider the processes in which the different groups have been involved. The aim here is to encourage a "meta" stance to the procedures involved in the inquiries and to the strategies that different individuals and groups have used to solve the problems they encountered. By making these matters explicit, there is an opportunity for students to learn about procedures and strategies of which they may not be aware and to add them to the tool kit of resources from which they can choose according to the demands of the particular tasks in which they are involved. This latter function of reflective discussion is particularly valuable, we have found, for the overall goal of fostering an inquiry orientation in all the activities in which the classroom community engages. This is also a feature of the classroom meetings described by Donoahue (Chapter 2) and Davis (Chapter 4).

Space does not allow me to include specific examples of this model in operation here, but several are included in other works (Wells, 1995, 1999; see also the list of DICEP publications at the end of this volume). However, the important point to make is that we do not see our inquiry model as a "method" of doing science, history, or any other subject, in which there is a linear sequence of stages to be traversed. Rather, it is an overall approach to the chosen themes and topics, in which the posing of real questions is positively encouraged whenever they occur and by whoever they are asked. Equally important as the hallmark of an inquiry approach is that all tentative answers are taken seriously and are explored as rigorously as the circumstances permit. Thus, inquiry should not be thought of as an approach to be adopted in occasional activities or in a single curriculum area. Although it may not always be possible to approach a curricular unit in the way suggested by the model, the aim should be to foster an inquiring disposition that influences the way in which *all* activities are approached and that is generative in the formation of students' identities. For this to happen, we believe, inquiry must become a central feature of classroom life. The class needs to become a *community of inquiry*.

TEACHERS AS INQUIRERS

How this is to be achieved, however, is not self-evident. Nor is there likely to be one single best way to proceed since, as emphasized earlier, each classroom consists of a unique collection of individuals, each with their personal experiential histories, current interests, and knowledgeable skills. We have found that regular class meetings (see Chapters 2 and 4) can play a significant role in this respect. We have also found some helpful pointers in the university-inspired initiatives mentioned above and in the increasing number of inquiries carried out by teacher researchers (Atwell, 1991; Gallas, 1994; Norman, 1992; Short & Burke, 1991; Wells et al., 1994). But, ultimately, each teacher has to discover how to proceed in his or her own specific situation and in collaboration with the students with whom he or she is working. It is for this reason that teachers themselves need to be inquirers, and they can do this most effectively when they belong to a community of teachers with similar concerns.

This, then, is the overriding aim of the DICEP community: to come to understand, in practice and in theory, how to create and sustain communities of inquiry, in which all concerned learn with and from each other about matters of individual and social significance through the dialogue of knowledge building. The chapters of this book represent our individual and collective attempts to achieve this aim. However, we do not present these chapters as universal answers. Each grew out of the situated practice of its author and its conclusions remain tentative and provisional. As in the classroom, dialogic knowledge building about learning and teaching is always in progress; it is always looking for further improvement.

CHAPTER 11

Look How We've Grown!

Monica McGlynn-Stewart

As TEACHER-RESEARCHER members of DICEP, we all agree that we have grown tremendously as a result of incorporating action research into our practice with the support of DICEP. And we have grown not just as practitioners of action research, but in our confidence as teachers, as authors, and as conference speakers. We have found our voice both in DICEP and in the wider educational community, and have found a place from which to critically examine both theory and practice in current educational thinking.

Many changes have taken place over the nine years since the first proposal was written to obtain funding for a "collaborative action research project," an almost completely unknown idea at the time. Many members have come and gone, our focus has altered, and our method of operating has evolved, but the most inspiring and fulfilling aspects of DICEP have remained constant. We recently had an e-mail conversation about the impact that doing action research with DICEP has had on us as teachers and learners. A strong theme that emerged during the conversation was the supportive mutual learning and teaching that DICEP offers. As Zoe Donoahue put it:

> Having a group with whom to talk, share my findings, hear about other people's inquiries, has kept me going with my research. Writing and presenting together, as well as presenting my current

Action, Talk, and Text: Learning and Teaching Through Inquiry. Copyright © 2001 by Teachers College, Columbia University. All rights reserved. ISBN 0-8077-4014-4 (pbk), ISBN 0-8077-4015-2 (cloth). Prior to photocopying items for classroom use, please contact the Copyright Clearance Center, Customer Service, 222 Rosewood Dr., Danvers, MA 01923, USA, tel. (508) 750-8400.

work at meetings, gives me a reason to analyze and think about my data on a regular basis. Getting feedback from others, answering their questions and hearing how my thinking links with other members of the group helps me to develop ideas and gives me ideas for future inquiries.

We also find DICEP a place to renew our excitement and enthusiasm about teaching. Here's Karen Hume talking about the early days of DICEP:

I felt enormous excitement during and after each meeting. I looked forward to attending the next meeting. In the first year, when we had a very active e-mail conversation, I spent hours and hours writing, reading, and responding. That communication was invaluable to me.

Greta Davis concurs:

I think the most important thing DICEP has brought to my practice is enthusiasm. . . . I always left the meetings enthused, filled with new questions and ideas, ready to head back to class the next day. This enthusiasm is something I can't find anywhere else.

While we were all convinced of the usefulness of action research prior to joining DICEP, either through our application of it in our practices or through graduate courses, it was the experience of engaging in research with others in a community with a shared theoretical framework and teaching philosophy that really made it come alive. Mari Haneda put it this way:

Before participating in DICEP, I had conducted a series of AR projects on my own and AR was synonymous for me with a solitary activity. Learning about DICEP members' AR projects was really exciting for me. This experience prompted me to realize other potential inherent in the AR approach (i.e., a form of teachers' professional development on an individual and collective basis in a community of inquiry).

As a collaborative action research group comprised of classroom teachers, university-based teachers, and graduate students, we have been part of the development of a new and exciting method of educational research. And like most groups exploring new territory, we have had our growing pains. The first funding proposal that was submitted in 1990 proposed to combine traditional university research, including expected outcomes, with collaborative action research, in which it would be the classroom teachers who would decide exactly what to investigate within the broad theme of classroom discourse. For this second component, no expected outcomes could be specified because the teachers could not predict ahead of time what would be a significant research question for a particular class. Some of those who reviewed the proposal were skeptical of this sharing of the role of researcher between university teachers and classroom teachers. However, the Spencer Foundation agreed to fund the project as long as there was systematic research on classroom discourse as well as teacher-initiated inquiries. The dual nature of the project—systematic traditional research and teacher-initiated action research—was the cause of some tension in the group.

While we have been working toward being truly democratic and egalitarian in our group, it is generally felt that we did not start out this way. As teachers in DICEP we had far more say in the focus of the research project than teachers in traditional research; however, a survey we conducted in 1997 revealed that there were still some traditional roles being played by members of the group.

Some members felt that the university-based members still exerted considerable control over research focus, budget, size and functioning of the group, leadership, and decision making generally. Many of the classroom-based members had been, or were currently, students of the university-based members and continued to act in the role of student. The discrepancy between these more traditional roles and the claim of democracy bothered some members more than others. There was a sense that the claim that we were truly collaborative in the early years was premature (McGlynn-Stewart, 1998). Mary Ann Van Tassell, a founding member, describes it this way:

> Certainly, in those earliest years, the university group set the agenda; they had applied for the funding and had set the ball rolling. I didn't have a problem with that, but I did feel that what we said was going on did not match what was really going on. . . . I liked how the group evolved to share responsibilities for the meetings. I can't remember if it was after one or two years, but that was a really significant shift. When we started to take turns chairing the meetings and posting the agenda and sharing e-mail conversation responsibilities, a shift happened in the group. It was becoming more collaborative.

Our recent self-reflective e-mail conversation highlights how we have grown both individually and as a group. By mid-1999, the tensions of the early days were a distant memory. Group members' recent discussion focused on our areas of growth. Karen Hume describes several ways in which DICEP has helped her grow:

> I gained confidence in my ability to write through our e-mail dialogues. . . . Presentations by other members of the group were really helpful to me in showing me ways to organize my thinking. Later, involvement in conference presentations and in writing articles/chapters solidified my ability to write with a purpose . . .

Greta Davis discusses her growth and the parallel growth of the group:

> I certainly had growing pains! It took a while to feel comfortable in the group and find my place. I did however find a voice in the group over time and this came from listening to others present their research and seeing that we were all exploring similar issues. Choosing to explore community as a group really helped our own community during that time. . . . I believe we have made a lot of progress toward equalizing power, if one can call it that, among the group.

My own e-mail contribution gives my view on my own growth in confidence and the evolution of the group:

> Over the years I think we grew in confidence (I know I did) and felt freer to discuss difficult issues, and to take the initiative in proposing other ways of doing business. . . . I think we all felt that, although there were tensions and areas of difficulty, we were making progress, and that the opportunities for professional growth outweighed the problems. The phase we are in now, in which we are writing our own grant proposal and carrying on under the leadership of Zoe, one of the teacher members, with Gordon, a university-based member taking an advisory role, will accelerate the pace of our evolution.

An important result of our growth as learners and teachers, speakers and writers, we believe, is that it has led to improved learning opportunities for our students. Zoe speaks about how she now sees everything through an action research lens, and how this is helping her students to do the same:

> Being involved in DICEP and doing teacher research has had a tremendous impact on my classroom teaching. I now approach my

teaching from an inquiry stance. I explain my questions to my students, enlist their help in finding answers, discuss what I am learning and ask them what they are finding out. Throughout the inquiry process I find that I am more explicit when teaching my students, and that I have become better at taking a metacognitive stance myself, and modeling it for my students.

Greta reports an increased sense of closeness and community in her classes through the use of action research:

DICEP/AR has also really affected my classroom community. I have felt the strongest connection with my students when I am engaged in action research in my classroom. The process of simply discussing my questions with them, what I am learning, and sharing my writing with them has drawn them into the process.

Karen reflects on how her own development through action research has led to an enrichment in her students' education:

Learning to do action research didn't help me to be a more observant or reflective teacher, nor did it help me to see myself as a learner—I'd been all of those things from the beginning—but it was hugely important in helping me to become a more thorough, organized, confident, and professional teacher. It helped me to become someone who could articulate thoughts about education beyond the level of daily practicalities. It helped my respective schools, through the development of school-based action research groups, to become places where discussions of those thoughts were not only acceptable but welcomed. And in the last couple of years that has extended to involving my students in our research efforts, thus elevating the quality of our classroom discourse and our classroom activity.

Finally, we feel that practicing action research has allowed us to use both theory and practice more effectively in creating appropriate learning opportunities for our students. And of course, the best learning opportunities are those that are tailored to the learners' situation. Maria Kowal explains it this way:

At first action research was a means of taking the theory I had been reading and applying it to my practice—a means of making theory useful; but it also quickly became a means of allowing me to see how the theory needed changing in my individual context. I also think that it then gave me the confidence to refute aspects of the research I was reading about and thereby to contribute to the theory base and develop it further. . . . It helped me to stop looking for the "right" way to do things and to recognize the many variables and factors that influence the teaching/learning context.

The action research that the members of DICEP have carried out collaboratively for nearly a decade has left us richer, both as teachers and as learners. We bring to our work a renewed enthusiasm, professionalism, and a set of research tools that aid us in providing more appropriate and effective learning experiences for our students. We feel that, beyond our individual sites of practice and beyond our DICEP group, we have become contributing members to an international community of educators through our writing and conference presentations. We eagerly look forward to the next decade of growth and highly recommend collaborative action research to other educators seeking to infuse new life into their practice.

Conventions of Transcription

Note: Not all chapters use all these conventions. Chapter authors have selected from them as appropriate for their data.

Layout	The stream of speech is segmented into tone units, with each tone unit starting on a new line. Speakers are indicated by the initial letter of their name.
_	Incomplete utterances or self-corrections are shown by a hyphen on the end of the segment that was not completed. Continuations after an intervening speaker are shown preceded by a hyphen.
.	One period marks a perceptible pause. Thereafter, each period corresponds to approximately one second of pause; for example, "Yes . . . I did" indicates 3 seconds pause.
? !	These punctuation marks are used to mark utterances that are judged to have an interrogative or exclamatory intention.
CAPS	Capitals are use for words spoken with emphasis, for example, "I really LOVE painting."
< >	Angle brackets enclose segments about which the transcriber was uncertain.
x	Passages that were insufficiently clear to transcribe are shown with this symbol, with one for each word judged to have been spoken.
___	When two participants speak at once, the overlapping segments are underlined and vertically aligned.
" "	Words that are quoted or passages that are read aloud are enclosed in quotation marks.
( )	Interpretations of what was said or descriptions of the manner in which it was said are enclosed in parentheses.
[ ]	Square brackets enclose descriptions of other relevant behavior.

CONVENTIONS FOR TABLE 5.3

Intonation

The following symbols are placed before the tonic syllable to indicate the direction of pitch movement:

/	Rising pitch
\	Falling pitch
\/	Fall-rise pitch
/\	Rise-fall pitch
--	Level pitch

Gaze

The focus is on the speaker's gaze: whether or not he or she looks at the addressee(s) for at least some part of his or her speaking turn and, if not, whether his or her gaze is directed to the current focus of joint attention. Initials are used to identify participants and X to indicate some other focus of joint attention.

<	Unidirectional gaze by speaker
<>	Mutual gaze between speaker and addressee

Gesture

Gesture is coded according to the categories in Table 5.1.

*	An asterisk is placed immediately preceding the word on which the gesture reaches its "point," for example, the word that is emphasized by an emphatic beat.

Spatial Orientation

Initials identify the human participants and X indicates the apparatus. A new coding is entered each time there is a major change in their relative positions. Thus, a typical configuration might be represented as:

$$J$$
$$T \quad X \quad A$$

Viewed from the position of the camera "below," this configuration is to be interpreted as Jasmin and Alex close to the apparatus on adjacent sides of the desk, and Teacher facing Alex, but further away than they from the apparatus.

References

Argyris, C. (1990). *Overcoming organizational defenses.* New York: Jossey-Bass.

Argyris, C. (1991, May/June). Teaching smart people how to learn. *Harvard Business Review,* pp. 99–109.

Argyris, C., & Schön, D. (1974). *Theory in practice: Increasing professional effectiveness.* San Francisco: Jossey-Bass.

Atwell, N. (1991). *Side by side: Essays on teaching to learn.* Portsmouth, NH: Heinemann.

Bakhtin, M. N. (1981). *The dialogic imagination.* Austin: University of Texas Press.

Bakhtin, M. N. (1986). *Speech genres and other late essays.* Austin: University of Texas Press.

Barnes, D. (1976). *From communication to curriculum.* Harmondsworth, England: Penguin.

Bennis, W., & Biederman, P. (1997). *Organizing genius: The secrets of creative collaboration.* Toronto: Addison-Wesley.

Bereiter, C. (1994). Implications of postmodernism for science, or, science as progressive discourse. *Educational Psychologist, 29*(1), 3–12.

Bereiter, C., & Scardamalia, M. (1987). *The psychology of written composition.* Hillsdale, NJ: Erlbaum.

Bereiter, C., & Scardamalia, M. (1994). Computer support for knowledge-building communities. *The Journal of the Learning Sciences, 3*(3), 265–283.

Bettencourt, A. (1990). *On understanding science.* Unpublished paper, Michigan State University, East Lansing.

Bien, E. G., & Stern, S. S. (1994, March 1–5). *Democracy as discipline.* Paper presented at the annual meeting of the National Association of School Psychologists, Seattle, WA.

Brazil, D. (1981). The place of intonation in a discourse model. In M. C. Coulthard & M. Montgomery (Eds.), *Studies in discourse analysis* (pp. 12–145). London: Routledge and Kegan Paul.

Britton, J. (1970). *Language and learning.* London: Allen Lane.

Britton, J., Burgess, T., Martin, N., McLeod, A., & Rosen, H. (1975). *The development of writing abilities, 11–18.* London: Macmillan.

Brooks, F. B., & Donato, R., (1994). Vygotskyan approaches to understanding foreign language learner discourse during communicative tasks. *Hispania, 77*(1), 2–14.

Brooks, J. G., & Brooks, M. G. (1993). *In search of understanding: The case for constructivist classrooms.* Alexandria, VA: Association for Supervision and Curriculum Development.

Brown, A. L., & Campione, J. C. (1994). Guided discovery in a community of learners. In K. McGilly (Ed.), *Integrating cognitive theory and classroom practice: Classroom lessons* (pp. 229–270). Cambridge, MA: MIT Press/Bradford Books.

Bruner, J. S. (1983). *Child's talk.* New York: Norton.

Bruner, J. S. (1986). *Actual minds, possible worlds.* Cambridge, MA: Harvard University Press.

Carr, W., & Kemmis, S. (1983). *Becoming critical: Knowing through action research.* Geelong, Australia: Deakin University Press.

Case, R. (1996). Changing views of knowledge and their impact on educational research and practice. In D. R. Olson & N. Torrance (Eds.), *The handbook of education and human development* (pp. 75–99). Cambridge, MA: Blackwell.

Cazden, C. (1988). *Classroom discourse: The language of teaching and learning.* Portsmouth, NH: Heinemann.

Chambers, A. (1985). *Booktalk: Occasional writing on literature and children.* London: The Bodley Head.

Chambers, A. (1988). *More treasure than they wanted: Children, literature and talk.* A talk given at the Victorian Reading Association Conference, Australia.

Christie, F., & Martin, J. R. (Eds.). (1997). *Genres and institutions: Social processes in the workplace and school.* London: Cassell.

Cohen, D. K., McLaughlin, M. W., & Talbert, J. E. (Eds.). (1993). *Teaching for understanding: Challenges for policy and practice.* San Francisco: Jossey-Bass.

Cole, M., & Wertsch, J. V. (1996). Beyond the Individual-Social Antinomy in Discussions of Piaget and Vygotsky. *Human Development, 39,* 250–256.

Connelly, F. M., & Clandinin, D. J. (1985). Personal practical knowledge and the modes of knowing: Relevance for teaching and learning. In E. Eisner (Ed.), *Learning and teaching the ways of knowing* (Eighty-fourth Yearbook of the National Society for the Study of Education, Pt. 2, pp. 174–198). Chicago: National Society for the Study of Education; distributed by the University of Chicago Press.

Dewey, J. (1916). *Democracy and education.* New York: Free Press.

Dewey, J. (1938). *Experience and education.* New York: Collier Macmillan.

Dewey, J. (1990). *The school and society* (P.W. Jackson Ed.). Chicago: University of Chicago Press. (Original work published 1900)

Diamond, J. (1998). *Guns, germs, and steel: The fates of human societies.* New York: Norton.

Dick, B. (1997, ongoing). *Action research and evaluation on-line* (a 14-week introductory course offered by e-mail each semester as public service by the graduate College of Management at Southern Cross University, Lismore, Australia). http://www.scu.edu.au/schools/gcm/ar/areol/areolhome.html

Donald, M. (1991). *Origins of the modern mind: Three stages in the evolution of culture and cognition.* Cambridge, MA: Harvard University Press.

Donoahue, Z. (1996). Collaboration, community and communication: Modes of discourse for teacher research. In Z. Donoahue, M. A. Van Tassell, and L. Patterson (Eds.), *Research in the classroom: Talk, text and inquiry* (pp. 91–107). Newark, DE: International Reading Association.

Donoahue, Z. (1998a). Giving children control: Fourth graders initiate and sustain discussions after teacher read-alouds. *Orbit, 29*(3), 18–21.

Donoahue, Z. (1998b). Giving children control: Fourth graders initiate and sustain discussions after teacher read-alouds. http://www.oise.utoronto.ca/~ctd/networks

Duckworth, E. (1987). *"The having of wonderful ideas" and other essays on teaching and learning.* New York: Teachers College Press.

Elliott, J. (1991). *Action research for educational change.* Milton Keynes, England: Open University Press.

Engeström, Y. (1990). *Learning, working and imagining: Twelve studies in activity theory.* Helsinki: Orienta-Konsultit.

Engeström, Y. (1991). Non scolae sed vitae discimus: Toward overcoming the encapsulation of school learning. *Learning and Instruction, 1*, 243–259.

Fullan, M. (1992). *Successful school improvement: The implementation perspective and beyond.* Toronto: OISE Press.

Gal'perin, P. Y. (1969). Stages in the development of mental acts. In M. Cole & I. Maltzman (Eds.), *A handbook of contemporary Soviet psychology* (pp. 249–273). New York: Basic Books.

Gallas, K. (1994). *The languages of learning: How children talk, write, dance, draw, and sing their understanding of the world.* New York: Teachers College Press.

Gallas, K. (1995). *Talking their way into science: Hearing children's questions and theories, responding with curricula.* New York: Teachers College Press.

Galton, M., Simon, B., & Croll, P. (1980). *Inside primary schools.* London: Routledge.

Gardner, H. (1983). *Multiple intelligences: The theory in practice.* New York: Basic Books.

Gardner, H. (1989). *Art, mind, and education: Research from Project Zero.* Urbana: University of Illinois Press.

Gibbs, J. (1994). *Tribes: A new way of learning together.* Santa Rosa, CA: Center Source Publications.

Gipps, C. (1999). Socio-cultural aspects of assessment. In A. Iran-Nejad & P. D. Pearson (Eds.), *Review of Research in Education* (Vol. 24, pp. 355–392). Washington, DC: American Educational Research Association.

Giroux, H. (1991). Democracy, border pedagogy, and the politics of difference. *British Journal of the Sociology of Education, 12*, 501–519.

Glasersfeld, E. von (1995). *Radical constructivism: A way of knowing and learning.* Washington, DC: Falmer Press.

Goodman, Y. M., & Goodman, K. S. (1990). Vygotsky in a whole language perspective. In L. C. Moll (Ed.), *Vygotsky and education: Instructional implications and applications of sociohistorical psychology* (pp. 223–250). New York: Cambridge University Press.

Hall, E. T. (1959). *The silent language.* Greenwich, CT: Premier Books.

Halliday, M. A. K. (1967). *Intonation and grammar in British English.* The Hague, Netherlands: Mouton.

Halliday, M. A. K., & Hasan, R. (1985). *Language, context and text: Aspects of language in a social-semiotic perspective.* Geelong, Australia: Deakin University Press.

Haneda, M., & Wells, G. (2000). Writing in knowledge building communities. *Research in the Teaching of English, 34*(3), 430–457.

Harste, J. (1993). Literacy as curricular conversations about knowledge, inquiry and morality. In R. B. Ruddell, M. R. Ruddell, & H. Singer (Eds.), *Theoretical models and processes of reading* (4th ed., pp. 1025–1047). Newark, DE: International Reading Association.

Holzman, L. (1995). Creating developmental learning environments. *School Psychology International, 16*, 199–212.

Hubbard, R. S., & Power, B. M. (1993). *The art of classroom inquiry: A handbook for teacher-researchers.* Portsmouth, NH: Heinemann.

Hume, K. (1998). A whole school approach. *Orbit, 29*(3), 7–9.

Hume, K., & Wells, G. (1999). Making lives meaningful: Extending perspectives through role play. In B. J. Wagner (Ed.), *Building moral communities through educational drama* (pp. 63–87). Norwood, NJ: Ablex.

Hutchins, E. (1995). *Cognition in the wild.* Cambridge, MA: MIT Press.

Kowal, M., & Swain, M. (1994). Using collaborative language production tasks to promote students' language awareness. *Language Awareness, 3*(2), 73–93.

Kress, G. (1997). *Before writing: Rethinking the paths to literacy.* London: Routledge.

Lampert, M. (1992). Practices and problems in teaching authentic mathematics. In F. K. Oser, A. Dick, & J.-L. Patry (Eds.), *Effective and responsible teaching* (pp. 295–314). San Francisco: Jossey-Bass.

Lave, J., & Wenger, E. (1991). *Situated learning: Legitimate peripheral participation.* New York: Cambridge University Press.

Lemke, J. L. (1990). *Talking science: Language, learning, and values.* Norwood, NJ: Ablex.

Lemke, J. L. (1993). Intertextuality and educational research. *Linguistics and Education, 4*(3/4), 257–268.

Leont'ev, A. N. (1981). The problem of activity in psychology. In J. V. Wertsch (Ed.), *The concept of activity in Soviet Psychology* (pp. 37–71). Armonk, NY: Sharpe.

Lotman, Y. M. (1988). Text within a text. *Soviet Psychology, 26*(3), 32–51.

Maguire, P. (1987). *Doing participatory research: A feminist approach.* Amherst: University of Massachusetts, Center for International Education.

Martin, J. R. (1993). *Genre and literacy: Modelling context in educational linguistics.* Sydney, Australia: University of Sydney.

McGlynn-Stewart, M. (1996). A language experience approach to elementary geometry. In Z. Donoahue, M. A. Van Tassell, & L. Patterson (Eds.), *Research in the classroom: Talk, texts, and inquiry* (pp. 65–80). Newark, DE: International Reading Association.

McGlynn-Stewart, M. (1998). Researching the researchers. *Orbit, 29*(3), 29–31.

McNeill, D. (1992). *Hand and mind: What gestures reveal about thought.* Chicago: University of Chicago Press.

Mehan, H. (1979). *Learning lessons: Social organization in the classroom.* Cambridge, MA: Harvard University Press.

Mercer, N. (1995). *The guided construction of knowledge*. Clevedon, U. K.: Multilingual Matters.

Moffett, J. (1968). *Teaching the universe of discourse*. Boston: Houghton Mifflin.

Mohr, M. (1996). Wild dreams and sober cautions: The future of teacher research. In Z. Donoahue, M. A. Van Tassell, & L. Patterson (Eds.), *Research in the classroom: Talk, texts and inquiry* (pp. 117–123). Newark, DE: International Reading Association.

Moll, L. C. (Ed.). (1990). *Vygotsky and education: Instructional implications and applications of sociohistorical psychology*. New York: Cambridge University Press.

Murphy, M. B., Amin, J. P., & Schelkun, R. F. (1991, March 16). *Pupils as Partners: Site-based management in elementary education*. Paper presented at the annual meeting of the Association for Supervision and Curriculum Development, San Francisco. (ERIC Document No. ED 329 368)

Nassaji, H., & Wells, G. (2000). What's the use of triadic dialogue? An investigation of teacher-student interaction. *Applied Linguistics, 21*(3), 333–363.

Nelson, J. (1981). *Positive discipline*. New York: Ballantine Books.

Newman, J. (1987). Learning to teach by uncovering our assumptions. *Language Arts, 64*(7), 727–737.

Newman, J. (1991). *Interwoven conversations: Learning and teaching through critical reflection*. Toronto: OISE Press; Portsmouth, NH: Heinemann.

Newman, J. (Ed.). (1998). *Tensions of teaching: Beyond tips to critical reflection*. New York: Teachers College Press.

Norman, K. (Ed.). (1992). *Thinking voices: The work of the National Oracy Project*. London: Hodder and Stoughton.

Nuthall, G. A., & Alton-Lee, A. G. (1995). Assessing classroom learning: How students use their knowledge and experience to answer achievement test questions in science and social studies. *American Educational Research Journal, 32*, 185–223.

Nystrand, M. (1997). *Opening dialogue: Understanding the dynamics of language and learning in the English classroom*. New York: Teachers College Press.

Nystrand, M., & Gamoran, A. (1991). Student engagement: When recitation becomes conversation. In H. C. Waxman & H. J. Walberg (Eds.), *Effective teaching: Current research* (pp. 257–276). Berkeley, CA: McCutchan.

Olson, D. R. (1994). *The world on paper*. Cambridge, U. K.: Cambridge University Press.

Owen, H. (1992). *Open space technology: A user's guide*. Potomac, MD: Abbott.

Palincsar, A. S., Magnusson, S. J., Marano, N., Ford, D., & Brown, N. (1998). Designing a community of practice: Principles and practices of the GIsML Community. *Teaching and Teacher Education,14*, 5–19.

Piaget, J. (1970). Piaget's theory. In P. H. Mussen (Ed.), *Carmichael's manual of child development* (3rd ed., pp. 703–732). New York: Wiley.

Popper, K. R., & Eccles, J. C. (1977). *The self and its brain*. Berlin: Springer-Verlag.

Raphael, T. E., & McMahon, S. S. (1994). Book Club: An alternative framework for reading instruction. *The Reading Teacher, 48*, 102–116.

Reddy, M. (1979). The conduit metaphor—a case of frame conflict in our language about language. In A. Ortony (Ed.), *Metaphor and thought* (pp. 284–324). Cambridge, U. K.: Cambridge University Press.

Resnick, L. (1987). Learning in school and out. *Educational Researcher, 16*(9), 13–20.

Rogoff, B. (1994). Developing understanding of the idea of Communities of Learners. *Mind, Culture, and Activity, 1*(4), 209–229.

Rosebery, A., Warren B., & Conant, F. (1992). Appropriating scientific discourse: Findings from language minority classrooms. *Journal of the Learning Sciences, 2*(1), 61–94.

Sacks, H., Schegloff, E. A., & Jefferson, G. (1974). A simplest systematics for the organizing of turn-taking for conversation. *Language, 50*(4), 696–735.

Scardamalia, M., & Bereiter, C. (1992). Text-based and knowledge-based questioning by children. *Cognition and Instruction, 9*(3), 177–199.

Scardamalia, M., Bereiter, C., & Lamon, M. (1994). The CSILE project: Trying to bring the classroom into World 3. In K. McGilley (Ed.), *Classroom lessons: Integrating cognitive theory and classroom practice* (pp. 201–228). Cambridge, MA: MIT Press.

Schön, D. (1987). *Educating the reflective practitioner: Toward a new design for teaching and learning in the professions.* San Francisco: Jossey-Bass.

Schwartz, S., & Bone, M. (1995). *Retelling, relating, reflecting: Beyond the 3 R's.* Concord, ON: Irwin Publishing.

Senge, P. (1990). *The fifth discipline: The art and practice of the learning organization.* New York: Doubleday.

Shechter, M. (1998). Mrs. Frisby and the grade four children. *Orbit, 29*(3), 22–25.

Short, K. G., & Burke, C. L. (1991). *Creating curriculum: Teachers and students as a community of learners.* Portsmouth, NH: Heinemann.

Stenhouse, L. (1975). *An introduction to curriculum research and development.* London: Heinemann.

Tharp, R., & Gallimore, R. (1988). *Rousing minds to life.* New York: Cambridge University Press.

Toronto Board of Education. (1995). *A curriculum for all students.* Toronto: Toronto Board of Education.

Vygotsky, L. S. (1978). *Mind in society: The development of higher psychological processes.* Cambridge, MA: Harvard University Press.

Vygotsky, L. S. (1981). The genesis of higher mental functions. In J. V. Wertsch (Ed.), *The concept of activity in Soviet psychology* (pp. 144–188). Armonk, NY: Sharpe.

Vygotsky, L. S. (1987). Thinking and speech. In R. W. Rieber & A. S. Carton (Eds.), *The collected works of L. S. Vygotsky, Volume 1: Problems of general psychology* (pp. 39–285). New York: Plenum.

Wells, G. (1986). *The meaning makers: Children learning language and using language to learn.* Portsmouth, NH: Heinemann.

Wells, G. (1993). Working with a teacher in the zone of proximal development: Action research on the learning and teaching of science. *Journal of the Society for Accelerative Learning and Teaching, 18,* 127–222.

Wells, G. (1994). Introduction: Teacher research and educational change. In G. Wells et al., *Changing schools from within: Creating communities of inquiry* (pp. 1–35). Toronto: OISE Press; Portsmouth, NH: Heinemann.

Wells, G. (1995). Language and the inquiry-oriented curriculum. *Curriculum Inquiry, 25*(3), 233–269.

Wells, G. (1996). Using the tool-kit of discourse in the activity of learning and teaching. *Mind, Culture, and Activity, 3*(2), 74–101.

Wells, G. (1997). From guessing to predicting: Progressive discourse in the learning and teaching of science. In C. Coll & D. Edwards (Eds.), *Teaching, learning and classroom discourse: Approaches to the study of educational discourse* (pp. 67–87). Madrid: Fundación Infancia y Aprendizaje.

Wells, G. (1999). *Dialogic inquiry: Towards a sociocultural practice and theory of education.* New York: Cambridge University Press.

Wells, G. (2000). Modes of meaning in a science activity. *Linguistics and Education, 10*(3): 307–334.

Wells, G., Bernard, L., Gianotti, M. A., Keating, C., Konjevic, C., Kowal, M., Maher, A., Mayer, C., Moscoe, T., Orzechowska, E., Smieja, A., & Swartz, L. (1994). *Changing schools from within: Creating communities of inquiry.* Toronto: OISE Press, Portsmouth, NH: Heinemann.

Wells, G., & Chang, G. L. (1997). "What Have You Learned?": Co-Constructing the Meaning of Time. In J. Flood, S. B. Heath, & D. Lapp (Eds.), *A handbook for literacy educators: Research on teaching the communicative and visual arts* (pp. 514–527). New York: Macmillan.

Wells, G., & Claxton, G. (Eds.). (in press). *Learning for living in the twenty-first century: Sociocultural perspectives on the future of education.* Oxford: Blackwell.

Wertsch, J. V. (1985). A sociocultural approach to mind: Some theoretical considerations. In *Vygotsky and the social formation of mind.* Cambridge, MA: Harvard University Press.

Whyte, W. F. (Ed.). (1991). *Participatory action research.* London: Sage Publications.

DICEP Publications

Allen, P. (1995). *The integration of ESL students into mainstream science classrooms: A Canadian case study.* Unpublished paper, University of Toronto, Ontario Institute for Studies in Education (OISE), Toronto, Canada.

Allen, P. (1998). Negotiating entry to the classroom community. *Orbit, 29*(3), 26–28.

Chang, G. L., & Wells, G. (1997). Modes of discourse for living, learning and teaching. In S. Hollingsworth (Ed.), *International action research and educational reform* (pp. 147–156). Philadelphia: Falmer Press.

Donoahue, Z. (1995). *One teacher's journey into classroom inquiry about science teaching and science writing.* Unpublished paper, OISE.

Donoahue, Z. (1996). Collaboration, community and communication: Modes of discourse for teacher research. In Z. Donoahue, M. A. Van Tassell, & L. Patterson (Eds.), *Research in the classroom: Talk, text and inquiry* (pp. 91–107). Newark, DE: International Reading Association.

Donoahue, Z. (1996). A collaborative project to develop a school-wide spelling program. In Z. Donoahue, M. A. Van Tassell, & L. Patterson (Eds.), *Research in the classroom: Talk, text and inquiry* (pp. 91–107). Newark, DE: International Reading Association.

Donoahue, Z. (1996, Fall). Making connections: First graders integrate music, math and reading. *Canadian Music Educator 96,* 3–4.

Donoahue, Z. (1997). *Methods of data collection for teacher research.* Newark, DE: International Reading Association.

Donoahue, Z. (1998). Giving children control: Fourth graders initiate and sustain discussions after teacher read-alouds. *Orbit, 29*(3), 18–21.

Donoahue, Z. (1998). Giving children control: Fourth graders initiate and sustain discussions after teacher read-alouds. *Networks, 1.* http://www.oise.utoronto.ca/~ctd/networks

Donoahue, Z., Van Tassell, M. A., & Patterson, L. (Eds.). (1996). *Research in the classroom: Talk, text and inquiry.* Newark, DE: International Reading Association.

Giles, J. (1995, December). Creating that special link—Resources for home and school partnerships. *OPSTF News,10,* 2. (Published by the Ontario Public School Teachers Federation).

Giles, J. (1998). The role of the resource teacher in supporting action research. *Orbit,* 29(3), 10–12.

Haneda, M. (1997). Second language learning in a "community of practice": A case study of adult Japanese learners. *Canadian Modern Language Review,* 54(1), 11–27.

Haneda, M. (1998). Action research and the role of the colleague. *Orbit,* 29(3), 16–17.

Haneda, M. (in press). Modes of student participation in an elementary school science classroom: From talk to writing. *Linguistics and Education.*

Haneda, M., & Wells, G. (2000). Writing in knowledge building communities. *Research in the Teaching of English,* 34(3), 430–457.

Hume, K. (1995). Concerns for the future. *Orbit,* 26(1), 48–52.

Hume, K. (1998). A whole school approach. *Orbit,* 29(3), 7–9.

Hume, K., & Wells, G. (1999). Making lives meaningful: Extending perspectives through role play. In B. J. Wagner (Ed.), *Building communities through drama* (pp. 63–87). Norwood, NJ: Ablex.

McGlynn-Stewart, M. (1996). A language experience approach to elementary geometry. In Z. Donoahue, M. A. Van Tassell, & L. Patterson (Eds.), *Research in the classroom: Talk, text and inquiry* (pp. 65–80). Newark, DE: International Reading Association.

McGlynn-Stewart, M. (1998). Researching the researchers. *Orbit,* 29(3), 29–31.

Measures, E., Quell, C., & Wells, G. (1997). A sociocultural perspective on classroom discourse. In B. Davies & D. Corson (Eds.), *The encyclopedia of language and education: Vol. 3. Oral discourse and education* (pp. 21–30). Dordrecht, The Netherlands: Kluwer Academic.

Nassaji, H., & Wells, G. (2000). What's the use of triadic dialogue? An investigation of teacher-student interaction. *Applied Linguistics,* 21(3), 333–363.

Shechter, M. (1994). "It was a real shame something wasn't done sooner." *Orbit,* 25(2), 46–47.

Shechter, M. (1994). *Learning science: Children's voices.* Unpublished monograph, OISE.

Shechter, M. (1998). Mrs. Frisby and the grade four children. *Orbit,* 29(3), 22–25.

Smith, B. (1996). *Constructing understandings of teaching and learning: An inquiry into peer teaching.* Unpublished Ph.D. thesis, University of Toronto, OISE, Toronto, Canada.

Smith, B. (1998). Students as action researchers. *Orbit,* 29(3), 13–15.

Van Tassell, M. A. (as Gianotti, M. A.) (1994). Moving between worlds: Talk during writing workshop. In Wells, G., et al., *Changing schools from within: Creating communities of inquiry* (pp. 37–59). Toronto: OISE Press; Portsmouth, NH: Heinemann.

Van Tassell, M. A., & Wells, G. (with Galbraith, B.) (1997). Aprendizaje y enseanza en la zona de desarrollo proximo [Learning and teaching in the zone of proximal development]. In A. Alvarez (Ed.), *Hacia un curriculum cultural: La vigencia de Vygotski en la educacion* (pp. 55–76). Madrid: Fundacion Infancia y Aprendizaje. (Reprinted, in English, as "On learning with and from our students," in *Dialogic inquiry: Towards a sociocultural practice and theory of education*, pp. 293–312, by G. Wells, 1999, New York: Cambridge University Press.)

Wells, G. (1993). Working with a teacher in the zone of proximal development: Action research on the learning and teaching of science. *Journal of the Society for Accelerative Learning and Teaching, 18*(1/2), 127–222.

Wells, G. (1994). Writing, reading, talking and thinking: Literacy in the schools. In S. P. Boardman, S. B. Straw, & L. E. Atkinson (Eds.), *Social Reflections on Writing* (pp. 60–75). Winnipeg, Canada: Literacy Publications.

Wells, G. (1995). Language and the inquiry-oriented curriculum. *Curriculum Inquiry, 25*(3), 233–269.

Wells, G. (1996). Using the tool-kit of discourse in the activity of learning and teaching. *Mind, Culture and Activity, 3*(2), 74–101.

Wells, G. (1996). Co-constructing meaning: Some roles for research in education. *English International.*

Wells, G. (1998). Some questions about direct instruction: Why? To whom? How? and When? *Language Arts, 76*(1), 27–35.

Wells, G. (1998). Working together to understand and improve practice. *Orbit, 29*(3), 4–6.

Wells, G. (1999). Reconceptualizing education as dialogue. *Annual Review of Applied Linguistics, 19*, 135–55.

Wells, G. (1999). *Dialogic inquiry: Towards a sociocultural practice and theory of education.* New York: Cambridge University Press.

Wells, G. (2000). Dialogic inquiry in education: Building on Vygotsky's legacy. In C. D. Lee & P. Smagorinsky (Eds.), *Vygotskian perspectives on literacy research* (pp. 51–85). New York: Cambridge University Press. (Original paper presented at the meeting of the NCTE, Detroit, MI, November 1997.)

Wells, G. (2000). From action to writing: Modes of representing and knowing. In J. W. Astington (Ed.), *Minds in the making* (pp. 115–140). Oxford: Blackwell.

Wells, G. (with Booth, D.) (1994). Developing communities of inquiry: Teachers as researchers. *Orbit, 25*(4), 23–27.

Wells, G., & Chang, G. L. (1997) "What Have You Learned?": Co-Constructing the Meaning of Time. In J. Flood, S. B. Heath, & D. Lapp (Eds.), *A handbook for literacy educators: Research on teaching the communicative and visual arts* (pp. 514–527). New York: Macmillan.

About the Editor
and the Contributors

GORDON WELLS is Professor of Education at the University of California at Santa Cruz. During the writing of this book, he was Professor of Education at the Ontario Institute for Studies in Education (OISE) of the University of Toronto, where as a member of the Curriculum Department and of the Joint Centre for Teacher Development, he researched and taught in the fields of language, literacy, and learning. Before emigrating to Canada, he directed the "Bristol Study of Language Development." This naturalistic longitudinal study of the language and literacy development of 128 children from 1 to 10 years old is reported in *The Meaning Makers: Children Learning Language and Using Language to Learn*. For the last 15 years he has been involved in several collaborative action research projects with educational practitioners in Canada. As an educator, he is committed to the development of an inquiry-oriented approach to learning and teaching, based on the work of Vygotsky and other sociocultural theorists. Gordon received his B.A. degree from Cambridge University and his Ph.D. from Bristol University. A worldwide lecturer and consultant, he has published widely in edited books and in journals such as *Curriculum Inquiry, Research in the Teaching of English, Language Arts*, and *Linguistics and Education*.

GRETA DAVIS is currently a Grade 5 teacher with the Durham District School Board, Ontario. She has been teaching for 10 years and has worked with students from kindergarten to Grade 8. During that time Greta has been an acting vice principal and chairperson of her school's primary teaching staff. She attended Brock University for her undergraduate work and obtained a Bachelor of Arts in Child Studies. She recently completed her Masters of Education in Curriculum Studies at OISE/University of Toronto.

ZOE DONOAHUE is an elementary teacher with the Toronto District School Board. She is currently teaching Grade 2 at Lambton Kingsway Junior Middle School. She received her Bachelor of Arts degree from McMaster University and her Master of Education degree from OISE/University of Toronto. Her recent research interests include examining how class meetings contribute to the development of classroom community and how she can help her students to initiate and control discussions after she reads to them.

KAREN HUME is a classroom teacher with 14 years of experience at all levels of elementary school as well as the school library. She obtained her teaching degree from the University of Toronto and, a number of years later, a master's degree in Curriculum and Teacher Development from OISE/University of Toronto. Karen's research interests are in the development of classroom communities centered around knowledge building and inquiry learning. Karen's interests in writing began as an undergraduate when she assisted a professor in writing a text about language development in children. Since then, she has published several articles and book chapters based on the action research activities in her classroom. Karen has been honored with the TVOntario Teacher of the Year award and the Educational Computing Organization Teacher of the Year award, both for her innovative use of technology in the intermediate classroom.

MARIA KOWAL is a teacher with the Toronto District School Board. She has also taught in preservice teacher education courses at the University of Toronto and continuing teacher education courses at York University, Toronto. She holds a B.A. degree and teaching certificate from Oxford University, a master's degree in Education from Harvard University, and a doctorate in Education from OISE/University of Toronto. As a researcher she is primarily interested in classroom-based research in first and second language classrooms.

MONICA MCGLYNN-STEWART is a former elementary teacher and high school teacher and principal. In her classroom-based work, she focuses on the arts, integrated curriculum, and student leadership development. Monica now works as an organizational learning consultant in education and in the corporate, not-for-profit, and public sectors. She specializes in large systems interventions, organizational assessment and clarification of organizational direction, leadership development, and conference and retreat design and facilitation. She obtained her teaching degree from the Institute for Child Study at the University of Toronto, and her master's degree from OISE/University of Toronto.

MARY ANN VAN TASSELL currently teaches second grade at North Bend Elementary School in the state of Washington. She taught first and second grades at the York School in Toronto, for 10 years before that. During that time, she completed her master's degree in Education at OISE/University of Toronto. Throughout her teaching career, Mary Ann has been interested in developing emerging literacy skills across the curriculum. As well as studying the role of language in elementary science, her research has also involved investigation of the role of talk in Writing Workshop.

Index